Alone at Sea

THE ADVENTURES OF JOSHUA SLOCUM

Ann Spencer

Published in cooperation with the
Old Dartmouth Historical Society –
New Bedford Whaling Museum

FIREFLY BOOKS

A FIREFLY BOOK

Published by Firefly Books Ltd. 1999

First Printing

Library of Congress Cataloguing in Publication Data
Spencer, Ann.
    Alone at sea : the adventures of Joshua Slocum / Ann Spencer ; published in cooperation with the Old Dartmouth Historical Society - New Bedford Whaling Museum.–1st US ed.
[322] p. : Ill.; [24x16] cm.
Includes index.
Appendix includes chronology, letters.
Originally published: Toronto : Doubleday Canada, 1998.
Summary: The story of Joshua Slocum, the first person to single-handedly sail around the globe.
ISBN 1-55209-394-8
1. Slocum, Joshua, b. 1844. 2. Sailors—Canadian—Biography.
3. Voyages around the world. 4. Spray (Sloop). 5. Sailing, Single-handed. I. Old Dartmouth Historical Society - New Bedford Whaling Museum–Massachusetts. II. Title.

910.4' 1' 092–dc21   1999   CIP

Published in the United States in 1999 by
Firefly Books (U.S.) Inc.
P.O. Box 1338, Ellicott Station
Buffalo, New York 14205

Cover design by Tania Craan
Cover photographs courtesy Old Dartmouth Historical Society –
    New Bedford Whaling Museum
Letters from Henrietta Slocum in Appendix 3 courtesy Nova Scotia
    Archives and Records Management/MG100 Vol. 94
Text and insert design by Heidy Lawrance Associates
Printed and bound in the USA

To Jo and Joe, who helped me understand the intricacies of solo sailing and the courage and skill it requires.

CONTENTS

Preface vii

Prologue: *On Beam Ends* 1

One: *The Call of the Running Tide* 12

Two: *Learning the Ropes* 22

Three: *True Love and a Family Afloat* 32

Four: *Ebb and Flow* 54

Five: *What Was There For an Old Sailor to Do?* . . . 74

Six: *All Watches* 96

Seven: *High Seas Adventures* 114

Eight: *Walden at Sea: A Solitude Supreme* 132

Nine: *Ports of Call* 152

Ten: *Booming Along Joyously for Home* 176

Eleven: *That Intrepid Water Tramp* 188

Twelve: *Swallowing the Anchor?* 206

Thirteen: *Seaworthy for the Last Time* 226

Appendices 251

Notes on Sources 273

Index 313

Preface

Early in September of 1997 I sat on the edge of a cliff where land ended and the Atlantic Ocean began. I was on Brier Island, Joshua Slocum's boyhood home in the Bay of Fundy. The smell of salt water was riding the wind, and seabirds were calling. I sat with closed eyes and listened to the rhythms of the island. A constant pattern was all around: waves lapped on the shore directly below me, and the high-pitched sigh of a foghorn punctuated the lull, which startled an island rooster to crowing. The sounds echoed softly, before the sequence started up again. I tried to imagine how this vital environment had shaped the spirit of young Joshua Slocum, how it felt to be a ten-year-old boy running through the wind to the edge of this very cliff. It was Brier Island that had given young Joshua the sense that adventure and escape would always be found on the water, and the belief that a larger world lay just beyond the horizon. The sea coursed through his veins, and it would always beckon him, whatever its mood.

Brier Island inspired me. By the time I boarded the ferry back to the mainland, I had already embarked on a voyage of discovery. I had begun to get a sense of Joshua Slocum's strength and his complexity. He was a master mariner who had followed his calling with an uncompromising spirit fueled by deep reserves of courage and humor. At the same time, he paid a high price for staying true to his passion: he was both a restless man and a profoundly sad one, and he was forever an outsider on dry land.

From Brier Island I traveled to New Bedford, Massachusetts, where the Whaling Museum houses the extensive Teller collection of documents about Slocum, as well as letters, photographs and other Slocum memorabilia. I owe a great debt to Walter Magnes Teller, Slocum's biographer in the 1950s, and envy him for being the first to undertake this research. In the foreword to his 1956 biography, *The Search for Captain Slocum*, Teller wrote that his journey started with "a chance reading of his [Slocum's] book, and a chance discovery, at Martha's Vineyard, that people who knew him were still alive. For Joshua Slocum had disappeared at sea some forty years before." Intrigued, Teller began collecting stories and memorabilia relating to Slocum. Sadly, other people's recollections were all that survived — Slocum's published books were still available, but his letters, logs and personal diaries and papers had been lost at sea with the *Spray*. It was also rumored that Slocum's widow, Hettie, had burned much of the captain's correspondence. Nevertheless, Teller pieced together a full and vibrant portrait of a determined man "living on the edge of the twentieth century." It was through Teller's research that I became fascinated by

Slocum the navigator, explorer, lecturer, shipwright, writer, and staunch individualist.

Some forty years after Teller, it was I who was searching for Captain Slocum. I felt certain there was more to be discovered, and new ways to approach what was already known about him. In my preliminary research at the Public Archives of Nova Scotia, I uncovered three letters that Teller had not seen. They were written by Slocum's second wife, Hettie, to a captain's wife in the Annapolis Valley, which was Slocum's birthplace. In a letter dated 1910, Hettie wrote that her husband had been missing since he first set out in November 1908. This intrigued me right away, as this date contradicted every published account of Slocum's disappearance, allegedly in 1909. It was quite possible that Hettie had her dates mixed up, but documents in the Teller collection almost exclusively mention the date of Slocum's last sail as November 1908. The captain's fate was now even more of a mystery than before.

The Teller collection is a feast of folk history. I pored over letters from Slocum's sons, daughter, and relatives. All had similar memories of their mother, Joshua's extraordinary first wife, Virginia. By all accounts, Virginia was a woman of tremendous spirit and strength of character as well as beauty and grace. Her strong sense of beauty breathed life into the rugged existence aboard her husband's commands. Her navigational skills and, perhaps more importantly, her guiding intuition were said to have been Slocum's mainstays. As Slocum's son Ben Aymar remembered, "one peep from her would have changed the whole picture."

The story of Joshua Slocum is of a man's life lived fully and uncompromisingly. He survived mutinies and shipboard epidemics of smallpox. He was challenged to duels, and shot and killed a member of his crew in self-defense. His wife and three of his children died in foreign ports, and he lost his fortune when he stranded an uninsured vessel. His three-year circumnavigation was, for him, as much a spiritual and emotional voyage as it was a quest to be history's first solo circumnavigator. His sad decline after the circumnavigation, and his mysterious death, add a mythic element to his life.

I wish to express my gratitude to the following people, who inspired and helped me along this literary voyage of discovery.

Many thanks to the people of Brier Island, especially to Phil Shea, Judy Joys, Nancy and Rolland Swift, and Carol and Bill Welch, who helped me understand what was indelibly etched in a boy's soul.

Thank you to the following sailors, who helped me understand what calls someone to the sea: Tom Gallant talked seadog lingo to me and answered my many questions about why a sailor does what a sailor does. Tom has the true storyteller's uncanny ability to find the choice words, explaining not only the mundane realities but the profound philosophy of a sailor's life. Ed and Lainie Porter shared stories of their experience in gales, becalmings and fine weather along the coast of Maine. Lainie sang me sea songs and Ed answered any and all technical questions. I spent a Sunday morning around a Portsmouth, New Hampshire, kitchen table with Dean Plager, who told me how he came to pack up his office job and sail alone. His stories of unbroken horizons, phosphorescence and mirages fueled the chapter on solitude. Cam Allbright in Annapolis Royal shared stories of the challenges of sailing the Bay of Fundy, as well as his knowledge of celestial navigation. However, it was Cam's thoughts on sailing as a spiritual discipline that helped me understand what Slocum meant when he wrote, "Everything in connection with the sea would be eminently respectable and be told in spirituality."

I am grateful also to Fred Lawrence of Cape Breton, who sails his homemade replica of the *Spray*, the *Double Crow*, and shared his thoughts on Slocum's forgiving old boat; and to Gary Maynard and his wife, Kristie Kinsman, of Martha's Vineyard, who gave me a tour of the captain's home in West Tisbury and loaned me videos of the Maynard family's replica of the *Spray*, the *Scud*, in which Gary's parents took their family around the world.

For historical and nautical information, thanks to Alton Barteaux at the Mount Hanley School Museum; and to Dan Conlin, Curator of Marine History at the Maritime Museum of the Atlantic in Halifax, Nova Scotia. The museum's permanent exhibit "Sailing Alone," which tells stories of four single-handers, including Slocum, was installed in June 1997. Dan's research and enthusiastic writing about nautical adventurers, along with the historical photos in the exhibit, gave me a solid footing to start my journey. Thank you to Garry Shutlak, Senior Archivist, Reference Services, at the Provincial Archives of Nova Scotia; to Carlton J. Pinheiro, Curator at the Herreshoff Marine Museum in Bristol, Rhode Island; and to Mike Martel and Phil Shea of the Joshua Slocum Society International Inc.

Judith N. Lund, curator at the Old Dartmouth Historical Society–New Bedford Whaling Museum, was an invaluable source of information and inspiration. Thank you, Judy, for your enthusiasm, thoroughness, detective work and care during the project. Judy drew my attention to new shipping information to be gleaned from the records filed away in the Teller Collection, which disputed all published reports of Slocum's early commands. Thanks also to Lee Heald and Laura Pereira.

I had the pleasure of talking with Ben Aymar's granddaughters, Carol Slocum Jimerson and Gale Slocum Hermanet, who told me of Virginia Slocum's Native American heritage, shared with me family stories of her bravery, and filled in details of the cultured life she left behind in Australia when she married Joshua. Gale Slocum Hermanet also sent me three unpublished photographs of Virginia and two of her sons, Victor and Ben Aymar. I thank them here for their insights into the captain and his wife and for their kind permission to use those three photographs in this book.

I also wish to thank Don Sedgwick for listening to my sea captain stories and encouraging me to turn that interest into a book about Joshua Slocum; and my editor, Anne Holloway, who sat at the helm when my self-steering mechanism took us into strange waters.

There was so much kindness along the way. I am grateful to Gerret Warner and Mimi Gredy, and to Dr. David Glover and Tina Balog, for opening their homes to me. Dr. Glover also shared his knowledge of ocean conditions, williwaws, and the treacheries of the Horn.

Thanks to Dr. Joseph Gabriel for his help in making sense of Slocum's way of thinking, to Joanna MacIntyre for her boosts to the creative spirit, and to Debbie Young for her insights into the past. Thanks also to Sandra Spencer, Kevin Fitzpatrick, Ray Imai and Klara Fassett for their thoughts on safe passage through storms. Thanks to my mother for all her help; to my sons Sam and Max for their patience and interesting suggestions; to Graham and Alecia Spencer for their computer know-how and for being on twenty-four-hour emergency standby; to Andy Manning for his patience and time teaching me the intricacies of my new computer; to Fred MacDonald for showing me his uncle's watercolors of ports at the turn of the century; to Chris van den Berg for helping with swift communications; to Gerrie Grevatt for the author photo; and to Uncle

Gordon for checking any odd fact at any odd hour.

Thanks to Linda Granfield, Paul McKenzie, and Gail Whiteside for their leads on tackling the initial research.

Thanks to those friends who cheered me on throughout the voyage: Belinda, Audrey, Katherine, Arlene, Dick, Charis, Lorry Anne, George, Lee, Rudi, Trevor, Rigel, Debbie and Chris, and Lynn and Ray; and to Christopher for sharing a parallel technological, artistic and soulful journey.

Ann Spencer
April 1998

Prologue: *On Beam Ends*

I had been cast up from old ocean.
— Joshua Slocum,
Sailing Alone Around the World

On a winter's day in 1892, the coastal village of Fairhaven, Massachusetts, was buzzing with speculation. Who was the newcomer, and what had brought him into town? The stranger had a weary look about him. He was surely someone down on his luck. His gaunt frame and balding head heightened the impression of an aging and weather-beaten soul dealt a heavy hand. He was not the approachable sort: one could not just saunter up to him and ask his business. He had a self-contained air, and his eyes were sad. Yet he was also clearly a proud man: his brown beard was neat and close-cropped, and he walked with a spirited step. He seemed to be in town for a purpose.

"Who's the old-timer?" was probably the question of the day, a puzzle to chew over around the dockyard and main crossroads in Fairhaven. That curious blend of smalltown guesswork, rumor and not always benign gossip would not die down until it had pieced together the identity of this enigmatic fellow making his way toward the shore. Soon they had the answer: the stranger was Captain Joshua Slocum. And their impressions were dead on: times were tough for the captain. He looked older than his forty-eight years and most certainly he was down on his luck. What was missing from the general scuttlebutt was sympathy for his plight. In many ways, Joshua Slocum was just another sea captain wandering jobless around the wharves, one of many captains who had not yet made their fortune or who made and lost it. Such men had established themselves on the sea but had since been left without a command, bypassed in the transition from sail to steam. But Slocum's career had been colorful, and he stood out from the crowd. Chances were that the Fairhaven villagers knew the old salt by reputation. He had been famous for his sailing exploits, and the most scandalous episodes of his career had been chronicled in newspapers and spiced up in the tales of the men who had sailed with him. Word was that Captain Slocum could be just plain bull-headed, and this trait had no doubt played a large part in his sad reversal of fortune.

The change had been a dramatic one. Three years earlier a very different Slocum would have come into port; eight years earlier Fairhaven folk would have encountered the epitome of nautical success. Back then Slocum had been a dapper skipper, the master and part owner of a full-rigged ship, *Northern Light*. She was a beauty, and the captain regarded her as "one of the finest American sailing vessels afloat." With her to command, he had

2

reached the pinnacle of his over twenty-year career as a master merchant mariner. He had sailed around the world five times. His career had been a steady rise with some lucky breaks along the way. Slocum had been made a captain in 1869 when he was just twenty-five years old. He was a spunky young fellow from away, a Canadian turned "naturalized" Yankee. He did most of his shipping in the Pacific trade and called San Francisco his home port. His life seemed charmed. He had even met the perfect life partner: on a stopover in Australia he had married Virginia Walker. Folks recalled her gumption with admiration. She could handle the rough life aboard ships and had traveled everywhere with her husband, raising their growing family. With Virginia at his side, Slocum was respected as a world-class captain with an important command.

Those happy years at sea were not free of shadows. Charges had been laid against Slocum late in 1883 over his harsh treatment of a mutinous crew member. The story was circulating freely that he had kept the man chained in irons for most of the voyage and nearly starved him to death. Virginia had stood by her husband throughout that episode, holding the mutineers at bay by pointing revolvers at them. People said that Virginia was his anchor, and that everything began to fall apart for him after her death in 1884.

They'd heard he had got married again, to a young woman from Nova Scotia — a cousin, they believed. Hettie and two of his boys, Victor and Garfield, had sailed with Slocum aboard his next command, during which more scandals arose. This time Slocum had been charged in Brazil with killing a crew member. He was acquitted, but it must have all been too much for him. Shortly afterward, he ran his ship aground on a sandbar, and lost his life savings with it. His "elegant bark" carried no insurance, and Slocum had to make his way home not only with a tarnished reputation but also in a state of financial ruin.

Even so, people marveled at the old seadog's ingenuity. He had sailed his family back all the way from Brazil in a homemade "canoe," as he called the small boat he had built in the jungle. He had spunk, but among seamen who knew him, the consensus was that he was a proud, sad fool. Didn't he know he had to change with the times? The age of grand sailing ships was over. To work in freight shipping in the 1890s a captain had to be able to guarantee that goods would arrive at an appointed time. Keeping to a schedule meant not being at the mercy of the wind. But "going steam" went against Slocum's grain. Most people thought that his resistance to inevitable change was the real reason for his sad decline.

Slocum, of course, would have told it differently. Sailing without Virginia had been a painful transition. Also, to give up what he was best at and surrender to machine-driven shipping was never a choice for him. He hated steamships — it was that simple. His unbending will and the troubles he had encountered on his final voyages had sealed his future in merchant shipping. Slocum was never given another command. His career marked the end of the age of sail.

Few knew how difficult his life had become. His family had no home in Boston, and the children and Hettie were boarding throughout the city with various relatives. The captain had worked for a time as a stevedore at the Boston shipyards, but his stubbornness resurfaced when he refused to pay a fifty-dollar union fee. Slocum later described the moment he decided to leave the humiliating life of the docks: "One day when I was doing a bit of an odd job on a boat and a whole lot of coal and dirt came down all about my face, I stood up, thought of the difference between my state and when I was master of the *Northern Light*, and quit the job."

His decision to quit left him scrambling for employment in a waterfront world that held few opportunities for a man like himself. But a winter's walk along the Boston wharves led to a chance encounter with an old sailing acquaintance. Former Captain Eben Pierce from Fairhaven was out for a walk that cold day. He had retired after a successful career in whaling and later designing whaling equipment. Now he saw another opportunity, and made Slocum an interesting proposition: "Come to Fairhaven and I'll give you a ship, but she wants some repairs." The very next day, Slocum was in Fairhaven on his way to Captain Pierce's.

Perhaps it was hope that was adding a bounce to his step as he walked along the Acushnet River shore road. Perhaps he felt that with the gift of this ship he was being given a second chance at life on the water. That she wanted some repairs was a trivial matter to Slocum, who had always loved shipwrighting only a little less than sailing and who had already built three boats. What were a few repairs? One can only imagine what daydreams were halted when Pierce took him to the "ship." Was this gift from his supposed friend just a cruel joke? There, hauled up in a pasture on Fairhaven's Oxford Point, was the derelict hulk of an old oyster sloop. Pierce figured her to be about one hundred years old. No one knew her origins — only that she had been employed along Delaware Bay before being moved to New Bedford and ending up in Captain Pierce's field. Her name was *Spray*. Obviously, Pierce hoped Slocum would find a way to rid him of this neighborhood eyesore.

Fairhaven people liked to mosey down to see what was happening on Oxford Point. "Poverty Point" is what the locals called that area of town, and the penniless captain and the dilapidated old fishing sloop fit right in. Both had somehow been "cast up from old ocean" to meet on Poverty Point. There was no missing the symbolism, or the sad irony: Slocum and the boat were both on their beam ends.

Slocum was surely confused, angered and desperate to maintain some dignity in his laughable situation. He had plummeted from owning the grandest of sailing ships to being stuck with an ancient craft sitting abandoned in a cow pasture. His reaction to all this was unexpected and no doubt gave villagers their first intimation of how determined and resourceful the old captain could be in heavy seas. The crowd gathered in the pasture shared the assumption that Slocum would be breaking up the *Spray* for scrap. His reply was quick and to the point: "No, going to rebuild her."

To the crowd the plan may have seemed impractical, and even crazy, but from that point on it became Slocum's mission. He had built the *Liberdade*, his Brazilian canoe, out of salvaged parts and whatever makeshift materials he could lay his hands on. Why not the *Spray*? Others would have thrown up their hands. Slocum couldn't afford to do that, so he threw himself at the intricate labor of shipbuilding. Rebuilding the *Spray* took Slocum thirteen months, including short interruptions while he raised whatever money he needed to keep working on her. The point was that Slocum *needed* to keep working on her: he had a purpose again, and it buoyed his spirits. The end of Poverty Point rang with the sounds of his determination. He felt reinvigorated by his outlandish dream of resurrecting the miserable old vessel. The entire boat needed overhauling, and Slocum went about it "timber by timber, plank by plank." In a nearby lot he found an oak tree that was solid and worthy of being the hull. All the wood was hauled in from nearby and seasoned.

Slocum kept his steambox boiling for when the wood needed to be shaped into arcs and hoops.

Winter turned into a spring marked by the ringing echo of the caulking mallet. The boat was taking shape, and it lightened Slocum's heart to see how "something tangible appeared every day to show for my labor." The neighbors, who had been scrutinizing the entire operation, had turned from skeptics into believers. Old whaling captains stopped by to chat as Slocum worked. In Fairhaven, the excitement grew. As the weather turned milder, Slocum claimed an added benefit: working on the deck of the *Spray*, he had only to reach out to pluck cherries from a nearby tree.

The *Spray* was looking good. She had new ribs, bulwarks of white oak, and Georgia and yellow pine for deck planking. He pitched the seams and sewed two sets of canvas sails by hand. He fitted a solid keel to make her more seaworthy than her original centerboarder design. He took pride in claiming that the "much-esteemed stempiece was from the butt of the smartest kind of a pasture oak." When she was finished, the change was remarkable, although according to Slocum the metamorphosis was slow: "The *Spray* changed her being so gradually that it was hard to say at what point the old died or the new took birth, and it was no matter."

Captain Slocum could have been writing those lines about himself. In the thirteen months of putting heart and soul into a beached vessel, he had rejuvenated himself.

Through his commitment to the resurrection of the *Spray*, he had also rebuilt himself — "timber by timber, plank by plank." He had made the connection with the one part of him that would always ring true, the part that really mattered. His labor had made the old girl and himself seaworthy once again. But for what purpose?

With the *Spray* finished, Slocum once again heard the question: "What was there for an old sailor to do?" Standing on the shore at Poverty Point, he gazed out to the one place where the answer could be found. As he pondered the waters, his breathing echoed the sea rhythm that was his constant meter, an ancient pulse as primal and familiar as his own mother's heartbeat. Saltwater winds had always blown over his soul. Surf and sea air were his heartbeat and his life force.

On both sides my family were sailors; and if any Slocum should be found not seafaring, he will show at least an inclination to whittle models of boats and contemplate voyages. My father was the sort of man who, if wrecked on a desolate island, would find his way home, if he had a jack-knife and could find a tree . . . At the age of eight I had already been afloat with other boys on the bay, with chances greatly in favor of being drowned.

— J.S., *Sailing Alone*

1

The Call of the
Running Tide

The wonderful sea charmed me from the first.
— J.S., *Sailing Alone*

Racing swift as lightning a young boy runs wild and free
along the one narrow footpath beaten down through the
grassy meadow. He stops only because the land ends. At
the foot of the cliff the sea begins. Rushing headfirst into
the seawinds is one of the glories of childhood on Brier
Island, off the westernmost tip of Nova Scotia. Like generations of Westport children before him, ten-year-old
Joshua Slocum probably made that mad-dash pilgrimage
every day, at least in gentler weather. At almost every
point of their four-mile-long, half-mile-wide island home,
land's end was marked and definite, a dramatic drop to
the sea, straight into the Bay of Fundy. The children of

12

Brier Island knew instinctively the boundaries of their coastal playground.

Perhaps Josh, as he was called by his school friends, would have wanted to stretch those boundaries a little, the abrupt halt to his breathless run filling him with an ache to go on. Perhaps he was bold enough to sit near the cliff's edge and let his legs dangle over, a posture assumed not in defiance but out of youth's remarkable combination of pluck, naiveté and sense of indestructibility. The jagged rocks formed a steep stairway to the rocky shore 120 feet down, the steps made of crumbling basalt columns. The long, deep grooves and cracks etched and beaten into the black cliff were testimonies to the sea's fury. The rocks on which he sat had been shifted and sculpted over aeons by the elemental forces of wind and water.

The sea's imprint was in evidence all around him. Directly below, visible from half ebb to low water, were rocks strewn with seaweed tossed by the turn of the tide. Rockweed and kelp torn free by gales clung to the shoreline. The rocks jutting from the meadow grass all around were covered in a brilliant yellow lichen that thrived in the salt air. The shingles on the village houses and the moose racks and deer antlers nailed proudly to porchways wore spreads of this yellow growth from years of facing the ocean. In all things animate and inanimate, the island answered to the sea and bore its harshness. On the cliff across from Josh, trees stood weathered and squat. Older islanders told tales of gnarled trees that hadn't changed one bit in sixty years. You could cut through a trunk of two and a half inches in diameter and discover the tree to be a hundred or more years old.

Even with his eyes closed, Josh could feel the sea's hold on the island. The air he breathed smelled of salt and tar and fish from the wharves. He heard the lapping waves and the high-pitched crying of gulls, all part of the constant drone underlying the melody of island life. On stormy days the usual sounds reached a more furious pitch and tempo. The surf pounded and the wind howled. He could hear the sea beyond the wall of white fog that now and again blanketed the island and hid the mainland across St. Marys Bay — fog that often lasted for six weeks at a time.

Josh's mother, Sarah Jane Southern, grew up an island girl. She was aware early in her life of the dangers of a thick fog. She would have known the anxiety in her father's voice and his fast actions whenever summer fog thickened or winter snow squalled. As keeper of the Southwest Point Light, he knew that when Brier Island was wrapped in darkness, ships were wrecked. Even in the best conditions, navigation is tricky between Brier Island and Long Island, off Digby. The sea passage is narrow and rough. It boasts colossal Bay of Fundy tides that completely empty out, only to rush back thirteen hours later with seemingly renewed strength. "There's all tide rips around here, right straight around the island everywhere" is how the islanders put it. "Rough water with a tide behind it driving it up over shoal water. When it goes down it makes the tide rip." This small island has seen scores of schooners and small boats washed up in pieces on its shore, their cargoes spilled out for beachcombers to find.

John Slocombe was one who brought in his ship to the island port safely. There he met, courted and married the lighthouse keeper's daughter, and together they sailed across to the mainland to live on his family farm. A son, Joshua, was born — the fifth of eleven children — on February 20, 1844, in Mount Hanley, Nova Scotia. Their homestead in this small Annapolis Valley community was exposed to the ocean winds blowing up their side of North Mountain. Later in life, Joshua would recall his beginnings: "I was born in a cold spot, on coldest North Mountain." The people of Mount Hanley still talk of snow often being on the ground "on the cold side" while the lee remains bare. On this harsh hillside the family tried to wrest a living from the land. Josh undoubtedly joined in as one of the farmhands helping with the chicken feeding, berry picking and small daily chores. From the Slocombe field he had a clear view down the steep hill to where the road was swallowed by the Bay of Fundy, whence he heard the pounding roar of the highest tides in the world.

Sarah Slocombe was caught up in the demanding life of farm wife and mother. After her eighth child she yearned to go home to Brier Island. One of her relatives described her as a "lovely, gentle soul" and added that her need to return to Westport stemmed from "too many children coming too closely." Her husband struggled stubbornly to make a living from farming, but the soil was poor and he could see commercial merit in the move to Brier Island. John Slocombe knew about tanning and boot making, so in 1852 he sold the family farm to set up a dockside shop on the island, specializing in fishermen's boots. Fishing and freighting were booming industries, and Westport, Brier Island, was an important stop for boats bound for distant ports. When Josh was eight, he and his family sailed across the Bay of Fundy to chart an easier life on what he later nostalgically recalled as "the island of plenty."

Their new home was on the southern tip of the island in a section dubbed Irishtown. A swampy meadow separated this part of the village from the Loyalist settlement the Irishtowners called Snobtown. So the bridge over the swamp spanned a social as well as a geographical divide. It was while defending the dignity of Irishtowners against the Snobtowners that Joshua Slocum first learned to scrap. His son Victor wrote years later that Westport taught his father "howling and fighting" — skills that one day would come in handy.

From his house, young Joshua could look out over Sweetcake Cove into the village harbor. Westport was bustling with fishermen's business. On sunny days Josh could probably have counted sixty dories at the moorings, with the bigger boats out fishing; on stormy days the waterfront would be full. The most common fishing schooners, the seakindly, double-ended "pinkies," sailed out of harbor to fish at the back of the island. Less prosperous fishermen went out in large dories that rode out with the tide and returned from the sou'west ledge with the tide whenever possible. Otherwise it was a long and tedious row home. There was a saying around Westport: "You sail by the Grace of God and the seat of your pants."

At age ten, Joshua's daily routine suddenly changed when he was taken out of school to help his father. The boy now spent long days cooped up in the boot shop, an unpleasant prospect for even the most passionately landlubber soul. Making fishermen's boots was not only a laborious task, but a smelly one. The cowhide first had to be softened by soaking. Every day, strips of leather were added to the vat to "marinate" until done. A terrible, sickening stench hung constantly in the air. On hot summer days the overpowering odor rivaled the other island stench, that of herring set out to rot in barrels for lobster bait. Josh's job of pegging the boots his father had fashioned was boring and physically demanding. He sat in the shop ten hours a day, tapping and hammering square pegs around the sole of each boot form.

The boot shop was a converted fish shack built on a wharf. Its windows looked out on the harbor, which was both the boy's salvation and his torment. From his window, Josh could watch his old school chums going out to fish in smacks on St. Mary's Bay. Until Josh began working for his father, he had been one of the boys patching up beat-up boats and sailing or rowing in and out of the bay on whatever might float. None of the island boys was a swimmer. "Can't swim a stroke" would surely have been their matter-of-fact way of putting it. There was a fatalism in their reasoning: "No difference around here. Water's so cold you wouldn't last five minutes anyway."

Aside from the dinghies and the makeshift boats that only boyhood dreaming could transform to clipper ships, Joshua had a taste of the real thing. Coming and going every day were tern schooners, the old name for a three-masted vessel, as well as full-rigged ships and lumber vessels bound for faraway foreign ports. Westport was their logical stopover. The Indies and European trading ships were part of the seasonal rhythm of the island. Every March the salt vessel arrived from Turks Island, and for a week islanders shoveled out its coarse glistening cargo into ox carts for delivery to each fish shop. But not too late in the spring, or the winding shore road would be "mud up to a fella's ankles." Early in the fall a vessel arrived with a cargo of coal, and boys and young men would be hired to dig into its filthy black hold, this time to load coal into horse carts to take door to door. Coal also fueled the steam-driven foghorn that guided ships safely on their way into the world.

Josh could only dream of being aboard. His fingers ached to do more than peg boots, and whenever the elder Slocombe left the shop, the younger took out his whittling knife to add more touches to his ship model. John Slocombe did not condone idle play and no doubt saw any straying as restless hands doing Beelzebub's work, so Joshua kept his "idling" a private matter. So secretive was he that he dared to work on the fine touches only in the cellar. And that was where John found his boy touching up rigging and masts instead of fitting square pegs. In his fury the bootmaker grabbed the twelve-year-old's creation from his hands and smashed it to the ground. Dreams were dashed in that instant, but they would resurface later with unbending strength and intent, like the Fundy tides.

Perhaps this incident aroused Josh's defiance and strengthened his urge to break free from the boot shop, his overzealous father and the confines of the island. He may have found some solace on the spectacular Green Head cliffs. Who knows what he dreamed? From his lofty vantage point he could slip effortlessly into the island's hypnotic spell. Below was the roaring gully where the tide flooded in, and beyond that the low blast of the foghorn. Ravens and seagulls flew by at eye level, and beyond them was only the sea, the sea with its ships he longed to sail away on.

Brier Island had attuned him to life on the water. He grew up governed by the tide, always aware of the time of day by the sound of rushing waters and the smell of seaweed-covered rocks in "a dead low." He knew how much time he had to scoot across the bay and get back before the currents swept his boat away. He knew the weather out to sea by the way the waves were breaking and by the hollow roar to be heard on calm days. The "rote" is what islanders called that roar, and it meant a storm happening somewhere out there. He reckoned hurricanes by the heavy swell and knew how many days out at sea they were. Joshua read those signs like a second language. He'd grown up hearing the local weather omens: "A solely sou'westerly wind drives the big ocean swell up the bay." "An easterly wind can blow a screaming gale, but when the wind is down, the sea is over."

Joshua longed to be at sea in whatever kind of weather, but for the next few years the sea came to him. He would learn its mysteries from his island. In many ways his island *was* his boat — but a boat that had gone hard aground.

I had a fair schooling in the so-called "hard ships" on the hard Western Ocean, and in the years there I do not remember having once been "called out of my name.". . . I did not live among angels, but among men who could be roused. My wish was, though, to please the officers of my ship wherever I was, and so I got on. Dangers there are, to be sure, on the sea as well as on the land, but the intelligence and skill God gives to man reduce these to a minimum.

To face the elements is, to be sure, no light matter when the sea is in its grandest mood. You must then know the sea, and know that you know it, and not forget that it was made to be sailed over.

— J.S., *Sailing Alone*

2

Learning
the Ropes

I came "over the bows" and not in through the cabin windows.
— J.S., *Sailing Alone*

The smashing of the ship's model had slammed shut a door between Joshua Slocum and his father. Two years later, at fourteen, Joshua tried to escape from his father's control by finding work as a cook on a fishing schooner, but the job was short-lived. As he recalled years later, "I was not long in the galley for the crew mutinied at the appearance of my first duff, and 'chucked me out' before I had a chance to shine as a culinary artist." So the teenager returned to the island and to his father's wrath at such an openly defiant and disobedient act. Josh received a good thrashing and was put back to the grueling bootshop routine.

Life would never be the same for Joshua Slocum. He had tasted independence and had tried out his sealegs on a voyage. He had a sailor's spirit, and his days on land were numbered. Once he had been across the bay, he wanted to go across the sea, and then around the world. But he remained under his father's watchful eye for another two years, until his mother, Sarah Jane, died on February 16, 1860, four days before Joshua's sixteenth birthday. Slocum never wrote about his mother or the role she played in making life with his father tolerable. Perhaps her soft presence provided a buffer for the angry lad, for his life changed dramatically with her passing.

When he turned sixteen, Slocum bolted from the island on the first schooner that would give him employment. He set out on the big sea adventure with an island chum named Cheney. Years later the two would meet again, this time as successful captains with their own commands. But now, as two green adolescents, they had to begin climbing the ranks from the very bottom. They signed on as foremast hands on a deal drogher sailing to Dublin from Saint John, New Brunswick. Deal droghers were ships, often old and in poor shape, that carried a full load of timber below and on deck. Because the ship's condition was considered precarious, the timber was often chained to the hull so that no matter what happened, the wood would stay afloat and the cargo would be saved.

Conditions were rough, and at sixteen the boys would have been shocked by the sight of the derelict crew that had been rounded up by the less than reputable shipping rings that controlled shipboard employment. Years later, Victor Slocum wrote about his father's first day on the drogher. According to Victor, the Brier Island teens were the first crewmen to board, and they watched as the crimps — the men who ran the rings — delivered roaring drunk sailors to the ship atop a wagon and threw them into their berths. Cheney and Slocum were the only sober crewmen. Sober or not, they were soon locked into the strict regimen and hierarchy of life aboard British ships.

In the nineteenth century that life was rigidly defined by class distinctions. Some young men began their sailing days as apprentices, coming "in through the cabin windows," as Slocum described their privileged status. In fact, apprentices had guaranteed their places on the ship's crew by paying a premium. In contrast, Slocum and Cheney arrived "over the bows," the hard way, and were classed as mere foremast hands. Apprentices' territory was the aft of the ship with the officers; foremast hands were relegated to the forecastle near the bow of the ship. In this often dirty area, the mates slept and relaxed during their free time. The fo'c'sle could be crowded, with sailors gathered to smoke, tell stories and do their mending. The captain lived aft, often in luxury, and visited the forecastle only for emergencies.

The sailors who came "over the bows" were expected to prove their sea worth at every turn. Cheney and Slocum were eager and earnest novices, and for them the sea was a kind of practical university. Slocum had left school at ten, and most of his education thereafter was firsthand, on the ocean. The sea, while a good teacher, could be a harsh one that made no allowances for inexperience. Slocum's immediate and keenest interest was navigation — a skill he was to develop to such a high level that in later years he seemed always to know intuitively where his boat was sailing. He practiced taking sights with the ship's sextant and calculating locations according to the positions of celestial bodies. Aboard his first ships, Slocum got to take measurements and to apply the theory he was teaching himself from a British book, *Epitome of Navigation* by J.W. Norie. Victor wrote that his father's first navigational equipment consisted of the more modern sextant and an ebony pig-yoke with an ivory arc — the old wooden octant that was still in use on ships, but limited in the range of angles it could measure. Slocum was an eager student and learned how to "shoot the sun and the moon" — that is, to measure the height of the sun and make lunar observations. As he became more proficient with celestial navigation, he became assistant to the captain and chief mate in making the daily sightings needed for determining longitude.

When it came to obeying orders, Slocum and Cheney were reliable workers. Slocum later wrote about some of their stern taskmasters. After his first voyage to Dublin, he sailed to Liverpool, where he joined the crew of the British vessel *Tanjore*, bound for China. Slocum chronicled the harsh working conditions imposed by Captain Martin. He recalled the crew's hardships of "working the ice cargo in the cool of the mornings and evenings and then aloft or, worse still, over the ship's side in the heat of the days, which in Hong Kong in the summer, as it was, was [so] intensely hot several of the crew died." Slocum and Cheney survived the inhumane treatment, although later Slocum sued and recovered three months' extra wages. After leaving Hong Kong, Slocum fell ill with fever and had to be left behind in a hospital in the next port, Batavia (now Djakarta). The *Tanjore* sailed on, and Slocum had to find another ship to join after he recuperated. Victor records that in Batavia "he found a good friend in Captain Airy of the steamship *Soushay*, who rescued him from that pest hole of the Dutch East Indies."

Slocum soon got his strength back. At 180 pounds he was considered a "husky youth," according to Victor. He was now eighteen years old, and his two years of sailing blue water had given him enough experience to become second mate. Again he was sailing between Liverpool and the Dutch East Indies. While he still preferred routine deck jobs, much of his work would have involved climbing the rigging to make continuous adjustments. This was often dangerous, especially in an uncertain sea. Slocum almost died when he was twenty, while working aboard the bark *Agra*. A later newspaper account reported, "He was on the upper topsail gathering in sail when a gust of wind pitched him off. He landed first on the main yard

26

and cut a gash over his left eye — and that's all that happened. He had [the eye] patched." He was to get rid of the patch shortly after, but the scar was always visible.

Slocum was moving steadily along toward what he referred to as "the goal of happiness." Part of the step-by-step climb was a break with his roots; he changed the spelling of his surname from Slocombe to Slocum to make it appear more American than the United Empire Loyalist spelling his family had retained. He declared San Francisco his hailing port and around 1865 became an American citizen, or what he called a "naturalized Yankee." There were exciting opportunities along the west coast, and Slocum saw his in the salmon fishery. His first business venture was with a boatbuilder named Griffin. Together they fished the Columbia River and successfully designed and built a gill-netting boat, which they sold at a good price at the end of the season.

Slocum never was much interested in the fishing end of things, but of boatbuilding he wrote, "Next in attractiveness, after seafaring, came ship-building. I longed to be master in both professions." Prophetic words from a twenty-year-old. His mastery of shipbuilding, however, would manifest itself mainly in an ingenious knack for recasting new from old. His time on the west coast gave him plenty of ideas about how to build efficient ocean-going craft. While heavily involved in sea otter hunting and fur trading along the Oregon and British Columbia coasts, he kept a journal of his daily observations. That journal has never been found, although Victor's keen descriptions of it suggest that his father's interest in writing began around this time. Victor also remembered Slocum's fascination with Native people. Slocum's acquired knowledge of Native boatbuilding techniques later served him well.

According to Victor, "The lure of his inshore adventure did not last long, though it was not without its profits. My father's real ambition was the command of a ship, which he had promised himself when first coming ashore in San Francisco." By twenty-five, Slocum had realized that ambition, having risen through the ranks — or as Slocum put it, having "come up through the hawse hole" — to become a captain. In October and November of 1869, Slocum was in command of the coasting schooner *Montana*, which ran between San Francisco and the pumpkin-growing town of Half Moon Bay. The vessel was about seventy-five feet in length and carried a cargo of potatoes, oats and barley back to the city. In his new capacity as ship captain, Slocum proved himself highly capable of commanding a vessel and overseeing a financial enterprise. It was his task to find cargo and transport it safely. His success led to the offer of a second command, this time working for Nicholas Bichard out of San Francisco. The 110-foot barkentine *Constitution* was a clear step up for the young captain. San Francisco shipping records for April 13, 1870, show Slocum in charge of a cargo of cotton seeds, lumber, machinery and shingles headed for Guayamas, Mexico. In August of that year his vessel headed for Carmen Island in the Gulf of California with a load of salt. By mid-October the *Constitution* was back in home port being loaded for Sydney, Australia, and Fiji. She was cleared to set sail on November 2, 1870. This was an eventful trip for Slocum. He arrived in Sydney as a bachelor with prospects and soon attracted the notice of Virginia Albertina Walker, whom he married, after a whirlwind courtship, on January 31, 1871.

Virginia was twenty-one years old, the eldest daughter of Mr. and Mrs. William Walker. She was born on Staten Island, New York. Soon after her birth her father caught gold fever and headed for California; later he followed his dreams again to the Australian gold mines. Virginia grew up in an adventurous and risk-taking but cultured household. Her father was active in amateur theatre, and her sister was an opera singer. According to Victor Slocum's memories of family stories, "Virginia was heard to remark that as soon as she saw Josh she knew he was just the kind of a man she wanted, not the stuffy sort she saw in conventional Sydney society."

Virginia's younger brother, George, sailed with the Slocums on their honeymoon trip. Early February saw the *Constitution* heading back to America from Sydney, arriving in San Francisco on May 4 with a cargo of coal and tomatoes. The newlyweds were in port for only two days before setting sail again in a new home. Shipping records show that Slocum assumed a second Bichard command, the *Washington*, a 110-foot, 332-ton bark. Slocum's proposal of a honeymoon fishing trip in Alaska would have been considered far from romantic by most young brides, but Virginia was intrigued. The salmon fishing went well, although Slocum and his crew were sailing in relatively unknown waters and the ship ran aground on unmarked shoals. Records indicate that around June 21, 1871, the *Washington* dragged her anchors. Two hundred miles from Kodiak, on the southern Alaska coast, she became stranded in a gale. She was pushed high up on a sandbar at Cook Inlet, and there she sat. Slocum set out immediately to solve the problem. Transporting the salmon catch before it spoiled was a mammoth task, but Slocum was undaunted. He thrived on challenges, and built the first of his makeshift rescue boats, a thirty-five-foot whaleboat, in the camp.

The Alaskan portion of the honeymoon ended with the appearance of a revenue cutter (a forerunner of the Coast Guard), which offered assistance. Virginia boarded the cutter and sailed on to Kodiak while her husband stayed behind with the *Washington*. He oversaw the transfer of the salmon catch from the bark to the whaleboat and into the holds of a couple of sealers. While the sealers left for San Francisco with his cargo, Slocum set out to rejoin Virginia. The newlyweds ended their honeymoon cruise aboard a Russian bark, which took them and their crew home safely.

Mrs. Slocum sat busily engaged with her little girl at needle-work. Her baby boy was fast asleep in his Chinese cradle. An older son was putting his room in order and a second son was sketching. The captain's stateroom is a commodious apartment, furnished with a double berth which one might mistake for a black walnut bedstead: a transom upholstered like a lounge, a library, chairs, carpets, wardrobe, and the chronomets. This room is abaft the main cabin, which is furnished like a parlor. In this latter apartment are the square piano, center table, sofa, easy chairs and carpets, while on the walls hang several oil paintings.

In front of the parlor is the dining room, which together with the other rooms, exhibit a neatness of which only a woman's hand is capable. The captain's baby is the captain's pride and bears an honored name. General Garfield acknowledged the compliment in an autographed letter to the child.

— From "An American Family Afloat,"
New York *Tribune*, 1882

3

True Love and a Family Afloat

Father took the wheel — mother stood by him. Her silence gave him confidence.
— Ben Aymar Slocum

Virginia Albertina Walker Slocum was as perfect a partner for Joshua Slocum as he could ever have imagined. She was beautiful and courageous, cultured and practical, strong-willed and gentle, and she was his strength. She was also adventurous enough to abandon big-city comforts and diversions for a rugged shipboard life as wife and mother. For as long as she lived, Virginia sailed the seas with her husband and stood loyally and inspirationally by his side through storms, mutinies, sorrows, blessings, losses and triumphs.

Virginia was an exceptional sea mate — and an able

navigator — but she was only one of scores of captain's wives who spent their lives at sea with their husbands. This trend was dictated in large part by the fact that the age of sail was dying. With steamers taking over the merchant trade, sailing vessels had to abandon their most common routes. Just to survive, captains had to take on freight wherever a cargo could be found and carry it to whichever out-of-the-way port it was bound. Captains and their crews were thankful for the work, but often it meant years sailing unpredictable routes, to ports too small and isolated to enjoy regular steamer service. Many captains had to spend years at a stretch at sea, and for them it made financial and emotional sense to take their wives along. Also, keeping a house on land was often an unaffordable luxury. Thus, many families had only the vessel to call their home.

Virginia was a willing traveling companion, even after the fiasco of her salmon-fishing honeymoon and her temporary separation from Joshua after the *Washington* was stranded in Alaskan waters. Contrary to all other published material regarding the newlyweds' life aboard the barkentine *Constitution*, the shipping records show clearly that after losing the *Washington*, Slocum never sailed for Bichard again. A listing of September 2, 1871, names a Captain Robertson as commanding the *Constitution*. However, in January 1872 the company must have allowed the Slocums to live aboard his old command at dock, as the city directory for that year gives their address as *Constitution*, Hathaway's Wharf, in San Francisco. There, the couple became new parents when Virginia gave birth to a son, Victor Joshua. The next nine years saw annual changes in the way of family additions and new commands.

It isn't until November 14, 1872, that Slocum surfaces as a captain on the Shipping Intelligence page in the *Daily Alta* in California. The small family moved aboard the *B. Aymar*, a slightly larger vessel than Slocum's previous commands, being 128 feet in length. That November the *B. Aymar* sailed for Burrard Inlet carrying coal and oil. During 1873 the Slocums made several Pacific crossings from San Francisco to the Orient. Again, the *Daily Alta* records the *B. Aymar*'s business and whereabouts: on June 17, 1873, she was bound for Swatow on the Chinese coast between Hong Kong and Amoy. Slocum reported strong winds in the South China Sea as his vessel began the sixty-four-day crossing back to home port. The *B. Aymar* arrived in San Francisco on August 21 with a cargo of 8,800 bags of sugar. The family stayed in port until September 24, when the vessel set sail for Melbourne carrying canned goods, lumber, salmon, broom corn and a pregnant Virginia. It was common for captains' wives to make a passage when they were pregnant, knowing they would probably give birth at sea. They accepted the possibility that their labour might be difficult and dangerous, and might begin in extremely rough conditions on a stormy sea. Depending on how threatening the sea was at the time, they would be lucky to have the help of even one of the mates. Such hardships were part and parcel of being a captain's wife. Virginia made it to Australia, where the Slocums enjoyed a stopover in Sydney with Virginia's parents. Here their second child, another son, was born on December 21, 1873; he was promptly named Benjamin Aymar in honor of their ocean home.

Victor's early impressions of family life aboard that ship were probably based on his mother's stories as she told them much later, as Victor would have been only two at the time. He recalled how his mother and father would stroll the deck during the second dogwatch before retiring below. It was on the *B. Aymar* that Victor got his toddler sealegs. His childhood memories included Christmas celebrations afloat. Santa Claus even came to Amoy (now known as Xiamen), where he found the children's stockings hanging around the cabin's mizzenmast. Victor recalled that Santa "never missed, no matter what the sea or the country." The child probably was not in the least surprised to find that the kindly old man had brought him Chinese toys and other Oriental goodies.

Victor was unaware of the many dangers of sailing in the early 1880s. There were still cannibals in the New Hebrides and on the Solomon Islands. In Sydney, locals still told the horrendous and tragic tale of John Williams, the missionary who was killed by cannibals in the New Hebrides in 1839. The sailing life on Chinese and Malaysian seas was rife with danger. Besides cannibal attacks, there were sudden typhoons to fear. On top of this, crews were always on the lookout for pirates, who preyed on boats that were in trouble — perhaps becalmed, or aground on a sandbar. Having found one, they would swoop down, vulturelike, and kill all on board. Pirate ships figured in many stories told on those waters. One was of the clipper ship the *Living Age*, bound for New York from Shanghai with a rich cargo of silks and teas. She ran aground on a reef in the East China Sea for almost two months, during which time a Chinese junk came into view. The crew's panic, while extreme, was justified by past accounts of the pirates' savagery. The second mate of the *Living Age* later recalled, "The cry arose at once: 'The pirates are waiting for daylight to come aboard and murder us.' . . . The crew gave way to despair . . . and one old sailor went raving crazy. The poor old man, with white hair streaming in the wind, stood up on a spar singing and shrieking at the top of his voice, adding to the terror of the rest." The sighting proved to be a false one, but such was the fear that pirates inspired. Slocum and Virginia well knew the treacheries found in those waters. Slocum met up with one renowned ruffian, Bully Hayes, who regaled the captain and his wife with tales of his unscrupulous deeds and pitiless acts. Hayes bragged about the part he played in South Sea slavery, which he called "blackbirding." At one point he lured an entire congregation aboard his ship in the name of fellowship, then immediately shackled them and boarded them up in the hold.

A third child was born to the Slocums in June 1875. Jessie Lena arrived while the boat was lying at anchor in a Philippine harbor. In Manila, shortly after the birth, the company sold the *B. Aymar* and asked Slocum to stay in the Philippines long enough to build a ship for inter-island trading. For the third time in his career, Slocum was happily employed as a shipwright. Since the best timber was most plentiful outside Manila, Slocum and his young family made a sixty-mile trek to the seaside village of Olongapo. Slocum's first task was to construct a safe and livable jungle hut. He built an elevated *nipa*-thatched house with a floor seven feet above the ground. There was ample room beneath it for pigs and fowl to roam, and its height gave some measure of security. Even so, Victor recalled their modest domain as creeping with venomous creatures: "Up through the cracks in the split bamboo flooring could crawl centipedes, scorpions, and even a small boa if it took a notion to come in at night and hang down from the rafters, tail first. We found that both centipedes and scorpions had a habit of crawling into our clothes and getting into our shoes while they were not in use, so it was routine to shake and search everything while dressing in the morning." The air was stifling, and everyone, especially the children, was cranky from the heavy, damp heat. Virginia not only had her everyday motherly duties but also had to keep her inquisitive little pack from touching or eating poisonous plants and tangling with boas and other reptiles. Victor remembered thick forest noises rising up from the crocodile-filled swamps, which only fueled his normal childhood fantasies and fears. He later recalled, "Only in forests like those in the Philippines can one hear such a nocturnal roar."

How Virginia survived such conditions with an infant, a toddler and a six-year-old is hard to fathom. Perhaps what saved her was her love of the wilderness. As a new bride she had been enthusiastic at the prospect of seeing Alaska, and she seemed to continue to welcome new and rugged experiences. She was part Native American on her mother's side, and her son Ben Aymar recalled her being proud of her "Indian blood." Virginia was a horse-woman and loved to be in the outdoors. Ben Aymar described horses as his mother's passion, one that began during her childhood in Australia, where she "was trained to ride horses and on weekends, she rode with associates into the Blue Mountains, exploring and sleeping on the ground much as the natives did. She told of cooking eggs in a piece of cloth held in a boiling hot spring."

In the oppressive Philippine jungle with her three small charges she was every bit as resilient. She was ever resourceful and alert to dangers, and her instincts were usually dead on. Some of the Chinese workers in the area resented Captain Slocum's shipbuilding commission and plotted to murder his family in their sleep while he was away in Manila. Virginia awoke to shouting and the light of torches all around the hut. To her relief, it was a group of friendly Tagals come to protect her and the children.

They had gotten wind of the plot and rallied to the family's defense.

The next target for the angry Chinese faction was the launching of Slocum's vessel. They blocked the launch by shifting the ways out of line. Again the Tagals came to the Slocums' rescue, this time with their teams of water buffalo, which they lined up to drag the ship down to the water. As payment for the steamer, Slocum was given a seventy-two-foot schooner, the *Pato*, which is Spanish for duck. The *Pato* had neither deck nor cabin, but the family agreed that life aboard a much smaller boat than they had been used to was preferable to life on shore in Olongapo. Virginia, pregnant with twins, boarded the *Pato*. Slocum picked up work immediately, and over the next months they made numerous inter-island trips. After salvaging a cargo of tea, camphor and silks from a British bark stranded on a reef, the *Pato* continued to Hong Kong, where Slocum decided to take the small boat and his family into the codfishing waters of the Sea of Okhotsk. During the fishing trip Virginia gave birth to her twins. In a letter to a business associate, Slocum betrayed little fatherly sentiment in his recollection of the event: "Two of my children were born on this voyage while at Petropolanska; they were two months old when we arrived at Oregon — four days old when we began to take in fish . . . Yes Sir, we had a stirring voyage and alto-gether a delightful time on the fishing grounds for every codfish that came in over the rail was a quarter of a dollar

— clear." Slocum pronounced the fishing trip "a great success"; the *Daily Astorian* for September 21, 1877, listed the *Pato*'s catch as 23,000 fine cod. But the rough fishing life had a price for Slocum's family — the twins died in infancy. Years later Ben Aymar could only reflect that "the ocean is no place to raise a family."

Slocum made life a little more livable aboard the *Pato*. With the fishing money he bought a small cargo of wood and built a good cabin for the vessel. He wrote that he also "made all comfortable outfits necessary." The *Pato* sailed from Oregon on March 30, 1878 bound for Honolulu. The Hawaii Public Archives place the schooner *Pato* on three runs between Honolulu and Kohala though May and early June. On one arrival in Honolulu, Slocum impressed a crowd on the docks. He raced to catch a departing mail boat that had left behind a bag of mail. She was sailing at a fast clip, but the *Pato* easily caught up to her. The small triumph brought this fast little schooner a moment of glory, and Slocum accepted an offer of five thousand dollars for her. He wrote to a friend that the payment was "all in twenty dollar gold pieces, ugh! if I had them now."

With their family home sold, the Slocums returned by steamer to their home port of San Francisco, where the captain bought his next command, the 109-foot bark *Amethyst*. For the next three years they travelled the Pacific with timber, coal, and even a hold full of gunpowder out of Shanghai. This voyaging was over many rough seas, and Slocum was well aware of the *Amethyst*'s age.

Built in 1822, she would have been one of the oldest American vessels still sailing those seas. These were difficult passages for Virginia, who was again pregnant. Slocum engaged his brother Ingram as the ship's cook and his sister Ella to be with Virginia. Virginia had a second daughter in 1879. The baby lived only a short time, her death coming in a small Philippine port where the *Amethyst* was loading a cargo of timber. The death of her child in this squalid foreign port hit Virginia hard. Her grief was excruciating and she made a slow recovery. She poured out her sorrow to the only person who might understand its depths — her own mother. On July 17, 1879, from Laguemanac in the Philippines, a frail and distraught Virginia wrote:

Dearest Mother & all

You must excuse for writing you so short a letter. I have been verey sick ever since the 15 of last month. I feel a little better now it is such a strange sicken. I have not been able to eat anything till lately. Dear Josh has got me every thing he can think of my hand shakes so now I can hardley write. Dear Mother my Dear little baby died the other day & I expect that is partley the cause. every time her teeth would start to come she would cry all night if I would cut them through the gum would grow togather again. the night she died she had one convulsion after another I gave her a hot bath and some medecine and was quite

41

quiet infact I thought she was going to come around when she gave a quiet sigh and was gone. Dear Josh embalmed her in brandy for we would not leave her in this horid place she did look so pretty after she died Dearest Mother I canot write any more
/s/ Virginia

Embalming a child in liquor, as Slocum did, was a common seafaring practice. Aboard a temperance vessel the method of preserving was to coat the child in tar. Both practices allowed a grieving family to bury their own in a home port. A return to San Francisco would probably have strengthened Virginia's health, but she improved without it. By the next year she was back by her husband's side on deck. As they sailed under full sail into Hong Kong harbor, they had to steer clear of three warships and a full-rigged vessel. Everyone expected an epic collision, but Slocum made it into port safely. Ben Aymar later wrote what had given him the courage: "Father took the wheel — mother stood by him. Her silence gave him confidence." Slocum apologized to one of the British admirals for the close call. He had cleared the warship only by inches. The admiral replied by commending his great navigational skills: "Any man who can sail a ship under full sail through a passageway too dangerous to contemplate need not apologize to the entire British Navy." Slocum and "the lady who stood beside" were invited aboard.

In March 1881, the seafaring couple and their three small children sailed again into Hong Kong harbor. Here Virginia gave birth to her last child, a son named James Abram Garfield Slocum. They were off again at the end of the month, and poor Virginia must have dreaded the destination — once again she would be in Laguemanac with an infant. But this time all went well, and early that May the family arrived back in Hong Kong with a load of lumber. On May 23, a Captain Kenney arrived in Hong Kong from Cardiff on a boat that caught Captain Slocum's eye. Slocum was smitten by her. She was the *Northern Light*, built in 1873 at Quincy, Massachusetts. The 220-foot ship indeed looked grand, with her three masts and three decks and the added elegance of a figurehead. "As beautiful as her name" is the way Slocum viewed her. The square rigger was easily five times the size of Slocum's vessel.

Slocum could not resist, and a transaction was made in Hong Kong harbor. Slocum sold his family's home, the *Amethyst*, and became part-owner of the *Northern Light*. Years later, Slocum would reflect on his years as captain of the tall-masted ship as "his best command." He added, "I had a right to be proud of her, for at that time — in the 1880's — she was the finest American sailing vessel afloat."

The succession of boats had been a strange environment for raising young children: livestock in pens on the deckhouse roof, a grand piano bolted to the floor, and

43

Slocum's vast library of over five hundred books. According to Victor, the orderly bookcases made the cabin "very much like the study of a literary worker or a college professor." Slocum also read poetry, the classics and essays, but his passion was for books of sea adventure: "He simply revelled in the tales of Sinbad the Sailor," Victor would remember.

At the age of thirty-seven, Captain Joshua Slocum seemed to be leading a charmed life. As a master mariner, he had reached the pinnacle of his career. His professional success had come without apparent domestic sacrifice. There is no doubt that his wife was the reason he had attained this rare balance and could live life on his own terms with few compromises. Virginia was the perfect wife for Joshua, an adventurous and hardworking traveling companion. She educated the children, holding lessons every day from nine until noon, and buying books at ports along the way. Victor recalled a German comic book being purchased in Hong Kong, for educational purposes. She also had the children memorize classical poetry. Slocum was their inspiration, as he was a great reciter and knew several verses of Coleridge's "The Rime of the Ancient Mariner" by heart. He also made scrapbooks with amusing and odd bits of news pasted in. Jessie remembered her father doing "a lot of chuckling over them" and that the books were used as part of their schooling. "Father and mother always encouraged us in reading any and all books," was Jessie's memory of her

English classes on board ship. Virginia was musical and played the piano, harp and guitar; she also sang and danced. On Saturdays she enforced a "field day," during which the children were expected not only to clean and tidy up but also to mend. And she taught them their Anglican catechism during the shipboard Sunday school. When it came to disciplining her lively charges and keeping order in the floating schoolhouse, Virginia kept a switch prominently displayed over a picture in the cabin.

Virginia's energy and verve were matched by her fearlessness. Ben Aymar remembered how he lured sharks to the stern of the boat with a tin can tied on a string; Virginia would then shoot them with her .32 caliber revolver. Her son wrote of her prowess: "How I loved to see her do it — and without any signs on her part of showing superior skill." Of her culinary abilities, he recalled, "She was an excellent cook of the rough and ready sort." Jessie wrote, "Mother was a remarkable woman, not many had the stamina she had and I might add, there are none today who lived as she had to. She lived truly as the Book of Ruth says . . ."

After Garfield's birth, the *Northern Light* sailed to Manila to load a cargo of sugar and hemp. The Slocums and their crew of twenty-five stopped in Java for supplies of fresh produce, and Victor recalled the bountiful spectacle of a "deck piled with yams, sweet potatoes, baskets of eggs and crates of chickens." He also remembered how the rat population was kept under control: "We had monkeys galore as well as musk deer and a civet, called a musk cat." The *Northern Light* made Liverpool by Christmas, boasting the largest single shipment of sugar into port. Victor recalled the glorious sound of church bells ringing through the fog and what a joyous effect it had on everyone aboard after six months at sea with little more than passing glimpses of land. Virginia, who never lost a teaching opportunity, took the children to see the sugar refinery as well as the factory where the hemp was made into twisted ropes and cordage.

After the *Northern Light* had her barnacles removed and bowsprit replaced, the vessel crossed the Atlantic for New York. She docked at Pier 23 after sailing under the new and soon to be opened Brooklyn Bridge. On their arrival back in the *Northern Light*'s home port, the Slocums were the toast of New York City. A reporter for the New York *Tribune* gave an account of their shipboard lifestyle in a feature titled "An American Family Afloat." Virginia and Joshua were glowingly portrayed as the "typical American sailor who has a typical American wife to accompany him on his long voyages, and to make his cabin as acceptable a home as he could have on shore." The article went on to give a rather glamorized account of life afloat for this "typical" American couple: "The tautness, trimness and cleanliness of this vessel, from keelson to truck and stem to stern, are features not common on merchant ships. The neat canvas cover over the steering-wheel bearing the vessel's name and hailing port, worked with silk, is the handiwork of the captain's wife. Descending to the main cabin, one wonders whether or not he is in some comfortable apartment ashore."

The New York welcome was a moment of glory for Slocum, and he wanted his father to witness this tangible evidence of his wayward son's success. John Slocombe, now in his seventies, together with his second wife and their teenage daughter, Emma, arrived from their home outside Lunenburg, Nova Scotia. The reunion of father and son was filled with pleasant memories from twenty-two years earlier, the last time they had seen each other on Brier Island. Emma stayed for seven weeks with the captain and his family and was moved by Virginia's hospitality. Years later, she recalled the impact that Virginia's generous and energetic spirit had on a young country girl: "Virginia was most kind to me . . . took me sight seeing to the Historical and Art Museums, also bought some nice things for me. I'd seen nothing but happiness between Josh and Virginia, perhaps I was too young to discern anything else." Virginia and the captain gave her a memorable vacation. "Two incidents come to mind — one was a visit to the Harper Publishing House with Captain Slocum, Virginia and myself. We were escorted all through the plant which was great to me. I understand Josh done some writings that Harper published — the other are going to Coney Island and Manhattan Beach and hearing Sousa's band of 100 pieces — that also was great."

47

Emma returned to Nova Scotia, and the *Northern Light* set sail in August 1882 for Yokohama with a hold full of case oil. The trip had minor troubles from the beginning. In the glowing account of life portrayed in the *Tribune* feature, one line stands out as foreshadowing the dangers ahead for the Slocum family on the *Northern Light*. The reporter reflected on "two striking thoughts, one that American sailing ships are becoming obsolete and the other, that so few American sailors can be found." The latter was a hard truth for Slocum. Finding a hardworking and reputable American crew was next to impossible, for young men with the gumption and necessary wit were heading West. Slocum was left with less than choice pickings: an array of social outcasts, from drunkards to ex-convicts. To make matters worse, the shipping rings found in every port were still in tight control, and the crews they recruited were often delivered to the ship drunken and unwilling. Slocum knew that these were the men who would accompany his young family around the world, and he may well have seen trouble on the horizon.

A malfunctioning rudder brought them into New London, Connecticut, for minor repairs. Once in port, a cocky portion of the crew took liberties with the rules outlined by the shipping rings. They argued that the voyage was technically over once they made port and that they were entitled to leave ship with their advanced wages. Hell broke loose, and mutiny was in the air. Within minutes, the chief officer of the *Northern Light* was fatally stabbed in a scuffle to subdue the mutineers' ringleader. A swift-thinking and courageous Virginia was at her husband's side, covering him with a revolver in each hand. The crew was searched, the Coast Guard was called in, the mutineers were arrested and the remaining troublemakers were incarcerated aboard ship. Slocum secured a new chief officer.

In December the discordant crew and their troubled captain were given a strange opportunity to bond together in a humanitarian act. Two weeks before Christmas, as they were sailing through the South Sea Islands, a small open craft was spotted floating in the middle of the ocean. As the *Northern Light* drew near, Slocum saw five desperate-looking souls aboard. When they were thrown a line and hoisted up to the *Northern Light*'s deck, the gravity of the situation became apparent. The four men and one woman were starving and near death. The survivors were offered brandy to warm them, but two refused, even in their weakened state, explaining that they were missionaries. (At that time in the South Seas, "missionary" meant anyone who had adopted the Christian faith.) After being given the chance to rest, they told their gruesome tale.

They had begun as a party of twelve Gilbert Islanders on a mission from their king to a neighboring Polynesian island. On their return trip they encountered a storm that set their twenty-one-foot open boat drifting. For over a month the islanders had been "at the scant mercy of a changing monsoon." All that time they had lived on dried bananas, what flying fish landed aboard and the diminished remains of their water supply. Over one-third of their water had been lost immediately when a jug smashed. Slocum wanted to return the survivors to their island, but the *Northern Light* was drifting westward on a strong equatorial current. The party refused to be put off on another island along the way, so Slocum took them to Japan. He felt he had no other moral choice in the matter and was inspired by the fictional adventures of Sinbad the sailor. The passage he recalled read, "When we behold a ship-wrecked person on the shore of the sea, . . . we take him with us and feed him and give him drink, and if he be naked we clothe him, and when we arrive at the port of safety we give him something of our property as a present, and act toward him with kindness and favor for the sake of God whose name be exalted."

They arrived in Japan in mid-January. The little band was impressed by the look of the snowy countryside, but the cold winter "racked their joints with pain." Virginia had been attending to the needs of the one lady islander; now, with this change of climate she found warmer clothing for the five of them. The odd assortment of old coats and poorly fitting mismatched suits for the men, and the dress and woollen shawl for the woman, came from the family's "slop chest." Slocum confessed that he was "at a loss to know what to do with these waifs of the ocean"; they seemed so helpless and out of place in Japan. Finally, he secured passage for them to their home island on the mission ship *Morning Star*.

After unloading the cargo of case oil in Japan, the *Northern Light* headed for the Philippines to pick up a cargo of hemp and sugar bound for Liverpool. Sailing through the Sunda Strait in August 1883, she passed by Krakatoa, a volcanic island that was then erupting. Although the initial eruption had been in May, "paroxysmal explosions" were still occurring. Stones and ash were shooting seventeen miles or farther out of the volcano's mouth, whipping up the seas and causing fifty-foot waves to crash around the *Northern Light*. Ben Aymar later reflected on the treacherous passage: "Had we been three days later in that region we would have been suffocated by the fumes." For many days to follow, an ash-covered *Northern Light* made her way in a dense haze through seas of floating pumice stone.

The spewing ash was visible around the world in the form of intensely brilliant red sunsets. Their seeming glory were an ironic portent for the captain and his beloved Virginia. Although reckoned to be a sailor's delight, those beautiful sunsets were really an illusion, an omen of an uncertain dawn.

Washington D.C. 10th Feb. 1885

Dear Mother

. . . I feel most of the time that Virginia is with me and help-ing me and that her noble soul is helping support her mother . . . and I doubt not at all but that she is with you and me more now than before — It has pained me tho to have to give up my beautiful wife when we wer gettin so many enjoyable friends and gettin in comfortable circumstances — I would have had some money in hand by this time if I hadnt got crazy and runn my vessel onshore. As it is now I am just swimming out of trouble on borowd money . . .

The children are just lovely and healthy. I shall strive to do well by my loved ones children I shall try mother to make her Happy in Heaven she was I know happy with me here — she knew that I loved her dearely, and always loved to be in her company — What a terrible separation this has been to me I sen you a photo of or dear ones grave — the name Virginia is in gold and shall be kept in gold as long as I live

Good bye Dear mother. We will write you from Brazil.

> *Yours in affliction*
> */s/ Josh*

— From Joshua Slocum's letter to Virginia's mother

4

Ebb and Flow

When she died, father never recovered. He was like a ship with a broken rudder.
— Garfield Slocum

Off the Cape of Good Hope, fierce seas twisted the *Northern Light*'s rudderhead completely off and she started leaking through the seams in the topsides. As water seeped into the lower hold, the cargo of sugar melted. Pumping the bilge was not feasible: it would have been like pumping out corn syrup. In an effort to lower the ship's center of gravity and prevent her from keeling over, Slocum jettisoned bales of hemp from the middle deck. Slowly, in heavy seas, the vessel righted. Eventually the *Northern Light* made it safely to a South African port, where she spent two months being overhauled.

Once again murderous trouble was brewing for Captain

Slocum. Before the *Northern Light* sailed, one of the crew took ill and the captain had to find a replacement — not an easy task in a foreign port. The new second mate was Henry A. Slater, an ex-convict who, it is believed, signed on after arranging with other crew members to murder Slocum and take over the *Northern Light*. Whatever the truth in this, Slater tried to incite a mutiny shortly after the vessel left port. Slocum could afford no further setbacks. Taking the law into his own hands, he imprisoned Slater. The *Northern Light* sailed for another fifty-three days to New York with the ship's prisoner in irons. Later, in a newspaper article, Slocum described his approach to matters of discipline at sea. He referred to himself as "not a martinet, but I have ideas of how to run a ship. The old shipmasters treated their crews like intelligent beings, giving them plenty of leeway, but holding them with a strong hand in an emergency. That's my style." Years later, a relative of Slocum's, Grace Murray Brown, recalled a family story she had heard regarding Slocum's discipline: "My brother met an old seaman in some Chinese port who had sailed under the captain. He said Captain Slocum was considered a hard man but no one ever felt unsafe under his command."

Slocum may not have considered himself a martinet, but the Slater affair was not about to blow over. As soon as his ship docked in New York harbor, Slocum was charged with false and cruel imprisonment, convicted on Slater's evidence and fined five hundred dollars. Slater was later to make apologies to Slocum. This sudden change of heart came about on January 12, 1884, in the form of a confession of sorts to B.S. Osborn, editor of the *Nautical Gazette*. Slater explained that he had learned later of some of the crew's manipulations in the whole ordeal: "I now see that both Captain Slocum and myself have been made the dupes of the very men who ought to have protected us, and the whole affair is made to get money out of Captain Slocum, to be distributed among them." His story made the Boston *Herald*, which reported, "'Slater said he came voluntarily,' said Mr. Osborn. 'He said he had put Slocum in a bad hole, and was in an equally bad hole himself. He said he did not know what he had been doing. He had signed lots of papers, but did not know what they were.'"

The confession did little to alter Slocum's image or end his plight. While he was busy defending himself in law-suits, another captain was employed to take charge of the *Northern Light*. Much more than Slocum's reputation had been affected; the episode at sea had cost him financially. Early in 1884, Slocum was forced to give up his part ownership in the beloved *Northern Light*. However, sell-ing his shares did little to alleviate his money problems. The ship needed a complete overhaul, and in the 1880s, doing such work on a sail-driven ship was no longer con-sidered economically practical. As sail gave way to steam, Slocum's career as a sailing master was fading. He would never again be master of a vessel to compare with "the magnificent ship." This point must have hit home when he got wind of the *Northern Light*'s fate: she had been reduced in size and put to work as a coal barge. Slocum reflected on the pitiful spectacle of his "best command" as she was "ignominiously towed by the nose from port to port." Her fate foreshadowed his own — Slocum's glory days had ended, and his fortunes had entered a downward spiral.

Slocum's pride in and love of sailing may have blinded him to his own best interests. Logically, he should have accepted the death of sail, adapted to the new technology of steam, and got on with his life. But the pathetic fate of the *Northern Light* did nothing to shatter his illusions. It would take a more dramatic event to make him recognize that his career as a sailing captain was over, and such an event was not long in coming. Slocum bought his final chance as a sailing master when he handed over the last of the gold pieces he had made from the *Pato* contract to purchase the *Aquidneck*, a bark a fraction of the size of the *Northern Light*. Built in Mystic, Connecticut, in 1865, the *Aquidneck* was only 138 feet long compared with the *Northern Light*'s 220 feet, and it had only one deck, to the previous ship's three. But Slocum was proud, and boasted that the fast and efficient little bark was "the nearest in perfection to beauty." While the *Aquidneck* was being made seaworthy, Virginia and the children stayed ashore with Slocum's sister in the Boston area. Her daughter, Jessie, would later reflect how important that break was for her mother: the perils of *Northern Light*'s tumultuous eighteen-month circumnavigation had exhausted her. Both Slocum biographer Walter Teller and Slocum's son Victor concluded that the "constant alarms" of the sea had undermined her health. Jessie herself wrote, "Her heart was not strong." Virginia's in-laws were impressed by the captain's wife, proclaiming her to be a "handsome woman." They noticed how in love Virginia and Joshua were and remarked that they "could be completely oblivious of everyone and everything if they could be together." This was after thirteen years of marriage, and after they had spent every day together in small quarters and under rough conditions.

Although Virginia had rested and relaxed, her health would never again be what it had been before babies, mutinies, strandings and court cases took their toll. Nevertheless, later that spring she sailed with her family aboard the repaired *Aquidneck*. Garfield, only three at the time, would remember the *Aquidneck* vividly and, years later, in a letter to Slocum biographer Walter Teller, he wrote down his impressions: "the stateroom doors painted light blue and gold . . . a skylight with colored glass, a canary that sang all day — a beautiful singer. Also a square grand piano bolted to the deck." The domestic arrangements of this floating home easily transcended the mundane. "The deck house was amidships: A fully equipped carpenter shop, galley, staterooms for the bosun, cook and carpenter. On the roof were pens for sheep, pigs and fowl." Victor also remembered the *Aquidneck*, and seems to have inherited his father's knack for embellishment when he proclaimed the bark to be "as close to a yacht as a merchantman could be."

The passage south to Pernambuco, on Brazil's eastern tip, was clear sailing. The young family even stopped to picnic in a coconut grove. But during the sail south along the coast for Buenos Aires, life aboard ship fell apart for the Slocums. Viriginia became ill, stopped all domestic work, and took to her bed. Her last sight of land was Santa Catarina Island. Garfield later remembered that his once vibrant mother had no energy or desire to take up her embroidery or her tapestry: "She left her needle where she stopped." In Buenos Aires, Slocum hoped to pick up a cargo bound for Australia. Virginia was weak, and she wished to go home to Sydney. Before he left for shore, he and his wife agreed on a signal that would call him back to the ship if the need arose. Ben Aymar later recalled that his mother got up for the first time in weeks and began to salt butter. Her conversation was filled with thoughts of going home. But it was not a call to her earthly home that had given Virginia her last few hours of renewed strength. She became increasingly weak and asked her twelve-year-old son to put up the signal. She knew Joshua would hurry back to the boat at the appearance of the blue-and-white letter "J" as soon as Ben Aymar hoisted it. Slocum returned by noon; Virginia was dead by eight o'clock that evening. It was July 25, 1884, less than a month before her thirty-fifth birthday. The cause of her death was not recorded, but family members speculated. While Virginia's brother, George Walker, felt that her early death was related to childbirth or possibly miscarriage, Ben Aymar remembered that "she often fainted when trouble disturbed her" and agreed with his sister that her death was a result of heart problems. Virginia Albertina Walker Slocum was buried in the English cemetery in Buenos Aires. Slocum recorded the details of her short life and death in Virginia's family Bible, adding the line, "Thy will be done not ours!"

Slocum was plunged into a state of utter grief. For fourteen years Virginia had been his guiding strength. He trusted her and had come to rely on her perceptive wisdom. Ben Aymar remembered the quiet power his mother's presence brought to family life: "Mother's eyes were a brilliant golden color — I have seen such eyes on our Golden Eagles — she knew how to use them, too, but very calmly." He later reflected that his mother "on many occasions had proved herself to be very psychic," and that Slocum "learned to understand her powers of intuition and . . . relied on them fully until she passed on." The young son and the other children watched helplessly as their father's "ill fortunes gathered rapidly from the time of her death."

The first of Slocum's "ill fortunes" came just a few days later when he ran his ship aground on a sandbar. He paid to clear the *Aquidneck* and quickly returned to

Boston with his little family, which was soon to split up. Ben Aymar vowed never to go to sea again — a decision perhaps fueled by grief and by the allure of a stable home life on land with his aunts, Joshua's sisters, who had known and liked his mother. He later recalled that his father wept at his young son's conviction. The youngest three Slocums remained with their aunts, Etta and Alice, in Massachusetts, while Victor stayed with his father on the *Aquidneck*. Slocum was stunned by his losses, and found that fending for himself without his wife's wisdom was a desperate struggle. He busied himself with fast passages between Baltimore and Pernambuco. On one voyage he was shipping a cargo of pianos and cordwood when the *Aquidneck* suddenly began pitching, which caused the cordwood to start rolling around and bowling into the pianos, causing their strings to snap. The symbolism is inescapable: Slocum, a man rocked by grief and ready to snap, was captaining a ship that was rocking and audibly snapping.

Garfield compared his grieving father to "a ship with a broken rudder." A ship without a rudder is at the mercy of the waves. If a big sea hits broadside, the ship broaches. A ship that cannot be steered can easily capsize or drift aimlessly. The only way to avoid disaster is to jury-rig some sort of rudder, and that is what Slocum did in the first year after Virginia's death, in his growing loneliness and melancholy.

In 1885, while he was visiting Ben Aymar, Jessie and

Garfield in Massachusetts, he met his twenty-four-year-old first cousin, Hettie from Nova Scotia. Henrietta Miller Elliott was her real name, and she was from Annapolis County, where Slocum had spent the first eight years of his life. The forty-two-year-old Slocum was attentive to his comely cousin and, as another Slocum relative observed, "Hettie was no doubt bedazzled by his attentions when he was considered successful." Joshua married Hettie on February 22, 1886, in Boston. Six days later the newlyweds began their married life together on the *Aquidneck*.

The young bride's honeymoon was a passage to Montevideo with a crew of ten and a cargo of case oil. The nightmare began with Slocum's decision to sail despite storm warnings. It's hard to imagine how Hettie must have felt about her new life with the middle-aged captain. She was not accustomed to life on ships, and she most certainly did not have Virginia's resilient spirit. The voyage to Uruguay was beset with frequent and terrible storms. A hurricane struck early out of New York and the *Aquidneck* started leaking. Victor, who was then fifteen, sailed as mate and remembered the heavy seas flooding the main deck and the pumps running continuously for thirty-six hours. Even Slocum, with his years of experience, reckoned it a bad storm, "for out on the Atlantic our bark could carry only a mere rag of a foresail, somewhat larger than a table-cloth . . . Mountains of seas swept clean over the bark in their mad race, filling her decks full to the top of the bulwarks, and shaking things generally."

Once the cargo was unloaded, Hettie got a small taste of how rough life could be among sailors, as Slocum had to bar and lock his hold, which was full of wine salvaged from a Spanish ship up river. The *Aquidneck*'s next cargo was bales of alfalfa hay bound for Rio de Janeiro. The trip began with near shipwreck due to a pilot's incompetence. In fact, the entire crew was suspect, having been delivered by a "vile crimp," according to Slocum. Subsequently, the *Aquidneck* was refused entry into Rio because of a cholera outbreak in Rosario, where the hay had been loaded; the ship was sent instead to a nearby quarantine station at Ilha Grande. Slocum was unable to gain clearance to Rio harbor and was turned away at gunpoint when he questioned the ruling. The Brazilian authorities refused even to allow him to take on provisions. With the gun pointed at his ship, and with his family aboard, Slocum had no alternative but to sail back to Rosario with the hay. There they waited until Rio lifted its quarantine restrictions.

Excitement stirred when it was announced on April 9 that all Brazilian ports were again open. The *Aquidneck* prepared to set sail a second time with the cargo of hay. It isn't clear whether Hettie was aware of the kind of rag-tag seamen she was sailing with, but Slocum knew at least some of the seedy details of his new crew: "Crew were picked up here and there, out of brothels that had not been pulled down during the cholera, and out of the street or from the fields. Mixed among them were many that had been let out of the prisons all over the country, so that scourge should not be increased by over-crowded jails." Slocum learned only later that four of his crew had been imprisoned for murder or highway robbery. Treachery was lurking, but before it surfaced the load of hay that had been sitting in the hold for nearly six months was discharged. Slocum provided his readers with a disturbing dockside image: "A change of rats also was made . . . fleas, too, skipped about in the hay as happy as larks, and nearly as big." Only once in his writings does Slocum mention Hettie having any fun on this doomed wedding voyage. In Rio she bought a fashionable tall hat, which caused Slocum concern at night, when while half-asleep he fancied it "looming up like a dreadful stack of hay."

Slocum's next cargo was three pianos. The *Aquidneck* hit a severe storm, and Slocum wrote that because his bark was thrown on her beam-ends, the pianos arrived "fearfully out of tune." Slocum shrugged it off, telling himself that the pianos, no doubt, were "suffering, I should say, from the effects of seasickness!" He learned later that the owners of the pianos had prayed fervently for the *Aquidneck* during the storm.

Slocum could recount the near calamities of this part of the voyage with levity, but what happened next could not be taken other than seriously, even by the drollest of Yankee wisecrackers. Hettie woke Joshua near midnight on July 23, 1887. She had heard footsteps above on the poop deck and whispers in the forward entry. She was so insistent that she had not been dreaming that Slocum ignored his first impulse to go up on deck by his usual route to investigate. "Arming myself, therefore, with a stout carbine repeater, with eight ball cartridges in the magazine, I stepped on deck abaft instead of forward, where evidently I had been expected." He surprised the "gang of cut-throats" and warned them he was armed. The traitorous crew members defied his authority and his warning, and one approached to attack him with a knife. Slocum recalled, "I could not speak, or even breathe, but my carbine spoke for me, and the ruffian fell with the knife in his hand which had been raised against me!" Immediately another of the mutinous pack advanced on the captain, and he too was felled with a single shot. That ended the drama. Slocum later concluded, "A man will defend himself and his family to the last, for life is sweet, after all."

One man, Thomas Maloney, lay dead; the second crewman, James Aiken, was severely wounded and was sent to hospital in Paranaguá, where he recovered. Slocum himself was arrested. While he was in detention, the *Aquidneck* was placed under the command of a Spanish master, with Victor remaining on board as mate. Slocum was entangled in the Brazilian legal system for the next month, but the trial itself was swift. He pleaded self-defense and was acquitted and released. He must have decided that Hettie had had enough high sea adventure, for he bade her to stay in Antonina, in Paranaguá Bay, with young Garfield, while he caught a steamer to Montevideo, where he recovered the *Aquidneck*.

Hettie may have been taking a breather, but Slocum would have little time for one. He gave his new crew a half-day's liberty on shore at Paranaguá. When they set sail the next morning they seemed content, except for one sailor, who complained of chills. Slocum dismissed his complaint, but a couple of days later, "his chills turned to something which I knew less about. The next day, three more men went down with rigor in the spine, and at the base of the brain. I knew by this that small-pox was among us!" Slocum found it hard to believe that the distress signals they hoisted for immediate medical attention were not answered until thirty-six hours later. In Maldonado, Uruguayan officials confirmed the diagnosis, then ordered the bark to leave port without further aid. The sick and seriously short-handed crew sailed through a gale that stripped the sails, leaving them with bare poles. Then came torrential rains, lightning and the realization that they were in the clutches of a hurricane. Almost everything was washed away but the virus; only three of the crew were unaffected — Slocum, Victor and the ship's carpenter. When the weather calmed, Slocum recalled, "wet, and lame and weary, we fell down in our wet clothes, to rest as we might — to sleep, or to listen to groans of our dying shipmates." They received medical aid along the River Plate, but it came too late for many. Slocum offers a poignant picture of the afflicted sailors. When they buried the first to die, a man called José, Slocum reflected on the sailor's honest smile, then cast him to the waves. "I listened to the solemn splash," he wrote, "that told of one life ended."

With José's death, Slocum's crew became increasingly demoralized. The sick begged Slocum to call for a priest if medical help was not to be given. The captain set the flags, but knew that no one ashore wanted to answer their call for fear of contracting the deadly contagion. He watched the padre, as he put it, "pacing the beach." Their plea was ignored.

After burying another sailor, Slocum decided his "drifting pest house" had no choice but to move on for Montevideo. There the sick were taken from the ship and the *Aquidneck* was disinfected with demijohns of carbolic acid. This cleansing cost the captain over a thousand dollars. For Slocum one of the most anguishing moments occurred when he had to destroy the dead sailors' property. The small gifts and trinkets they had purchased in Rio for their loved ones all met the fire or were ruined by carbolic acid. The captain later wrote that "what it cost me in health and mental anxiety cannot be estimated by such value."

Once again, he shipped with a new crew and headed for Antonina and reunion with his wife and son. Sailing past Santa Catarina, Slocum was transported to a happier time three and a half years earlier. "We came to a stand, as if it were impossible to go further . . . a spell seemed over us. I recognized the place as one I knew very well; a very dear friend had stood by me on deck, looking at that island, some years before. It was the last land that my friend ever saw." Gripped with sadness mixed with renewed strength and hope, Slocum sailed on. With Hettie and Garfield back on board, the *Aquidneck* began another business venture, this time carrying a load of Brazilian wood. The final disaster for the ill-fated *Aquidneck* came soon after it headed out into Paranaguá Bay. Slocum recalled the final moments: "Currents and wind caught her foul, near a dangerous sandbar, she mis-stayed and went on the strand. The anchor was let go to club her. It wouldn't hold in the treacherous sands; so she dragged and stranded broadside on, where open to the sea, a strong swell came in that raked her fore and aft, for three days, the waves dashing over her groaning hull the while till at last her back was broke and — why not add 'heart' as well!" The *Aquidneck* was lost. Slocum sold the wrecked ship on the spot and paid off the crew. She was uninsured, and as Garfield later wrote, "Father lost all of his money and our beautiful home." Slocum strug-gled with the paradox of this loss: "This was no time to weep, for the lives of all the crew were saved; neither was it a time to laugh, for our loss was great."

To let go of his anger over the loss took years of letter writing to the President of the United States, the Depart-ment of State, the American consul at Rio and the consul at Pernambuco. Slocum cited the initial refusal of clearance at the quarantine harbor outside Rio as the decisive blow in his loss of fortune. In his view he had become enmeshed in the politics of a change of government in Brazil, and he blamed the competing factions for holding him stuck, which in turn caused him to be in the wrong place at the wrong time when the devastating storm struck. He pursued his campaign to right this perceived injustice from October of 1887 to its futile conclusion on December 9, 1893. In January 1888, when the U.S. consulate in Rio offered to do its duty and bring the shipwrecked family back to the United States, a proud and disgruntled Slocum decided they would find their own passage home.

Stranded in Brazil, Slocum set his mind to a plan to build a boat to sail his family home. It didn't have to be a beauty — seaworthiness was all he wanted. He knew it would be primitive at best, made up of salvaged parts of the wrecked *Aquidneck* plus whatever he could afford or alter or make do with. He worked out a design and tackled it with optimism, deciding that "she should sail well, at least before free winds. We counted on favorable winds." His boat was certainly an original — a strange blend of Cape Ann dory, Japanese sampan, Chinese junk and native canoe designs. Slocum himself referred to the vessel as a canoe.

From the *Aquidneck* Slocum salvaged "a megre kit" of basic tools, his compass and charts, and his chronometer.

He was able to use some of *Aquidneck*'s hardware, and he was ingenious at adapting the rest. For example, he pounded charcoal into a fine powder that, mixed with water, served for chalk. He made boat clamps from guava trees, and melted down ship's metal for fastenings and cast some of it into nails. He punched holes through the local copper coins, cut them into diamond shapes, and used them as burrs for the nails. This improvisation, together with a rough-and-ready approach to hewing local trees for boat timber, took place during an epidemic of jungle fever, which made its rounds among the Slocums and the workers. They were undaunted, and Slocum reflected on the spirit of the day: "But all that, and all other obstacles vanished at last, or became less, before a new energy which grew apace with the boat, and the building of the craft went rapidly forward." Victor served as carpenter and ropemaker. Even Hettie got into the spirit of the adventure and sewed the sails. She had been a dressmaker, and Slocum was pleased with the finished product: "Madam had made the sails — and very good sails they were, too!" When finished, the canoe was thirty-five feet in length. Rigged with full-battened sails, which Slocum considered "the most convenient boat rig in the world," she took on the appearance of a Chinese junk. She was christened *Liberdade*, as she was launched on the day that Brazilian slaves were given their freedom. All that remained now was the voyage home.

At the outset of the voyage back to the United States,

the captain, who had suffered such grueling misfortunes, felt invigorated: "The old boating trick came back fresh to me . . . the love of the thing itself gaining on me as the little ship stood out: and my crew with one voice said: 'Go on.'" They hit a storm immediately, and Hettie's new sails were completely shredded. They were towed into Rio by a steamer, which Hettie had boarded by this time. Garfield remembered how his father and Victor stayed on the disabled *Liberdade* and managed to work with the steamer. "Father had a lot of nerve, strength, and will power. He steered all day and all night. Victor sat in the fore-peak under a tarpaulin, an ax in his lap to cut the hawser in case the *Liberdade* turned over. Father had a lanyard tied to Victor's wrist. Father would pull on it and Victor responded with a pull." After they set out again with new sails, there were several further mishaps. On a late July day, just out of Rio, a whale got a little too friendly with the craft and interrupted everyone's supper with its churning up of the waters beneath and around the *Liberdade*. There were several close calls coming up the coast of South America, but they continued north with a growing appreciation for and confidence in "the thin cedar planks between the crew and eternity." Upon arriving back in the United States, he recalled the passage home as "the most exciting boat-ride" of his life, to that point at least.

The voyage of the *Liberdade* covered 5,500 miles and took fifty-five days. It had taken them up the coast of South America, through the Caribbean, past the Carolinas, up to Norfolk and then to Washington. When the family arrived on December 27, 1888, Hettie must have wanted to kiss the ground. Asked if she planned to go on another voyage, she quickly answered, "Oh, I hope not. I haven't been home in over three years, and this was my wedding voyage." Perhaps Hettie's reluctance to set sail again with Joshua was due to more than the discomforts and hardships of her voyage. She may have realized by then that her husband's heart was too often with his "dear friend" Virginia. As the *Liberdade* came to the equator he said a poignant goodbye. Of his gaze heavenward to the stars, he wrote that he had "left those of the south at last, with the Southern Cross — most beautiful in all the heavens — to watch over a friend." Virginia haunted him on at least one other occasion on that voyage north. He wrote of a specter that appeared to him one night while on watch. It was of the vessel she had died on: "A phantom of the stately *Aquidneck* appeared one night, sweeping by with crowning skysails set, that fairly brushed the stars."

As Slocum made this final leg of the trip to bring his family back home, he must have felt mixed emotions. There would have been, of course, a sense of triumph and personal satisfaction in pulling off such an adventure, but he must also have felt a certain emptiness. He was closing the book on his youth and his professional career. Adjusting to life on new terms was to be his next challenge.

Mine was not the sort of life to make one long to coil up one's ropes on land, the customs and ways of which I had finally almost forgotten. And so when times for freighters got bad, as at last they did, and I tried to quit the sea, what was there for an old sailor to do? I was born in the breezes, and I had studied the sea as perhaps few men have studied it, neglecting all else . . . Thus the voyage which I am now to narrate was a natural outcome not only of my love of adventure, but of my lifelong experience.

— J.S., *Sailing Alone*

<u>5</u>

What Was There for an Old Sailor to Do?

*With all its vicissitudes I still love a life on the broad, free
ocean, never regretting the choice of my profession.*
— J.S., *Voyage of the Liberdade*

When Slocum left the United States over three years
before, he had been a gainfully employed captain and the
owner of his own command. On his return in a homemade
canoe, he was an unemployed drifter. Years later, Joseph
Chase Allen recalled the impact the eccentric appearance
of the *Liberdade* made on the people of Martha's Vineyard.
"She was canoe-shaped, sharp at both ends with some
sheer. The predominating color on and about her was
brown, the brown of plug tobacco, or dried autumn leaves
. . . Her cabin was a hut, of the type seen in pictures of
tropical countries, for its rounded 'crowned' top was

thatched with some variety of broad leaf, lapping and over-lapping to make it weatherproof, although why these leaves did not lift as the wind struck them seemed remarkable."

The *Liberdade* may have looked like an alien craft, but it got the Slocums home, and in doing so it brought them some notoriety. After wintering in Washington, D.C., the *Liberdade* and her crew sailed down the Potomac and into New York harbor. There the press was waiting, but the New York *World* reporter did not want to talk to the captain; he was on the waterfront that day to capture his wife's thoughts on this unique voyage. Hettie was in the spotlight for once, and the article provided a curious yet complimentary portrayal of her as a strong young woman of gentle manner with "full brow, bright hazel eyes, a remarkably well-formed 'nez', a frank smiling mouth, and a chin expressing both firmness and tenderness . . . Here is the face of a woman who would be capable of the most devoted, intrepid deeds, done in the quietest and most matter-of-fact way, and never voluntarily spoken of afterwards." The interview was conducted in the "wee cabin on a plank running the length and raised about three inches from the deck. A sitting posture was the only attitude possible unless one chose to lie down." This article showed just how very different the second Mrs. Slocum was from the first. Virginia had brought a sense of aesthetics to a grand ship. Readers of "An American Family Afloat," about the Slocums' voyages on the *Northern Light*, were surely enchanted by the romance of being a captain's wife; readers of the *Liberdade* article must have shaken their heads and muttered "that poor Mrs. Slocum." Virginia was portrayed as a goddess of efficient domesticity and motherhood in a vessel that the reporter compared to a "comfortable apartment ashore." Hettie gave the *World* reporter a tour of her domestic setup, and readers got the picture: "'Just there' — pointing outside the entrance — 'stood two big water casks. Behind them provisions were stowed. There's the stove over which we did our cooking.' It was a small iron pot on three legs, in which a handful of charcoal could be kindled." When asked how she felt about the voyage, she said, "It is an experience I should not care to repeat." Asked if she intended to go on another, she answered, "Oh, I hope not," and added, "I have had enough sailing to last me for a long time."

Hettie had reflected on the voyage earlier that winter in a letter to her friend Mrs. Alfred McNutt, dated January 28, 1889. The Slocums had met Captain and Mrs. McNutt in Barbados before their wild canoe excursion. Considering their hair-raising voyage, the letter was a rather bland account. Hettie wrote that Josh thanked her for the stockings and that the voyage was full of interest to them. She cited one pleasurable family moment: "Xmas day was spent in the Chesapeake bay. We ate our Xmas dinner on board the *Liberdade*. The weather was fine and wind fair. So we enjoyed our sail up the Chesapeake and Potomac very much." She then shared an adventurous moment:

"We had a big storm off the coast of Cuba and some bad weather on this coast. We came through everything nicely. It surprises me more and more when I think of all we have come through." Slocum seemed oblivious to the anxiety the perilous voyage had caused his young wife. He said she was "brave enough to face the worst storms," then added that she was not the worse for wear. He even made it sound like a beneficial trip for her, claiming his wife had "enjoyed not only the best of health, but had gained a richer complexion."

When they arrived back in Massachusetts, the family unit was again split apart. They had no home on land, so Hettie took lodgings with her sister in Boston — the same sister who had expressed her disapproval of the marriage and hadn't the time of day for the captain. Hettie may have secretly been in agreement, for years later one of Slocum's cousins recalled Hettie's feelings on returning home from her wedding trip. As Grace Brown remembered it, "Hettie found she was not wholly for that life. It was bad all around taking Virginia's place as a wife and trying to do right by the children." Slocum stayed with his aunt on his father's side, Naomi Slocombe Gates, at 69 Saratoga Street, East Boston. Victor and Ben Aymar found their own lodgings, while young Jessie and Garfield stayed with Hettie. Garfield confirmed that the family split involved more than a need to find lodgings when he wrote, "Father did not come to the house." As Grace Brown saw it, Slocum sorely missed Virginia: "His love for Hettie was not as vital but he seemed very kind and courtly. His children I am told came second to his great love for Virginia."

Slocum, now forty-five years old, found himself staring down his shortcomings and failures at every turn. He was effectively penniless, but perhaps the most humiliating aspect of the whole miserable turn of events was that he had to accept the shameful end of his lengthy career — he would never again be hired by a shipping company. The undeniable fact was that he had stranded his last command. Author and sailor Joseph Conrad wrote of the powerful sense of loss a sailor experiences in such circumstances: "More than any other event does stranding bring to the sailor a sense of utter and dismal failure . . . To keep ships afloat is his business; it is his trust; it is the effective formula at the bottom of all these vague impulses, dreams, and illusions that go to the making up of a boy's vocation . . . but saved or not saved, there remains with her commander a distinct sense of loss, a flavour in the mouth of the real, abiding danger that lurks in all the forms of human existence. It is an acquisition, too, that feeling. A man may be the better for it, but he will not be the same."

From East Boston, Slocum continued his letter-writing battle with the State Department to take on the Brazilian government for the *Aquidneck*'s loss. Perhaps he was displacing the blame for stranding his vessel, or at least trying to diffuse it. His arguments were lengthy and self-serving; he began to sound like a tedious crank. Ben

Aymar recalled his father searching for employment during this period and said that Slocum "spent much of his time in contacting his former business associates, seeking a lead to something acceptable." This was a tough mid-life transition for the captain: the job he was most qualified for simply no longer existed. His experiences in tramp freighting had given him some preparation for this change in status. His years wandering between ports hustling for jobs had helped him develop the driven yet flexible attitude he would need to survive as a freelancer. To make money or return to the water, he would have to rely entirely on his own wiliness. Anyone who knew Slocum was aware that he was not only inventive but also awesomely tenacious.

Slocum decided to cash in on the attention that had come his way with the *Liberdade* adventure. He wrote a chronicle of the trip, although he had his reservations about his abilities as an author. He claimed that he wrote with "a hand alas! that has grasped the sextant more often than the plane or pen." His 175-page self-published book, *Voyage of the Liberdade*, was copyrighted in 1890. The Yarmouth *Herald*, out of his native Nova Scotia, gave the captain's first book a fine review: "It is a very interesting narrative of thrilling adventure, pluck and endurance rarely to be met with. It is a story of chances, privations and hardships which are not generally encountered in voyages between South America and U.S. ports." The same reviewer praised Slocum for his nautical skills, adding that the story was "a record of skilful seamanship and perils encountered with ready resource." As for his skills as an author, the reviewer remarked, "The book is written in a rollicking spirit, and shows considerable literary ability." Slocum, although not entirely comfortable telling sea stories with his pen, was to go on to greater literary fame. *Voyage of the Liberdade* sowed the seeds for his future endeavors.

Aside from writing, Slocum picked up whatever work he could find on the Boston waterfront. He was offered a job on a steamer but told Garfield that accepting such employment would be his undoing: "I would have to get used to steamships and I do not like steamships." There was no budging him on this point. He was immovable on other issues as well. When asked to pay the fifty-dollar union fee to work as a stevedore, he flatly refused. He was then asked which church he belonged to, and was indignant that the question was even raised: "It didn't seem to suffice that I belonged to God's great church that knew no bounds of creed or sect."

One day in the winter of 1892, Slocum was pacing the waterfront weighing his options when he met up with a wealthy, retired whaling captain, Eben Pierce. Pierce's offer to give him an antiquated sloop was the best opportunity he had had for almost two years. His hopes raised, he went off to Fairhaven the next day to meet the *Spray*, which lay beached on a pasture on Poverty Point. Once again he was facing a seemingly impossible venture —

just the kind that inspired him. He thrived on the challenge of defying unbeatable odds. Captain Pierce invited Slocum to live at his house while he rebuilt the boat. Ben Aymar often visited, and Hettie came for weekends when she could get away. Besides keeping up her duties as a stepmother, she helped make financial ends meet by working as a dressmaker and gown-fitter in Boston. Slocum's arrangement with Pierce, who had made part of his fortune inventing whaling gear, gave Slocum the freedom to devote large amounts of time and his own passionate determination to reconstructing the *Spray*. But he did have to pick up work to cover his building costs, which in the end totaled $553.62.

Heaven only knows what the villagers thought when he stopped work temporarily to tow an iron gunboat from New York to Brazil. The *Destroyer*, which Slocum referred to as "the first ship of the strong right arm of future Brazil," was just one of the warships the Brazilian president had purchased to defend himself against opposing forces within his own country. Of his time as navigator-in-command of the ship under tow, Slocum later wrote, "Frankly it was with a thrill of delight that I joined the service of Brazil to lend a hand to the legal government of a people in whose country I had spent happy days." There were several other, less humanitarian reasons why the job offer had appealed to the captain. For one thing, he needed the money to continue with his building. But there was an even more compelling reason:

if Slocum had a bee in his bonnet, as the Fairhaven neighbors sensed, it was over the loss of the *Aquidneck*. So when the opportunity presented itself to sail back to the country he blamed for his decline, Slocum jumped at it: "Confidentially: I was burning to get a rake at Mello and his *Aquideban*. He it was who in that ship expelled my bark, the *Aquidneck* from Ilha Grand some years ago . . . I was burning to let him know and palpably feel that this time I had in dynamite instead of hay." Bravado aside, Slocum clearly did not want to get embroiled in the ordeals of the war, nor did he wish to dirty his hands as a soldier of fortune. "Being a man of a peaceful turn of mind, however, no fighting was expected of me, except in the battle with the elements." His position aboard the gunboat was of "navigator in command." His job, as it had been when the *Liberdade* was under tow, would be to keep the *Destroyer* on course and stable.

The trip proved futile. Slocum sailed on December 7, 1893, probably with his head full of just how he would deal forcefully with the *Aquidneck* issue. The irony was that a letter written by the State Department two days later would just miss the tenacious — and by this time vengeful — captain. It contained their final word on the *Aquidneck*, direct and conclusive: "This Department therefore, does not feel warranted in taking any further action." Another bit of irony followed after he arrived in Brazil. The *Destroyer* was accidentally, though some felt quite deliberately, sunk. Not only was Slocum without compensation for the loss of the *Aquidneck*, but he would have to head home by steamer, unpaid for his job on the *Destroyer*. On his return, he vented his frustration at this misadventure by writing his second book. *Voyage of the Destroyer from New York to Brazil* ended up being so poorly produced that Slocum decided against selling the copies he had self-published. He gave them away, and even then he had a hard time getting rid of them. As to the *Destroyer*, Slocum wrote, "Alas! for all our hardships and perils! The latest account that I heard said that the *Destroyer* lay undone in the basin. The tide ebbing and flowing through her broken hull — a rendezvous for eels and crawfish — and now those high and dry sailors say they had a 'narrow escape.'"

There was one more piece of strange news about Slocum to keep the tongues wagging in Fairhaven. Their strange neighbor had been challenged to a duel by a British soldier of fortune. It seems that Lieutenant Carlos A. Rivers felt he had been misrepresented in *Voyage of the Destroyer*. According to the Boston *Sun* of August 3, 1894, Rivers was charging that the captain had "ridiculed and defamed him in his recently published book by declaring he was worsted ignominiously in a bout with the colored cook, and that his sword was not the historic Toledo blade which the owner claimed it to be." Rivers promised Slocum he would meet him "anywhere at any time and place, and with any weapons." Slocum didn't appear fazed, and replied that his wife's feelings had to

be considered and that in general "duellists should con-
sult their wives." He backed out of the confrontation,
declaring, "My wife would be disturbed to be left a widow
. . . It is better that I catch fish than fight him."

When Slocum spent any length of time on dry land he
quickly became embroiled in legalities, unpleasantness
and trouble. Escape to the sea constantly beckoned, and
now he put his mind to what he might do with the *Spray*,
which he had launched on a trial sail in Buzzards Bay,
with just himself and Captain Pierce aboard. Slocum was
proud of his accomplishment, boasting that "she sat on
the water like a swan." This captain, who had once commanded a 220-foot vessel, was describing a sloop thirty-
six feet nine inches long, fourteen feet two inches wide,
and four feet two inches deep in her hold, with net ton-
nage of nine tons and almost thirteen tons gross. The
Spray was plain and rough in her construction, but seaworthy with her oak keel and frames, pine hull planking,
white pine deck and concrete ballast. Slocum had replaced
her centerboard with a stout keel, which he had cut from
an oak in a local pasture, and had fashioned the mast
from "a smart New Hampshire spruce." Once again he
was master of his own vessel.

Slocum's next task was to answer the question that
haunted him: "What was there for an old sailor to do?"
For Slocum was an "old" sailor; now fifty-one, he had
spent over two-thirds of his life on the ocean. As a merchant mariner he had been around the world five times

over every kind of sea. His knowledge of ocean conditions, weather and navigation was vast — far beyond the grasp of an ordinary seaman. He knew the sea intuitively. After a year of trying to make a living by fishing and chartering small party cruises, Slocum felt himself beckoned by a plan to surpass all his previous adventures. He pined to be back on the ocean, where, as he well knew, he functioned best. He was tired of struggling to make a living, tired of defending and justifying himself to others. In the year following the launch, the *Spray* became his home; he had no other, and no ties to keep him on land. Life with Hettie in Boston held no appeal. In a letter to a friend, biographer Walter Teller reflected on Hettie's part in Slocum's decision to embark on a solo voyage around the world: "I'm glad you're quite frank about Hettie. As she had no children nothing said about her will hurt anyone. Perhaps the world owes her something — that is, if she had been more companionable the Captain might never have sailed alone and a great adventure of the human spirit might have come off quite differently." According to Slocum, when he invited Hettie to join him on his latest adventure, she answered curtly, "Joshua, I've had a v'yage."

Once he had made up his mind to sail alone around the world, Slocum was filled with purpose and drive. It was a means to display his daring and his impressive navigational skills. The plan also had a practical purpose, which he explained to a reporter from the Boston *Daily Globe*: "The object of the trip? Well, it is mainly to make

85

money. I see money ahead if I get through safely. I shan't carry much cargo, but I expect the *Spray* will be pretty well filled with curios of various kinds before she gets back." For well over a year before the voyage he had been busying himself with plans to finance it, partly by writing a syndicated newspaper column. Roberts Brothers in Boston agreed to be his agent, and Slocum hustled to find newspapers that would run his dispatches. The positive response excited him, and he wrote enthusiastically to Eugene Hardy at Roberts Brothers: "My Syndicade is filling up . . . This morning I got the great Mr. Watterson: The *Louisville Courier Journal*." Slocum's reading of Watterson's letter was too optimistic: all the *Courier* editor had conveyed was an interest in paying Slocum for what the paper chose to print. His reply to Slocum had been clear: "I can not contract with you for the whole of your series of letters. Knowing your reputation I can count on the letters being of interest but our using them might depend on other contingencies."

As he continued to court financial support, the captain looked after the physical preparations. One of his first concerns was to stock his library. Just as in his earlier sailing days, he considered a library on board a necessity. He wrote to Hardy again to ask for books, explaining, "Mr. Wagnalls of the house of Funk and Wagnalls told me the other day that he would also put me up some. I may be able to pay for all this kindness at some future time but not now." He added that he wasn't fussy about the condition of the books, and that "a 'shop-worn' book would be as good for me as any; so far as the outside goes." When the books arrived, Slocum sent Hardy a note of gratitude signed "A thousand thanks." He enthused over Hardy's choices, noting a "Mr. Stephensons" (Robert Louis Stevenson) and praising in particular a new book called *A Strange Career*. This biography of the bold English prospector and frontiersman John Gladwin Jebb obviously struck a deep chord with Slocum. The book's foreword, by H. Rider Haggard, made this acknowledgment of Jebb: "Rarely if ever in this nineteenth century, has a man lived so strange and varied an existence. 'Adventures are to the adventurous,' the saying tells us, and certainly they were to Mr. Jebb. From the time he came to manhood he was a wanderer." Surely Slocum, with his life of romance and adventure, not only identified with Jebb but was inspired by his success. In anticipation of quieter moments, Slocum created a poets' corner featuring the works of Burns, Tennyson, Longfellow, Lamb and Cervantes. He was a voracious reader, as the Boston *Herald* noted in a feature it ran before he left: "The library of the *Spray* includes such books as Darwin's 'The Descent of Man' and 'Expression of the Emotions,' 'Boswell's Life of Johnson,' 'Newcomb's Popular Astronomy,' 'The Life of Macaulay,' Mark Twain's 'Life on the Mississippi,' Todd's 'Total Eclipses of the Sun,' Bates' 'The Naturalist of the Amazon,' Shakespeare . . ."

In stark contrast to his well-stocked library, Slocum sailed with a bare minimum of navigational tools. He planned to circle the globe with what odds and ends he had gathered from years on the water: a sextant and a compass, his charts, and the most current of Massey patent taffrail logs, which he would trail behind the *Spray* to calculate her speed and determine distance. He planned to buy a clock along the way. He told a reporter, "I don't go out like the dumb and blind. Understanding nautical astronomy, I will, of course, navigate the world around with some degree of precision natural to any first-rate navigator."

He carried few medicines, and some disinfectants; according to Victor, on the *Liberdade* the family medicine chest had consisted of Brazil nuts, pepper, cinnamon and table salt. Slocum had always enjoyed a strong constitution, with unusual stamina and strength. The Boston *Herald* stated that the Captain never had sick days and observed that "Capt. Josh is a kinky salt, 51 years old, as spry as a kitten and as nimble as a monkey." As for the condition of the boat that would transport him, Slocum boasted of the *Spray*'s seaworthiness, and especially of her ability to steer herself. He claimed his little sloop was "very easily managed, even in a breeze."

Over the years the seaworthiness of the *Spray* has been the subject of many a spirited debate among sailors and marine historians. In the May 1940 issue of *The Rudder*, John Hanna wrote a cautionary note to those sailors who wished to build a copy of the *Spray*, referring to them as "the suicide squad." He spelled out a few facts: "A big lurching cross sea, that would scarcely disturb a properly designed hull, can — especially if it coincides, as it often does, with an extra-savage puff of a squall — flip over a *Spray* hull just as you would a poker chip . . . Perhaps I can save a life or two by explaining, as simply as possible, the basic reason (skipping many other good reasons) why *Spray* is the worst possible boat for anyone, and especially anyone lacking the experience and resourcefulness of Slocum, to take off soundings." He then points out that boats fashioned after the famous sloop are stiff, and should they ever heel beyond a critical point, "they flop right over as inevitably as a soup plate, which they resemble."

Howard Chapelle, a curator in the Smithsonian Institution's Division of Transportation, was every bit as harsh: "The *Spray* was a poor job, badly framed and fastened. Slocum was not a boat carpenter, of course. The *Spray* had been a typical Long Island Sound centreboard oyster sloop originally, and [Slocum] added a little to the outside depth of her keel, doing all rebuilding himself, without adequate funds . . . It is sheer ignorance to tout this damned bucket as a 'splendid ship' for she was not even a good oyster sloop with her board out."

Whatever the *Spray*'s virtues and shortcomings, no one has ever questioned Slocum's exceptional seamanship.

Slocum considered the *Spray* his home, so he valued her function, safety and comfort and wanted things snug aboard. The *Spray* had two cabins. The fore cabin, which measured six feet square, was the galley; aft was the larger cabin, roughly ten feet by twelve, which was the main living quarters. Here he had his meals, did his mending and passed his time reading. Both cabins rose more than three feet above deck, so the captain had adequate headroom. A hatch between the two let Slocum crawl between them. Under the deck, along the side of the cabin, the captain fitted his berth and storage shelves. Around the base of a stanchion in the middle of the cabin was a circular table, within reaching distance of the bunk. Between this main cabin and the galley was the midship hold, which provided ample storage room for several months' supplies. The wheel was handy to the companionway, which had a pine rail leading down into the cabin.

For provisions, Slocum laid in a large supply of staples. In a later article about his cooking aboard the *Spray*, Slocum noted what he started out with: "I laid in two barrels of ship's bread, or pilot bread, as some call it. In appearance this bread is like a large thick cracker of rather coarse quality. There's no nonsense about it, though. It was made for keeps. It isn't fine and white like the crackers most people like to buy. You could eat a bushel full of those and get no substance. But this old-fashioned hard bread is a kind of whole wheat. There's good stuff in it and you couldn't do better than to take some of it if you were going into the woods camping. My two barrels full lasted me the voyage through. I put them up in tin cans while they were dry and crisp, and I sealed the cans with solder so the bread was as good three years old as it was new." Slocum also laid in a good quantity of flour, codfish, potatoes, butter, tea and coffee. Aware that he would need to guard his possessions and his personal safety in waters still traveled by cannibals and pirates, Slocum armed himself with a Martini-Henry rifle and a revolver.

It was April of 1895, and Slocum was ready to set sail. Eight days before he departed, the Boston *Daily Globe* announced his plans: "To Sail Around World / Capt Joshua Slocum Has a Trim Craft Fitted Out." The reporter who visited the "builder, owner, skipper, crew, cook and cabin boy" aboard the *Spray* when it was docked in East Boston was stunned by the small size of the boat: "There now lies a little sloop which looks about large enough for a longshore fisherman, but which is, nevertheless, booked for a voyage around the world."

This newspaper article, dated April 16, 1895, illustrates how unsettled the captain's plans were. The lettering on the *Spray*'s stern at this time said "Spray Fairhaven," but before leaving on April 24, the captain had decided on a more visible hailing port: "Spray Boston." Slocum shared his early ideas on how the *Spray* would be rigged: "Her present rig is the ordinary one of the sloop, with mainsail and jib, a short topmast being carried only for signaling. Later, however, her rig may be changed to something like that of *La Liberdate* [sic], with a battened sail in place of the mainsail, and a smaller sail of the same kind on a mizen mast aft." Slocum indicated that this change would be made at the end of the week before the sloop started out from New York. Neither the New York departure nor the early change of rig happened as outlined.

As for the route and the time it would take, Slocum was completely off in his estimates. "From New York I shall sail for Panama," he predicted. "That is, if I can get the boat taken across the isthmus. If I cannot get transportation for her, I shall sail for the Straits of Magellan and so on into the Pacific. It will be a long way to the straits, so I shall do my best to get the boat across the isthmus. Once in the Pacific I shall make all my longitude in the trade winds, either north or south of the equator as it may happen. Then I shall touch many of the South Sea islands and thence head home across the Atlantic. It is quite a trip but two years ought to see it finished." In fact, the voyage would take three years and two months to complete.

In another article that ran in the Boston *Herald* at around the same time, Slocum said he hoped to find the Gilbert Islanders he had rescued on the *Northern Light* twelve years earlier. He also insisted that his craft was stable and reliable. The story described him just before the voyage as five feet nine and a half inches tall, 146 pounds and in remarkable health.

When Slocum was asked how he planned to carry out this venture single-handed, he explained that he intended to "sleep in the day time and keep the boat going at night . . . When it blows too hard I shall get out my sea anchor, batten everything down tight, and go below for a sleep and let the gale blow itself out." The Boston *Daily Globe* reporter, who had at first commented that Slocum and the little *Spray* were setting out on "an adventure from even the prospect of which many handy mariners might be excused from shrinking," left the interview a believer in the captain: "Capt. Slocum apparently regards it with no feeling of misgiving, and talks about it in a matter-of-fact way which shows confidence not only in his determination, but also in his ability to bring the adventure to a successful conclusion."

The old seadog received a vote of confidence from another staunch believer. Slocum's dealings with Funk and Wagnalls had brought him into contact with a young supporter of his voyage, whose enthusiasm perhaps partly made up for Hettie's coolness. Mabel Wagnalls, the daughter of publisher Adam Willis Wagnalls, was twenty-four and unmarried. She came to see Slocum on the *Spray* just before he sailed, bringing a box of books from her father, as well as a book she had written, "a musical story" titled *Miserere*. Mabel was cultured and had dreams of becoming a writer. She and Slocum quickly forged a close connection. Regarding Mabel's eagerness to cheer Slocum on, biographer Walter Teller could only conclude, "The enterprise the old knight of action was about to embark on touched her imagination and heart." Teller's editor agreed, and wrote back to Teller, "Do you think he ever really focussed on her as a woman — I'm inclined to think not. I think she was simply his writing home in the sense we've discussed." Whatever their relationship, Slocum was touched by her visit and cherished Mabel's parting words: "The *Spray* will return."

On April 24, 1895, with the noon-hour whistles blowing a noisy fanfare, the *Spray* left East Boston under full sail. This was the moment Slocum had long anticipated. In his memoir of the voyage, *Sailing Alone Around the World*, he recalled the beauty of that day: "Waves dancing joyously across Massachusetts Bay met the sloop coming out, to dash themselves instantly into myriads of sparkling gems that hung about her breast at every surge. The day was perfect, the sunlight clear and strong. Every particle of water thrown into the air became a gem, and the *Spray*, making good her name as she dashed ahead, snatched necklace after necklace from the sea, and as often threw them away. We have all seen miniature rainbows about a ship's prow, but the *Spray* flung out a bow of her own that day, such as I had never seen before. Her good angel had embarked on the voyage, I so read it in the sea."

I used to soak my hardtack and make bread pudding of the very nicest kind and it had strength and nourishment, too. It was something that would stand by you. I soaked the bread about six hours to get it thoroughly soft, then added sugar, butter, milk and raisins, put it on my lamp-stove and in a few minutes it was done.

My stores included coffee, tea, flour, baking powder, salt, pepper and mustard — yes, and curry, I mustn't forget that. Curry powder is great stuff aboard a vessel. It was just what I needed to give the final touch to my venison stews that I made out of the salt beef and salt pork I carried along. Besides those meats I had ham and dried codfish. Very few persons know how to treat a salt codfish properly. To freshen it they let it stand in water half a day or more, very likely, and it may be, use several waters. That takes all the goodness out. You can get rid of the extra salt just as effectively and without hurting the fish by picking it to pieces and washing it with your hands — just shaking it up and down in the water. Then put it right into the pot and boil for fifteen minutes. When you get it ready for the table, add butter and pepper and chop a hard-boiled egg and put on top. You make codfish that way and I want to sit down prepared to hoist in a meal of it; and all I want besides is potatoes, coffee, and bread and butter.

— From "The Cook Who Sailed Alone,"
Good Housekeeping, February 1903

6

All Watches

Sleeping or waking, I seemed always to know the position of the sloop.
— J.S., *Sailing Alone*

The *Spray* and Slocum were off and away, but the route they had embarked on was not even remotely the one the captain had mapped out in newspaper interviews just the week before. From the beginning he sailed as the spirit moved him. Even after the "thrilling pulse" of a send-off fanned by plenty of hype in the local press, Slocum set his own deliberate pace. His first straying from plan, while minor, suggested how important mulling and moseying were to be in the overall scheme of the voyage. Slocum made first for Gloucester, Massachusetts, where he stopped in the cove part of the harbor to "weigh the voyage, and my feelings, and all that." He also wanted to

check out the *Spray* after her initial run. Here he had his
first experience of coming into port alone in a sizeable
boat. He stayed in port for close to two weeks, the first of
the many delays that were to aggravate his literary agent.
But Slocum already had the kind of audience that mattered to him. Old captains gathered to hear his plans and
gave him a "fisherman's own" lantern as a bon voyage gift.
He also took on dry cod, a barrel of oil and a gaff, pugh
and dip-net, as well as some copper paint, with which he
coated the bottom of his sloop. Before leaving, he made
a dinghy of sorts by sawing a dory in half and boarding
up the ends. A full-size dory was too big for the *Spray*,
but this half-dory would do perfectly, and Slocum, ever
resourceful and inventive, planned to put it to good use:
"I perceived, moreover, that the newly arranged craft
would answer for a washing-machine when placed
athwartships, and also for a bath-tub."

On leaving Gloucester, he sailed up the coast for a
nostalgic visit to his childhood home of Brier Island. It
had been thirty-five years since he left, and he'd forgotten how to navigate through the passage and "the worst
tide-race in the Bay of Fundy." He asked a fisherman for
directions and realized in hindsight that he shouldn't have
paid attention, for the man was clearly not an islander:
"He dodged a sea that slopped over the rail, and stopping
to brush the water from his face, lost a fine cod which
he was about to ship. My islander would not have done
that. It is known that a Brier Islander, fish or no fish on

his hook, never flinches from a sea." Slocum got caught in the "fierce sou'west rip" and was glad to reach Westport. He felt reconnected to his home almost immediately, and stayed on Brier Island long enough to overhaul the *Spray*.

As he worked, he again reconsidered the route he would take. Soon after, he wrote to Eugene Hardy to let him know where he planned to sail when he left on the next full tides: "I think Pernambuco will be my first landfall, leaving this. Then touching the principal ports on S.A. coast on through Magellan Straits where I hope to be in November. So many courses to be taken after that, I can onlly then go as sircumstance and my feelings dictate. My mind is deffinately fixed on one thing and that is to go round . . ." Hardy and the newspaper syndicate must have wondered just when his drive to do what his mind had "fixed on" would kick in.

A month later, Slocum was still in his home province. After the Westport overhaul and a test run of the sou'west rip, Slocum made one more stop before sailing for open sea. In Yarmouth, on the southwest tip of Nova Scotia, Slocum loaded up on food and water. He also made an important purchase. He had been sailing without a chronometer, as his old one had been so long in disuse that bringing it up to scratch would have cost him fifteen dollars — an amount he found alarming. But he needed a chronometer aboard, as he explained in his typical tongue-in-cheek fashion: "In our newfangled notions of navigation it is supposed that a mariner cannot find his way without one; and I had myself drifted into this way of thinking." Now, in Yarmouth, he found a cheap solution and bought his famous tin clock with the broken face. It was a good deal: "The price of it was a dollar and a half, but on account of the face being smashed the merchant let me have it for a dollar." The tin alarm clock was to become a kind of running joke on the trip: to mask his true talents as a celestial navigator, Slocum used the gag of boiling his clock to keep it working.

Before setting out on the Atlantic, Slocum figured he had better let his Boston agents know what he was up to. First he explained the delay, citing "an attack of malaria at Gloucester, from working at the Sloop on the beach there in a sickning ooze." Then he announced a major change of plans that must have mystified Hardy and the people at Roberts Brothers: "After all deliberations and careful study of rout and the seasons, I think my best way is via the Suez canal, down the Read [sic] Sea and along the Coasts of India, in the winter months, calling at Aden and at Ceylon and Singapore taking the S.W. Monsoon next summer up the China Sea, calling at Hong Kong and other treaty ports in China thence to Japan and on to California From California I believe I shall cross the Isthmus of Panama The freight agent of the Panama road wrote me that I could not get over the isthmus — we'll see!"

On July 1, to the relief of his agent, Slocum finally "let go of my last hold on America." After eighteen days' sailing he reached the Azores. It was three months since he had set out on his world voyage. From Horta, on the island of Faial, he wrote to Hardy: "[I have] been trying to scribble a few lines for the newspapers but find it almost impossible to do or to think." In Gibraltar, Slocum was informed that the Mediterranean was unsafe and that he would have to cross the Atlantic again. Forty days' sailing brought Slocum to Pernambuco, in Brazil, where he wrote an anxious letter to Hardy. The Boston *Globe* had published three of his travel letters, but Slocum was unable to provide the newspapers with the regular, exciting copy they needed. What copy he did send contained dubious grammar and atrocious spelling and wasn't spectacular enough to entice readers. The *Globe* was his most important customer, and Slocum, now six months into his circumnavigation, could no longer implore them to be patient. He must have realized his syndicate days were numbered: "I send one more letter I dare not look it over If it is not interesting, I can not be interesting stirred up from the bottom of my soul . . . It was the voyage I thought of and not me. No sailor has ever done what [I] have done. I thank you sincerely for giving my son the money."

The journalistic venture was to founder quickly. In the fall he wrote Hardy another letter in which he said he had been obliged to sell some of the library he had been given simply to keep himself solvent. It was the last letter Hardy would receive from him. Giving up the syndicate gave Slocum back a sailor's freedom to simply roam — to live each day in the rhythm of the voyage.

100

In many ways a sailor is like an actor: if he's been in the business a long time, he can improvise just about anything. He makes it look easy, but there are years of solid training and practical experience behind his moves. He works with few props, knowing for each given scene what will spell success or disaster. The sailor's stage is ever changing, and he learns how to conduct himself against sunny, tranquil and stormy backgrounds. He learns to hear the cues, to trust his gut, to respond to each moment as it is given. His work on the ocean captures the joy, the tragedy, the humor, and the ordinary and the extraordinary experiences of life as it is lived in the moment.

Slocum's mind had been formed by years of ocean living. He was astute at reading the winds and currents. He could anticipate what would happen if the wind should fail or the current went against him. With his quick mind and sharp instincts, he was able to maintain a safe position while anticipating all eventualities. He understood that sailing was a free-form dance of boat, sail, wind and water. "A navigator husbands the wind" was how Slocum saw it.

The old captain went about his nautical tasks with grace, certainty and accuracy. He knew every inch of his boat. She was part of the internal calculations he made with every move on deck or up the rigging. He had the gift of being able to gauge which way to jump to grab the right rope, and of knowing precisely what to do at the right moment.

Slocum knew that the sea is completely impartial. It

doesn't care who or what sails over it. It makes no distinctions, and there is nothing personal in its actions. If it wants to make steep, thirty-foot waves and break them down on a boat, it will do just that. All a sailor can do is react with what he knows. He reefs his sails and keeps his hatches tight. He sails as hard as he can. Once he makes his pact with the sea, there is no negotiation. Off the coast of Samoa, Slocum put his skills to work with an uncompromising sea: "The *Spray* had barely cleared the island when a sudden burst of the trades brought her down to close reefs, and she reeled off one hundred and eighty-four miles the first day, of which I counted forty miles of current in her favor. Finding a rough sea, I swung her off free and sailed north of the Horn Islands, also north of Fiji instead of south, as I had intended, and coasted down the west side of the archipelago."

There was hardly any buffer between Slocum, his vessel and the elements. He absorbed all her movements. At every moment he knew whether she was on course. He always listened to how the *Spray* "talked" to him; she spoke to him in creaks and flapping sails, and he was always listening, and acting on what she was telling him. Early on in the voyage, he had had to poke about in her workings to discover her problems, but later on he probably just knew what needed greasing or tightening up, and what needed to be repaired or replaced. She let him know when she was overtaxed and tired, and he knew enough to respect her limits.

Slocum wrote of the strength and peace his hard-earned sailing knowledge gave him: "To know the laws that govern the winds, and to know that you know them, will give you an easy mind on your voyage round the world; otherwise you may tremble at the appearance of every cloud."

But Slocum knew more than the science of the wind. He could read water and sky — a task that demanded more instinct than skill. On his boyhood island he hadn't needed a wind to let him know a hurricane was happening out to sea. He even knew how many days out the storm was by the swell that struck the shore. Clouds, winds, smells and currents were his second language, and he thought in their terms all his life. Sailing just off the Keeling (Cocos) Islands, Slocum noted, "I saw antitrade clouds flying up from the southwest very high over the regular winds, which weakened now for a few days, while a swell heavier than usual set in also from the southwest. A winter gale was going on in the direction of the Cape of Good Hope. Accordingly, I steered higher to windward, allowing twenty miles a day while this went on, for change of current; and it was not too much, for on that course I made the Keeling Islands right ahead."

Slocum knew how to navigate gingerly when he had to. He watched the weather carefully and made decisions as he went concerning what route he had to take to avoid storms and rough waters. Contemplating the Cape of Good Hope, which is notorious for its stormy weather, he wrote, "I wished for no winter gales now. It was not that I feared them more, being in the *Spray* instead of a large ship, but that I preferred fine weather in any case."

Above all, Slocum believed in his good ship *Spray*. She wasn't a sleek greyhound of a vessel that would slip through the water; instead, she was beamy and broad and comfortable. And in heavy seas a broad, buoyant vessel is ideal for sailors with plenty of time. She didn't take green water on deck, so Slocum didn't worry greatly about being washed overboard. And *Spray* was a forgiving ship. Because she could carry her press of sail in a heavy air, Slocum could not endanger himself by putting on too much sail. She was very stiff, and had a stable platform, so he didn't face the difficulties that arise from excessive heeling. *Spray* was also easy on the helm. He was thrilled by one remarkable feature she possessed: she could self-steer. Without a good self-steering setup, Slocum would have had to heave to or just stop sailing when he was tired or needed to attend to other matters. Most vessels will balance to some extent, on certain points of sail, for a certain amount of time; what Slocum was talking about was a boat that he didn't have to steer. He boasted that while most boats will steer close-hauled on the wind, the *Spray* could self-steer dead down wind, wind on the quarter, or whatever. She was perfectly balanced, so he claimed.

Self-steering is achieved mostly through sail balance. A sailor steers the boat against the water's pressure on the rudder, usually countering the wind's pressure on the sails with the movement of the rudder. With constant wind pressure, a constant angle for the rudder can be found. Self-steering is simply a matter of taking the beckets, or lines, to the spokes of the wheel and tying them to hold the wheel in exactly the position where the rudder is perfectly countering the force on the sail. If the rudder is held over too far, it will start to operate like a brake, so finding the optimum position is key. Slocum explained the secret of working his dependable old sloop: "It never took long to find the amount of helm, or angle of rudder, required to hold her on her course, and when that was found I lashed the wheel with it at that angle."

Slocum made a fantastic claim concerning his passage from Thursday Island, off the north coast of Queensland, 2,700 miles to the Keeling Islands in the Indian Ocean. He arrived in July 1897, just over the two-year mark in his journey. This leg of his trip was one of his finest stretches of sailing: "During those twenty-three days I had not spent altogether more than three hours at the helm, including the time occupied in beating into Keeling harbor. I just lashed the helm and let her go; whether the wind was abeam or dead aft, it was all the same: she always sailed on her course. No part of the voyage up to this point, taking it by and large, had been so finished as this."

For Slocum, self-steering was not a luxury but rather a necessity, for it freed his hands for other business around the sloop. To other passing boats, the *Spray* must often have seemed like a ghost ship. While Slocum was below, tending to whatever needed doing, the *Spray* was able to sail along under full canvas with no sign that anyone was on board.

In fair winds, Slocum looked after routine domestic matters, acting as minion, messmate and chief cook and bottle washer. And because he was the captain, it was also he who called the orders. Slocum had some wry musings over his many hats aboard: "I found no fault with the cook, and it was the rule of the voyage that the cook found no fault with me. There was never a ship's crew so well agreed." He cooked on "a contrivance of my own, with a lamp to furnish the heat." In Montevideo he refitted himself with a stove fashioned out of an oil drum with a chimney on it and a small opening to put in wood. Although he boasted of making curried venison stews, most of his meals were really variations on the theme of boiling water. He boiled water for tea. He made chowder from boiled potatoes and boiled fish. Dried salt cod was a staple of his diet. Occasionally he baked soda bread; otherwise, at least twice a week he ate the sea biscuits he had brought along. He did have his particulars when it came to getting meals on the table. "My way is to cook my victuals as near the meal hour as possible and not allow the food to lose much time between the stove and the table," he told *Good Housekeeping* magazine. And he was a connoisseur when it came to making the perfect "at sea" cup of coffee: "Ground coffee isn't worth as much by a great deal if you've let it stand for a day. Add your hot water and serve at once. You mustn't boil it." What he didn't point out was how complicated — in fact dangerous — even a simple operation like pouring a cup of coffee can be on a boat that is rolling and lurching.

His diet varied by happenstance, and he often made a meal out of anything edible that floated by. Spotting a lolling sea turtle, he got out his harpoon and jabbed it in the neck. He had to work hard for his supper that night: "I had much difficulty in landing him on deck, which I finally accomplished by hooking the throat-halyards to one of the flippers, for he was as heavy as my boat . . . But the turtle-steak was good." Roasted turtle is said to have the consistency of a good pork chop and a delicious taste more like meat than fish. While stranded in the Strait of Magellan, he found large quantities of mussels. Slocum ate the kind of fish he didn't have to cast a line for: "The only fresh fish I had while on the open sea was flying fish that came aboard of their own accord. I was in tropical waters most of the time and had flying fish for breakfast pretty constantly — ah! such breakfasts as I used to have! Often I'd get up in the morning and find a dozen of those flying fish on the deck, and sometimes they'd get down the forescuttle right alongside the frying pan."

Slocum had no worries about scurvy on the trip. At every stop along the way he was certain to find local fresh vegetables and fruit. The captain drank unsweetened condensed milk, and when he had eggs aboard he'd let them sit for a minute in boiling water, claiming that this technique "hermetically sealed the pores." Slocum kept butter fresh by dipping it in brine and sealing it. He boasted that his pickled variety was "butter that will keep as long as you want."

When Slocum wasn't acting as ship's cook, there was always some chore to command his attention. A boat has a way of letting a sailor know how well he's doing his job. If the rig is looking tatty, it's because he's not keeping up with his work; if the boat is looking down in the heels, it's because he's not paying enough attention to her. A ship's captain is not the master of the vessel, but her servant. Any sailor gains deep satisfaction from being aboard a well-founded vessel in good condition and knowing that he's responsible for her soundness; and this was certainly true of Slocum.

In order to carry out solo maintenance of a thirty-seven-foot wooden boat with canvas sails, Slocum had to be adept in a wide range of nautical skills. He had to be able to repair the rigging — to know how to do splicing and reeve off tackles. He had to be able to repair his own sails, and know exactly how strong to make their stress areas. Perhaps most importantly of all when it came to sail repairs, he had to be able to sew a uniform stitch so that the finished sail was smooth and even. His sail-making skills were well tested in the Strait of Magellan, after several weeks of storm damage: "I was determined to rely on my own small resources to repair the damages of the great gale which drove me southward toward the Horn, after I passed from the Strait of Magellan out into the Pacific." Blown back into the strait, he "set to work with my palm and needle at every opportunity, when at anchor and when sailing. It was slow work; but little by little the squaresail on the boom expanded to the dimensions of a serviceable mainsail with a peak to it and a leech besides." Slocum showed his satisfaction with a job well enough done, and not without some self-effacing humor concerning his handiwork. "If it was not the best-setting sail afloat, it was at least very strongly made and would stand a hard blow. A ship, meeting the *Spray* long afterward, reported her as wearing a mainsail of some improved design and patent reefer, but that was not the case."

As a mechanic, Captain Slocum was on twenty-four-hour call. The situation often required whatever makeshift maneuver he was wily enough to envision at the time. Caught in a blustery snowstorm off Port Angosto, nearing Cape Horn, he put his skills to the test: "Between the storm-bursts I saw the headland of my port, and was steering for it when a flaw of wind caught the mainsail by the lee, jibed it over, and dear! dear! how nearly was this the cause of disaster; for the sheet parted and the boom unshipped, and it was then close upon night. I worked till the perspiration poured from my body to get things adjusted and in working order before dark, and, above all, to get it done before the sloop drove to leeward of the port of refuge. Even then I did not get the boom shipped in its saddle. I was at the entrance of the harbor before I could get this done, and it was time to haul her to or lose the port; but in that condition, like a bird with a broken wing, she made the haven."

This haven gave Slocum a brief hiatus from wind and weather, and time to catch his breath. He tidied his cabin, lay in wood and water, and made a technical change in the *Spray*: "I . . . mended the sloop's sails and rigging, and fitted a jigger, which changed the rig to a yawl, though I called the boat a sloop just the same, the jigger being merely a temporary affair."

Slocum's carpentry and shipwrighting skills came into play more than once on his three-year voyage. The water did its share of wear and tear on his beloved sloop. Besides repairing strategic parts of the rigging and caulking, he had to scrupulously maintain the hull below the water line. That vigilance was especially important in tropical waters, where he had to deal with barnacles, which threatened to coat the underside inches deep. In Tasmania he hauled out the *Spray* to check her "carefully top and bottom" for teredo, a destructive wood-devouring worm that can grow up to eight inches long. Another coat of copper paint was slapped on to further ensure that the wood would not be eaten away from under him.

Slocum made a number of adaptations on the voyage. At Buenos Aires he "unshipped the sloop's mast . . . and shortened it by seven feet. I reduced the length of the bowsprit by about five feet, and even then I found it reaching far enough from home; and more than once when on the end of its reefing the jib, I regretted that I had not shortened it another foot." Later, in Keeling (Cocos) Islands waters, he changed the boat's ballast, replacing the three tons of cement ballast with mammoth tridacna shells.

The captain wasn't always racing around deck. The *Spray*'s self-steering abilities afforded him the leisure to read in his cabin. "In the days of serene weather," he later wrote, "there was not much to do but to read and take rest on the *Spray*, to make up as much as possible for the rough time off Cape Horn, which was not yet forgotten, and to forestall the Cape of Good Hope by a store of ease."

But where the sloop avoided one danger she encountered another. For one day, well off the Patagonian coast, while the sloop was reaching under short sail, a tremendous wave, the culmination, it seemed of many waves, rolled down upon her in a storm, roaring as it came. I had only a moment to get all sail down and myself up on the peak halliards, out of danger, when I saw the mighty crest towering masthead-high above me. The mountain of water submerged my vessel. She shook in every timber and reeled under the weight of the sea, but rose quickly out of it, and rode grandly over the rollers that followed. It may have been a minute that from my hold in the rigging I could see no part of the Spray's *hull. Perhaps it was even less time than that . . . Not only did the past, with electric speed, flash before me, but I had time while in my hazardous position for resolutions for the future that would take a long time to fulfil.*

— J.S., *Sailing Alone*

7

High Seas
Adventures

For under great excitement, one lives fast.
  — J.S., *Sailing Alone*

From the moment he set out on his around-the-world
voyage, Slocum knew that adventure awaited him over
every horizon. "Take warning, *Spray*, and have a care,"
he bellowed prophetically as he sailed his sloop out of
Massachusetts Bay at the beginning of the voyage. It was
not long before the *Spray* encountered her first sea adventure, when she was battered and tossed around in the
temperamental tide rips off Brier Island. When Slocum
arrived on his childhood island safe and sound, he showed
that even an experienced seadog like himself was prone
to superstitious thinking in nautical matters, "It was the
13th of the month, and 13 is my lucky number — a fact

Three previously unpublished photographs given to the author by Joshua Slocum's great-granddaughters (Benjamin Aymar Slocum's granddaughters), Carol Slocum Jimerson and Gale Slocum Hermanet.

Virginia Albertina (Walker) Slocum, taken in Manila, some time between 1875 and 1880

Victor Slocum, taken in China (circa 1875)

Benjamin Aymar Slocum, probably age six (circa 1880)

All other photographs courtesy Old Dartmouth Historical Society — New Bedford Whaling Museum

Captain Slocum and the Gilbert Islanders he rescued in the Pacific Ocean. Unknown Japanese photographer (1882)

The homemade "canoe" *Liberdade* in which Slocum sailed home from South America
with his second wife, Hettie, and their two sons, Garfield and Victor.
Unknown photographer (1889)

A watercolor by Charles Henry Gifford of the *Spray* as a derelict at Poverty Point,
Fairhaven, Massachusetts. Informally titled "She wants some repairs" (1889)

A portrait of Slocum taken about the time he had just self-published *Voyage of the Liberdade*. Unknown photographer (circa 1890)

A rare photograph of the interior of the *Spray*'s cabin. Note the rudimentary navigational instruments that Slocum used on his voyages. Unknown photographer (circa 1900)

Spray moored at Gibraltar in August 1895. Slocum was on the first leg of his journey, before he decided to sail westward around the world. Ernest Lacy (1895)

Slocum aboard the *Spray* in South America, after sailing from Gibraltar through the doldrums and arriving in Pernambuco, Brazil. Unknown photographer (circa 1896)

An unusual photo of the *Spray* hauled out at Devonport, Tasmania.
The bottom was coated with copper paint to protect it from damage by mollusks.
Unknown photographer (1897)

Spray under sail in Australian waters. Slocum was into the second year of his circumnavigation of the globe, having spent Christmas 1896 in Melbourne.
Unknown photographer (1897)

registered long before Dr. Nansen sailed in search of the north pole with his crew of thirteen." Luck may have been with him, but there were to be many more challenging seas in which Slocum's boat would be "whirled around like a top." The old sailor expected and accepted these as an inevitable part of blue water sailing. He may have been less prepared for the adventures that arose not from weather and ocean but from other seafarers, among them pirates, brigands, cannibals and curious natives.

The first unusual predicament came as he sailed west from Gibraltar in late August of 1895 after being forced to backtrack across the Atlantic, owing to the dangers of Mediterranean pirates. The irony of this change in route was evident immediately. Just out of Gibraltar, off the coast of Morocco, Slocum spied a felucca carrying pirates and thieves. It seemed to be in hot pursuit of the *Spray*, so the captain changed direction. The confirmation of his fears came swiftly: the felucca changed direction and remained in pursuit. By Slocum's calculations, it was gaining on him. He wrote later that the ship came within a whisker of catching up to him: "I now saw the tufts of hair on the heads of the crew, — by which, it is said, Mohammed will pull the villains up into heaven, — and they were coming on like the wind." They were such a fierce-looking crew that Slocum reckoned them to be "the sons of generations of pirates." One glance at them and he knew they planned to do him harm. What happened next was like a gift from heaven. Slocum was stunned to

115

see the felucca, with far too much sail on for the conditions, broach to on a wave. But Slocum had little time for their sudden setback to register: in an instant he was hit by the same wave. With the shudder of impact, one that "shook her in every timber," the *Spray*'s mainboom broke at the rigging. Slocum turned his attention from outracing scoundrels to downing jib and mainsail. He later told a newspaper reporter, "You can just imagine that the one-man crew had to skip around pretty brisk to get the jib and mainsail secure."

Having saved the *Spray*, he turned his mind quickly back to matters of self-defense. He raced below to his cabin and grabbed his loaded Martini-Henry, assuming the pirates were almost ready to board. Back on deck, he watched a frantic spectacle: the pirates were not only much farther off but also completely out of the race. The elements had neutralized their blood-hungry greed. Instead of pillaging, they were scrambling to stay afloat in a dismasted boat: "I perceived [the] thieving crew, some dozen or more of them, struggling to recover their rigging from the sea." Slocum later noted sardonically, "Needless to say I did not stop to help them." He found a certain amount of justice in this moment. This first pirate adventure, and the quick repair of his broken boom, left the captain "too fatigued to sleep."

Slocum would have other perilous encounters with the wild side of humanity when he sailed through the Strait of Magellan. But before he entered those hazardous waters, he had his share of threatening moments in seas farther to the north. One night he found himself tossing miserably for hours and felt "heartsore of choppy seas." Slocum may have been a pragmatic sailor, but he maintained an optimism and a clear vision of his goal: "I will not say that I expected all fine sailing on the course for Cape Horn direct, but while I worked at the sails and rigging I thought only of onward and forward." At the same time, however, he noted that "where the sloop avoided one danger she encountered another."

He later confessed that one of the dangers had been avoidable and that it was his own error that had got him into trouble. He misjudged the distance to the Uruguayan coast, and December 11, 1895 found the *Spray* beached. Slocum surveyed the situation and determined his sloop to be hard and fast ashore. Next he looked out to sea and noted that a strong swell was running. To get his boat back in the water, he devised a plan that involved taking his small auxilliary anchor, the kedge, and attaching a light line to it. With one end of the line made fast to the *Spray*, he rowed out in his sawed-off dory until the line was taut, and then dropped the kedge anchor. But the tide was falling, and the *Spray* could not be budged. He resorted to a second strategy, and here is where he really got himself into trouble. This time he went out with his heaviest anchor, which weighed 180 pounds. The weight of the anchor and its cable swamped his little dory immediately, and Slocum quickly jumped out before he reached deep water. He then cut the cable in half and got back in the dory. He rowed out farther, but the dory was leaking and sinking fast, so he raised the anchor over his head and tossed it clear of the boat. At the same moment, the dory rolled over. Slocum could only hold on for his life. As the captain later told the story, it was while he was clinging to the gunwale that he suddenly remembered he could not swim. Three times he tried to right the dory and each time she rolled completely around. Slocum was seized by the determination not to give those who had scoffed at him the opportunity for a posthumous "I told you so." On the fourth try, he righted the dory and hauled himself back on board, with the help of a well-placed oar.

Back on the beach, after securing the two parts of his cable, he let himself collapse on the warm sand for a rest while he waited on the tide. At the sound of horse's hooves on the sand, Slocum opened an eye and saw a young boy looking over the *Spray* as if he had just found buried treasure. The young fellow attempted to move the sloop by tying it to his horse to haul, but failed as dismally as Slocum had with his kedge. The boy still hadn't seen the old seadog watching him. The interloper gave up the idea of towing the *Spray* and instead eyed the dory. At this point, Slocum made his presence known, telling the boy that he and his ship had come from the moon to take back a cargo of boys. His jest was perhaps taken seriously, for the boy whirled his lariat and tried to rope the captain. This made yet another tall tale for Slocum to tell later.

A great moment of high seas adventure was waiting over the horizon — one that would show off Slocum's expert seamanship and quick thinking. It came just over a month later, at the end of January 1896. Slocum was sailing cautiously down the treacherous Patagonian coast. In choppy waters, he looked out to sea and saw a huge wave heading toward him. From years of sailing in every kind of sea imaginable, he had learned to read the patterns and intervals between waves. Now and again those rhythms can synchronize to create one horrendous, monumental wave. And that was what was coming straight for the *Spray*. Slocum knew what he had to do, and fast: "I had only a moment to get all sail down and myself up on the peak halliards, out of danger, when I saw the mighty crest towering masthead-high above me. The mountain of water submerged my vessel." Because the sails were down, the *Spray* presented no surface for the massive wave to strike. Had it hit canvas, the sloop would probably have rolled over and been lost, for she did not have a self-righting hull. To be able to react perfectly in the moment and arrive at the only workable solution to a serious threat must have been satisfying to Slocum. He still had what it took to survive in tempestuous seas, and sailing south toward the Horn, he would need every ounce of his skill.

On February 14, 1896, having entered the Strait of Magellan, he arrived at the Chilean port of Punta Arenas. This part of the voyage provided him with a taste of the dangers that he would be facing for the next two months.

The seas beyond the southern tip of South America are the only part of the planet where the ocean goes all the way around the earth along a constant line of latitude without running into a land mass. Slocum described the effect: "At this point where the tides from the Atlantic and the Pacific meet, and in the strait, as on the outside coast, their meeting makes a commotion of whirlpools and combers that in a gale of wind is dangerous to canoes and other frail craft." Slocum was able to wax poetic over the ancient power of the Horn, the place where "the waves rose and fell and bellowed their never-ending-story of the sea."

While resupplying himself in port, Slocum got a sense of what other dangers might be lurking in those waters. He observed the Patagonian and Fuegian natives and felt that they were "as squalid as contact with unscrupulous traders could make them." He blamed their degraded state on the unlawful sale of "fire-water," which he thought was "poisonous stuff to the natives." At the customhouse, Slocum learned there was serious trouble brewing. Just before Slocum arrived in Punta Arenas, the governor had ordered an attack on a Fuegian settlement, as a swift sign of retribution for the natives' massacre of a schooner's crew. In light of the potentially explosive situation, the port captain strongly advised Slocum to take on a small crew while he sailed through the strait. But the feisty Captain Slocum had pledged himself to a solo voyage and would have none of it — he would not even consider having a watchdog on board. An Austrian captain presented the Yankee sailor with a bag of carpet tacks. Captain Pedro Samblich was a cryptic sort, and when Slocum protested that he had no use for this bizarre gift, Samblich told him bluntly, "You must use them with discretion, that is to say, don't step on them yourself." Slocum would later reflect that Samblich's gift was "worth more than all the fighting men and dogs of Tierro del Fuego."

He did, however, sail with loaded guns and rifles, mindful of the port captain's advice to shoot at the first sign of trouble, but to try not to kill any Fuegians in doing so. Slocum was worried, and later reflected, "It was not without thoughts of strange and stirring adventure beyond all I had yet encountered that I now sailed into the country and very core of the savage Fuegians." In Fortescue Bay he saw his first signs of trouble: native signal fires burning all around him. He anchored in a bed of kelp for two and a half days to wait out a heavy gale. On sailing out, he noticed he was not alone — canoes manned by "savages" were gaining on the *Spray*, but this time it was not to terrorize. They yelled out to Slocum the word "yammerschooner," which, he thought, was their term for begging. His reply to them was negative. What worried Slocum was the opportunity the encounter had given the Fuegians to study his situation. He could not afford to let them know he was sailing alone, and his mercurial mind arrived at an ingenious solution. He ran "into the cabin, and passing through the hold, came out at the forecastle changing my clothes as I went along. That made two men." He also fashioned a crude marionette from a sawed off piece of bowsprit, dressed it as a seaman, stuffed it on the lookout, and attached lines, so that he could manipulate the puppet as needed. Three on board was the message the Fuegians would get. However, this did not deter them. Slocum fired his first shot when the nearest canoe was about eighty yards from his boat. The incursion ended, but only for a moment. He fired a second shot close enough to one of the paddlers that they would think he had been aiming for him. The Fuegians took off for an island, leaving Slocum to write, "So much for the first day of savages."

On those days on the strait when he was forced to take shelter from storms and gales, Slocum was alert: "I reasoned that I had all about me the greatest danger of the whole voyage — the treachery of cunning savages." When he collected firewood, he carried his rifle, and always chose shores that seemed to be free of natives. He read the signs of the land as he did those at sea. The presence of birds and seals on the rocks gave him some assurance there were no cruel men about, but he was determined never to be surprised.

Early March found him in the Cockburn Channel, with time to reflect on the nautical excitement of the preceding days. He anchored on March 8 off Thieves Bay, where he was unable to shake the tormenting feeling that he was not alone. Even after a hot and comforting meal, he felt uneasy about giving in to his physical exhaustion.

Perhaps it was his stew, made from venison that Captain Samblich had given him, that reminded him of the good Austrian's other gift. Before allowing himself to fall asleep, Slocum sprinkled the carpet tacks over the *Spray*'s deck. He minded where he set foot, as the tacks were standing "business end" up. Around midnight, Slocum was jolted from his sleep by a cacophony of wild howls, "like a pack of hounds." The Fuegians had tried to sneak aboard in the dark; being barefoot, they had gotten the point (literally) that they were unwelcome aboard the *Spray*. Slocum looked up through the companionway to witness a frantic sight: "They jumped pell-mell, some into their canoes and some into the sea, to cool off, I suppose, and there was a deal of free language over it as they went." Slocum added to the spectacle by coming up on deck and firing his guns. Another calamity was averted, but the captain knew that unless he moved on, retaliation was only a matter of time.

Slocum would have yet another round with the Fuegians, just off Port Angosto. Working on the deck, he was spooked by the sound of something zipping through the air. He looked up to see an arrow sticking in the *Spray*'s mainmast, not far from where he was working. Slocum started firing to smoke the natives out of hiding. There were three of them, and Slocum aimed under their feet as they ran, to encourage their hasty retreat. They would never return, but while Slocum stayed in those waters he never slept without a liberal sprinkling of carpet tacks above him on deck. As for the arrow, he dubbed it "a Fuegian autograph." Once fairer weather arrived, he sailed away from the treacherous scene, noting that "had I been given to superstitious fears I should not have persisted in sailing on a thirteenth day."

Slocum recounted in *Sailing Alone Around the World* that he survived several other bizarre encounters with the hostile natives of Tierra del Fuego. At one point they appeared in what was obviously a stolen boat. Two of them stood up defiantly, and Slocum noticed that they were wearing sea boots. Quickly he pieced together the murderous story: not only had they attacked and pillaged a ship passing through the strait but they were warning Slocum that his carpet tacks were now useless as a means of defense. The captain was becoming unnerved. When he noticed natives armed with bows and spears hiding among the bushes on shore, he began working furiously to free the *Spray* from the mass of kelp her anchor had become tangled in. He worked until his fingers bled, in the hope of making a quick getaway from lurking native treachery. All the while he kept "one eye over my shoulders for savages. I watched at the same time, and sent a bullet whistling whenever I saw a limb or a twig move."

On another occasion he recognized one of the members of the boat party. It was none other than Black Pedro, the leader of many of the bloody massacres reported and a man, Slocum wrote, who was considered to be "the worst murderer in Tierra del Fuego." Officials had been hunting him down for over two years. Slocum was to meet the unscrupulous leader face to face during the days he was stuck in the strait. Throughout that encounter Slocum would keep his gun ready in hand.

Slocum may have embellished his tales of the native Fuegians; but the stories he told of his incredible seamanship through the waters off the tip of South America were, if anything, modest and self-effacing. He was blown back into the Strait of Magellan; for over two months he battled elemental forces. When the *Spray* first entered the Strait of Magellan on February 11, 1896, her captain would already have known full well that extreme weather was the norm in that desolate region. Squalls, gales and downpours were constant, and any wind not much over thirty knots was considered moderate. Even without a horrendous squall, the days could be tough going, and Slocum had to be ready at any time to shorten sail. He immediately observed the unruly nature of the waters he was about to venture through. He caught sight of two tide races and calculated that the *Spray*'s best hope was to charge through the channel between, under close-reefed sails. The tactic paid off. On a rare day when the sailing was smoother, he had almost relaxed when he spotted a steamer wrecked on a beach. He took the sight of it as a stern word of warning, and in fact he was not to be let off easy. During an especially bad rain squall, he found that all he could do was reef sail, and sit below in the *Spray*'s cabin to rest his eyes and wait out the conditions.

"I was so strongly impressed with what in all nature I might expect that as I dozed the very air I breathed seemed to warn me of danger. My senses heard '*Spray*, ahoy!' shouted in warning."

What he saw in the pitch-black of night was a white arch, which he gleaned immediately was "the terror of Cape Horn." What gave the experienced captain such a start was that he was nearing it at alarming speed, driven forward on a strong southwest gale. Without hesitation he downed sail to reduce the chances of catastrophe when the gale struck full force. For Slocum, who had sailed through many a wild gale, the first half-hour of this storm was an almighty blow, one to be long remembered. Diminished but wild winds nonetheless continued blowing for well over a day. Slocum fought to keep the *Spray* from being blown back, and was relieved when he cleared the narrows three days later.

But as he left Punta Arenas, he was barely off on his second leg of the trip through the strait when he met up with williwaws, which he described as "compressed gales of wind that Boreas handed down over the hills in chunks." These fearsome winds arise when cold descending air masses follow the elevated coastal topography and then hurl themselves out to sea. These extremely strong gusts off the land are challenging for even highly experienced seamen, and Slocum knew their awesome power: "A full-blown williwaw will throw a ship, even without sail on, over her beam ends." He rested from their numbing blows

126

whenever he could. Finally he anchored at Port Tamar and looked out on Cape Pillar. Although he thought of Cape Pillar as "the grim sentinel of the Horn," he also perceived it as a sign that he would soon be clear of the strait. He mused, "Here I felt the throb of the great ocean that lay before me. I knew now that I had put a world behind me, and that I was opening out another world ahead." It was only early March, and he was to be in a furious limbo for another six weeks in this hellish four-hundred-mile passage.

As he neared Cape Pillar in the heavy rains, Slocum remained optimistic. The *Spray* even got her first "bath" in Pacific Ocean water, from seas tossed up in the building storm. He responded to the moment and fought to keep his boat sailing before the colossal winds. He crowded on sail, but there was a sudden shift from southwest back to northeast. Now the fierce winds demanded that Slocum sail with bare pole — a testimony to their terrifying force. The boat was at the complete mercy of the wind. Simply by pushing on the cabin, the hull and the exposed masts, it was driving the *Spray* at top speed. For good reason, Slocum was afraid of the waves crashing side-ways down on the deck, with their potential to roll the sloop over and break its masts. Far worse even than this was the possibility that he might "pitch pole" — that is, that the *Spray* might go down the face of a wave so fast that it turned over, stern over bow.

Slocum resigned himself to turning eastward to keep

ahead of the wind. This route was unsettling and unnerving, for he was now sailing in the direction he would take if he were intending to round Cape Horn. Four days of wind found the *Spray* nearing the pitch of the Horn. By this time the mainsail was so battered and Slocum so tired that he actually welcomed the prospect of re-entering the strait and working his way through again. Even at this distance from the Horn, the exposed coastal sailing was demanding. He went to sleep that night wondering exactly where his sloop was in these dangerous waters. When darkness descended he was still "feeling his way in pitchy darkness." He was startled and puzzled by the sound of breakers where there shouldn't have been any. He awoke the next morning to a frightening discovery: the *Spray* was making its way straight through the dreaded Milky Way of the Sea.

During this treacherous passage, just to the northeast of Cape Horn, Slocum found himself engulfed by churning, furious seas crashing everywhere over slightly submerged rocks. These rocks have always been navigational hazards, for in the whipped-up foam of the Milky Way, it is unclear to sailors just where the jagged dangers lie. Slocum had read an account of this phenomenon by Charles Darwin, who had observed the fury of these seas from aboard the *Beagle*. "Any landsman seeing the Milky Way would have nightmares for a week," Darwin had written. Slocum called his adventure through this maze of rocks and crashing seas "the greatest sea adventure of my life." He was alone in horrendous weather, terrible visibility and the most treacherous of seas. He had no choice whatsoever except to keep on sailing till he was through the rocks. His face was bleeding from the assault of spray, hail and sleet, but he kept changing sail around the clock. He had set his sights on and steered for Fury Island. He simply kept going, and when he had made it, he could only wonder, "God knows how my vessel escaped."

Just as the captain was starting to breathe easy, he found himself back in the Cockburn Channel, whose waters would lead him back into the Strait of Magellan. It is no surprise he had gotten confused. Because of all the yawing and pitching, his measurements with the sextant had gone awry. He was determined not to return to Punta Arenas for repairs, and at the first small stretch of quiet, he set to work mending his ripped sail with scavenged bits of canvas.

Moving through the Cockburn Channel meant few anchorages, plenty of opportunities to get trapped, and tacking through narrow passages with adverse currents. Perhaps the most taxing aspect of this passage was that it offered little in the way of rest or sleeping time. His only relief came in the lee of a mountain or in a snug cove or inlet. He had to stay alert for hours on end and retain the stamina and the smarts to react wisely. He sailed through a gale and a snowstorm en route to Port Angosto. Having reached it, he had great difficulty leaving it. Finally, on April 13, 1896, on his seventh try, he put to sea and was able to sail free of Tierra del Fuego. He stayed at the helm the whole time, "humoring my vessel." A final wave broke over the sloop; it would be the last of the treacherous Cape Horn waters to hit the *Spray*'s deck. Slocum speculated optimistically, "All my troubles were now astern; summer was ahead; all the world was again before me."

Still in dismal fog I felt myself drifting into loneliness, an insect on a straw in the midst of the elements. I lashed the helm, and my vessel held her course, and while she sailed I slept.

During these days a feeling of awe crept over me. My memory worked with startling power. The ominous, the insignificant, the great, the small, the wonderful, the commonplace — all appeared before my mental vision in magical succession. Pages of my history were recalled which had been so long forgotten that they seemed to belong to a previous existence. I heard all the voices of the past laughing, crying, telling what I had heard them tell in many corners of the earth.

The loneliness of my state wore off when the gale was high and I found much work to do. When fine weather returned, then came the sense of solitude, which I could not shake off.

— J.S., *Sailing Alone*

8

Walden at Sea:
A Solitude Supreme

Even when I slept I dreamed that I was alone.
J.S., *Sailing Alone*

For all the exhilarating moments fed by the sheer adrenalin rush of adventure and life-threatening danger, there was a constant and more grueling aspect to Joshua Slocum's voyage: the stark reality of solitude. For more than three years Slocum sailed over the earth's waters by himself. The paradox of a sailor's life is that he lives out his freedom within the confines of a very small space. Slocum's world was thirty-seven feet long and held no form of companionship. His circumnavigation was a journey into unimaginable solitude and was filled with the psychological perils that arise from such an experience. Early on in the voyage Slocum got a stiff glimpse of the intense loneliness of his undertaking and of the personal demons that surface during prolonged solitude.

Although Slocum eventually came to embrace what he called his "solitude supreme," he had first to sail through the fearful isolation that came soon after he left Nova Scotia behind and entered the Atlantic. Slocum wrote of his final farewell to the land, "I watched light after light sink astern as I sailed into the unbounded sea, till Sambro, the last of [the beacons] was below the horizon." On his first solo day, Slocum found himself enveloped by fog so thick "one could almost 'stand on it.'" It was as if his loneliness had been made visible as the thick fog "lowered over the sea like a pall. I was in a world of fog, shut off from the universe." He knew the whole sea was ahead of him, but for the time being he could only hear and imagine the ocean beyond. He and the *Spray* were one small speck on an all-encompassing sea, invisible to the rest of the world. Slocum pondered his invisibility with a growing awareness of his insignificance in the universe: "In the dismal fog I felt myself drifting into loneliness, an insect on a straw in the midst of the elements."

He triumphed on this voyage's first test of emotional stamina, and later reflected, "The acute pain of solitude experienced at first never returned. I had penetrated a mystery, and, by the way, I had sailed through a fog. I had met Neptune in his wrath, but he found that I had not treated him with contempt, and so he suffered me to go on and explore." Although his loneliness lifted with the fog during that first week on the water, it would return later at intervals throughout the voyage. Often when he had left good company in port, he faced a small battle to readjust to his solitary life. Samoa was one of his most pleasant stopovers, and on leaving the island he was brought face to face with his isolation. During his stay he had been lulled into that island's tropical rhythms and ease of life: "While the days go thus in these Southern islands we at the North are struggling for the bare necessities of life." He had enjoyed a camaraderie with the Samoans, and of that departure he wrote that a "sense of loneliness seized upon me as the islands faded astern." Although he may have felt a twinge of homesickness for this island paradise, the truth was that Slocum had no place to call home. No strong ties pulled him anywhere or hurried him on his way. His only home was on his boat, wherever it sailed and whatever conditions it faced.

Slocum was also reminded of his solitude by the isolated and barren spots he sailed past. On seeing a light beaming from a hill in Port Tamar on the Strait of Magellan, he mused on what that remote island beacon signified. Speculating that someone had actually lived on that godforsaken spot, he asked, "How could one tell but that he had died of loneliness and grief? In a bleak land is not the place to enjoy solitude." In moments of profound isolation, a sailor fears that everyone has forgotten about him, and that if anything were to happen to him out on the water, no one would ever know. The possibility of becoming ill or being injured far out to sea arouses anxiety in any sailor. But once the fog lifted, Slocum would begin to exult in his solitude. "All distracting uneasiness and excitement being now over, I was once more alone with myself in the realization that I was on the mighty sea and in the hands of the elements. But I was happy, and was becoming more and more interested in the voyage."

Having confronted his insignificance, Slocum was free to appreciate, without self-pity, the marvels that surrounded him. For great stretches of time, Slocum saw only water and sky. His world for the most part was a palette of blues with touches of white and grey. In every direction at all times, he was exposed to the horizon. He had his cabin for relief, but spent most of his time in the open air. "Then was the time to uncover my head, for I sailed alone with God. The vast ocean was again around me, and the horizon was unbroken by land."

Slocum sailed through a world in which the potential for wonder was constant. At every turn he was exposed to the elements. His senses were finely attuned to the clouds, the waves and whatever might move through the water. Astronomical and meteorological events that most people would not notice were played out before him. The sky encircled him. Nights could bring light shows: shooting stars trailing through the sky, mirrored in and then vanishing into the water. A lightning bolt would be hurled into the distant sea, and he could only imagine what besides his small boat could be its target. A light rain might bring with it a vaulting rainbow, giving the *Spray* a prism to sail through until it came to the rainbow's end.

On the open sea, sailors often encounter strange phenomena. It is these sightings that fuel tales of the supernatural — of burning phantom ships and mystical green flashes. The phosphorescence created by microscopic phytoplankton, which begin to glow when the water is agitated, resembles a fire in the crashing waves. To sailors, a porpoise swimming through this fire often looks like an alien being, like a glowing apparition trailing streaks of sparks. Slocum came upon this spectacular sight and was moved to write, "For days she sailed in water milky white and green and purple. It was my good fortune to enter the sea on the last quarter of the moon, the advantage being that in the dark nights I witnessed the phosphorescent light effect at night in its greatest splendor. The sea, where the sloop disturbed it, seemed all ablaze, so that by its light I could see the smallest articles on deck, and her wake was a path of fire."

After weeks in this world of wonders, a sailor's grip on reality can start to loosen. Size becomes difficult to judge, and weird optical illusions abound. Slocum wrote about his frequent problems with seeing things: "The weather became fine and the sea smooth and life tranquil. The phenomenon of mirage frequently occurred. An albatross sitting on the water one day loomed up like a large ship; two fur-seals asleep on the surface of the sea appeared like great whales, and a bank of haze I could have sworn was high land. The kaleidoscope then changed, and on the following day I sailed in a world peopled by dwarfs."

Slocum came to realize that he could not trust his eyes in this world, where whales could look like steep breakers, and where real waves rising up in a fog could look like huge steamers making straight for his boat. When Slocum ran the *Spray* ashore on a Uruguayan beach, the accident was an abrupt and humbling reminder not to trust his eyes: "The false appearance of the sand-hills under a bright moon had deceived me, and I lamented now that I had trusted to appearances at all."

As he sailed alone through nights as black as hell, Slocum communed with those who had sailed the same seas centuries before him. His mind turned to Columbus on the *Santa Maria*. He looked on these ghosts from the past as fellow sailors traveling with him in spirit. At one point he came to the head of a cove, which appeared to him as "a sort of Calvary . . . where navigators, carrying their cross, had each set one up as a beacon to others coming after. They had anchored here and gone on . . . I read the other names of many other vessels; some of them I copied in my journal, others were illegible. Many of the crosses had decayed and fallen, and many a hand now still. The air of depression was about the place, and I hurried back to the sloop to forget myself again in the voyage."

His reading Washington Irving's *Life of Columbus* may have led to one ghostly encounter on the *Spray*. It

137

happened early, as he crossed the Atlantic heading to Gibraltar. Slocum had just left the island of Faial in the Azores, and made a supper from the Pico cheese and plums he had been given as gifts. That night found him sick and wretched in his cabin, bent over with painful cramps and delirious with fever. At one point he looked out the companionway, concerned about how the *Spray* was managing on her own. To his amazement, he saw a tall, ethereal form at the helm. Slocum thought the apparition was a pirate, as he was dressed like a foreign sailor with a "large red cap . . . cockbilled over his left ear, all was set off with shaggy black whiskers." Slocum feared for his life, and the stranger seemed to sense it. The man told him he was "never worse than a contrabandista," and identified himself as Martin Alonso Pinzòn, the pilot of Columbus's ship the *Pinta*. As he steered, he yelled into the wind, "Yonder is the Pinta ahead; we must overtake her. Give her sail! Vale, vale, muy vale!" He chanted a wild sea ditty about roaring tempests, fierce waves and screaming seabirds, and didn't vanish until he gave Slocum a word of advice to prevent future "pains and calentura," as he diagnosed the seadog's stomach cramps. He told Slocum, "You did wrong, captain, to mix cheese with plums. White cheese is never safe unless you know whence it comes." When he regained consciousness, Slocum dumped the plums into the sea.

The *Pinta*'s commander, or whoever or whatever had steered the *Spray* that night, was just one of Slocum's fellow travelers. Slocum looked for companions wherever they might appear. Early in the voyage he welcomed into his circle of friends the "smiling full moon" sitting at the end of his bowsprit. He confided that "many long talks since then I have had with the man in the moon; he had my confidence on the voyage." Throughout, he took delight in these interactions with nature. Making his way to Samoa, he reveled that "there was no end of companionship; the very coral reefs kept me company, or gave me no time to feel lonely, which is the same thing." Sometimes his encounters were startling. A great whale swam directly underneath the *Spray* as the boat sailed from Juan Fernández to Samoa, and Slocum bolted up on deck. He was greeted by a snort, great turbulence and a thorough drenching as the whale spouted.

Visitors from the animal kingdom also lived for a time aboard the *Spray*. Along with a cantankerous goat, which he marooned after one thousand miles of tedious travel, Slocum sheltered smaller, more cooperative stowaways. From the voyage's beginning there had been, as Slocum dubbed them, "the spider and his wife, from Boston." He observed later that their offspring had become part of the cruise. Slocum brought a Tierra del Fuego spider on board for the family to meet. The consequences for this visitor were disastrous: "In my cabin it met, oddly enough, a spider of its own size and species that had come all the way from Boston — a very civil little chap, too, but mighty spry. Well, the Fuegian threw up its antennae for a fight;

but my little Bostonian downed it at once, then broke its legs, and pulled them off, one by one, so dexterously that in less than three minutes from the time the battle began the Fuegian spider didn't know itself from a fly."

But Slocum's closest and most constant companion throughout his voyage was the *Spray* herself. He had given her shape and made her a thing of beauty, at least to his eyes. At times he seemed to treat the *Spray* as a living, breathing entity. He respected her part in his grand undertaking and considered her needs along the way. At Mauritius he paused and found a moment, "where I drew a long breath, the *Spray* rested her wings, it being the season of fine weather." To him, the *Spray* had a unique personality, and he knew her every eccentricity. He wrote about his boat as if she had a mind of her own. And always he captured *Spray*'s spirited moments with fondness and humor. "When I found myself, for instance, disentangling the sloop's mast from the branches of a tree after she had drifted three times around a small island, against my will, it seemed more than one's nerves could bear, and I had to speak about it, so I thought, or die of lockjaw, and I apostrophized the *Spray* as an impatient farmer might his horse or ox. 'Didn't you know,' cried I — 'didn't you know that you couldn't climb a tree?'" Then he reflected on what she had just come through making her way in the Strait of Magellan, and compassion overcame him: "Moreover, she had discovered an island. On the charts this one that she had sailed around was traced as a point of land."

Besides conversing with the *Spray*, the man in the moon, Neptune and various ghosts and sea creatures, Slocum shouted orders to imaginary crew and belted shanties and hymns into the salt winds. He had been warned before leaving that he could lose his voice from misuse. At first he talked incessantly, crying out "Eight bells," but that grew wearisome, and he probably saw the threat to his sanity in this approach to preserving his vocal cords. He also noted that his speaking voice "sounded hollow in the empty air, and I dropped the practice. However, it was not long before the thought came to me that when I was a lad I used to sing; why not try that now, where it would disturb no one? My musical talent had never bred envy in others, but out on the Atlantic, to realize what it meant, you should have heard me sing." Slocum fancied that porpoises leaped when "[I] pitched my voice for the waves and the sea and all that was in it." Choruses of old music hall tunes charmed old turtles out of their shells. "The porpoises were, on the whole, vastly more appreciative than the turtles; they jumped a deal higher. One day when I was humming a favorite chant, I think it was 'Babylon's a Fallin',' a porpoise jumped higher than the bowsprit. Had the *Spray* been going a little faster she would have scooped him in. The sea-birds sailed around rather shy."

Slocum's accounts of many of his solitary experiences show a strong gift for whimsy. He mixed his adventurous pioneering spirit with a good dose of lighthearted play.

He had some fun in his role as explorer of new territories. He named the *Spray*'s newly discovered island in the Strait of Magellan Alan Erric Island, "after a worthy literary friend whom I had met in strange by-places, and I put up a sign, 'Keep off the grass', which, as discoverer, was within my rights." Earlier in his adventures near the storm-lashed Horn he had sought shelter at midnight in the lee of an island. There he prepared a well-deserved cup of coffee — a birthday present to himself on the day he turned fifty-two. The drink was such a boost to his spirits after a day of beating heavy squalls and sailing against the current that he named the soulful shelter Coffee Island.

Though a practical man, Slocum heard poetry in the waves that lapped around his boat, referring to them whimsically as "gossiping waves," and he fancied that they "doffed their white caps beautifully." He yearned for the romantic, unhurried era of sailing. He recalled the good old days when ships stopped in ports for a "gam," or chat, with the locals, and fired their guns as a salute upon parting, and he bemoaned the changes in sea etiquette: "There are no poetry-enshrined freighters on the sea now; it is a prosy life when we have no time to bid one another good morning."

Passing boats and storms brought home the practical realities and quickly tamed his solitary flights of fancy. He had only to feel the salt spray smart in his eyes after hours of sailing through screaming gales. With no one on board to relieve him during stormy spells, Slocum knew all about the strange states of mind that come after uninterrupted hours at the helm. He had a rare stamina, and during one storm off the Horn, he stayed at the helm for thirty hours. Sometimes he continued sailing hours after his body and mind had been driven to a state beyond tiredness. His body worked automatically, registering and responding to the hiss of each wave: Was this the one that would break over the boat? He knew what extremes of exertion were required for solo sailing, and what it was like to deprive himself of sleep. He fought to stay awake by any means he could find: a reviving splash of water, a mouthful of pilot bread, a song to belt out. No doubt he often entered the next level of exhaustion, the moment when fatigue lifts and a sailor feels as if he could continue sailing for days. At this point he is functioning like a machine, and it often takes a sudden emergency to shake off any illusions of invincibility. He must then take stock and find a way to master his exhaustion. He must keep sailing.

Slocum thrived on the challenge of rough sailing; it was spells of becalming that tried his temper and patience to the limit. He hit one such spell in the horse latitudes. When sailing through a storm, sailors sense they are at the mercy of wind and water, but they also feel that it is within their power to affect the situation. A sailor who is becalmed quite literally has the wind taken out of his sails. He must sit helplessly on the spot where the sails went slat. A boat that is becalmed doesn't enjoy the regular patterns or predictability of a boat that is moving through the water. For days on end the boat may never sit level. With no wind to keep the sails filled, the booms, gaffs and sails slam about aimlessly; this puts an incredible strain on the canvas, which in turn strikes the halyard, which gives a shock to the mast. That shock is transmitted down the mast and the standing rigging to the hull; thus, with each blow a shock is registered throughout the hull.

A spell of becalming is even harder on the nerves. Bang! every four or five seconds when all the sails go slat. Clunk! because the waves are still rocking the boat but there's not enough wind to fill the sails and keep the pressure on them. This destructive and infuriating inertia can bring out the "Type A" personality traits that lurk in many sailors. Some react by frantically trying to tighten sails and looking for ways to keep them from slatting. Then after a time the frustrated sailor realizes that he can't make the wind blow. He just has to make the best of it and manage his boat properly while he waits for conditions to change. And waiting in a flat calm on a hot humid day under a blazing sun feels like slow torture.

Slocum knew the kind of attitude that becalming required, and he found a certain amount of pleasure in the surrender. Of his enforced stay, he waxed philosophical, comparing this trial to earlier ones he had suffered: "I had almost forgotten this calm belt, or had come to regard it as a myth. I now found it real, however, and difficult to cross. This was as it should have been, for, after all of the

Walden at Sea: A Solitude Supreme

dangers of the sea, the duststorm on the coast of Africa, the 'rain of blood' in Australia, and the war risk when nearing home, a natural experience would have been missing had the calm of the horse latitudes been left out. Anyhow, a philosophical turn of thought now was not amiss, else one's patience would have given out almost at the harbor entrance. The term of her probation was eight days. Evening after evening during this time I read by the light of a candle on deck. There was no wind at all, and the sea became smooth and monotonous. For three days I saw a full-rigged ship on the horizon, also becalmed."

During moments of clear sailing the captain found a deep peace, and a connection with a greater power. On fine days he sailed by the positions of the stars, the sun and the moon. He had his sextant for taking early morning, noon and twilight sightings. Slocum was well versed in the subtleties of celestial navigation. Along with his skillful readings, he trusted his intuition to guide him with accuracy: "I sailed with a free wind day after day, marking the position of my ship on the chart with considerable precision; but this was done by intuition, I think, more than by slavish calculations. For one whole month my vessel held her course true: I had not, the while, so much as a light in the binnacle. The Southern Cross I saw every night abeam. The sun every morning came up astern; every evening it went down ahead. I wished for no other compass to guide me, for these were true. If I doubted my reckoning after a long time at sea I verified

145

it by reading the clock aloft made by the Great Architect, and it was right."

Slocum's accuracy was astonishing. When he first sighted the Marquesas group of Polynesian islands, he was confused by a reading that told him the *Spray* was hundreds of miles west of where he knew she was. He took a second set of readings an hour later that confirmed the first. Frustrated by information that clashed with his intuition, Slocum consulted the logarithm table and there found the error that had thrown off his calculations. He corrected the tables and felt he could continue to sail with his "self-reliance unshaken, and with my tin clock fast asleep." He was delighted with his skill and couldn't help but boast: "I found from the result of three observations, after long wrestling with lunar tables, that her longitude by observation agreed within five miles of that by dead-reckoning."

Slocum gloried in the precision of the universe and marveled at man's ability to read its signs. Of the skills of the lunarian — the old-fashioned navigator who without a chronometer could ascertain the longitude of his ship by calculating the angle between the moon and certain fixed stars — Slocum wrote simple words of praise: "There is nothing in the realm of navigation that lifts one's heart up more in adoration." Out in the middle of the Pacific, the connection to nature was heightened, and Slocum came to a deep understanding of how things were and had always been for sailors who really knew the ocean and the sky. And this feeling of perfect knowledge filled him with satisfaction: "I was en rapport now with my surroundings, and was carried on a vast stream where I felt the buoyancy of His hand who made all the worlds, I realized the mathematical truth of their motions, so well known that astronomers compile tables of their positions through the years and the day, and the minutes of a day, with such precision that one coming along over the sea even five years later may, by their aid, find the standard time of any given meridian on the earth."

Slocum's deepening connection with nature affected his view of the creatures he encountered. In the Strait of Magellan, as he watched ducks flying past the *Spray*, he contemplated the joy of a good stew. But even this mouth-watering thought was not enough to make him pull the trigger: he simply did not have the mind to take a life in such a desolate landscape. He countered a native Samoan's suggestion that he carry caged chickens on board for slaughtering when desired: "To kill the companions of my voyage and eat them would be indeed next to murder and cannibalism." His dietary code of ethics had its limits, however; he drew the line when hungry-looking sharks circled the *Spray* as she traveled close to islands and coral reefs. His justification for killing them was self-defense and a kind of unspoken creed that he adhered to as a member of the nautical brotherhood: "Nothing is more dreadful to the mind of a sailor, I think, than a possible encounter with [these] 'tigers of the sea' . . . In the loneliness of the dreary country about Cape Horn I found myself in no mood to make one life less in the world, except in self-defense."

Slocum's long journey was as much an inner voyage through the psyche as an outward voyage over ocean waters. Pondering both depths brought him face to face with his own strengths and shortcomings. Alone at sea, he had to know who he was. Surviving such a plunge into solitude required courage and honesty. As he stripped away the sea's layers and penetrated its mysteries, a deep spirituality awakened that had always been part of him. By the end of the voyage, he was embracing each descent into solitude as an opportunity for spiritual growth: "I was destined to sail once more into the depths of solitude, but these experiences had no bad effect upon me; on the contrary, a spirit of charity and even benevolence grew stronger in my nature through the meditations of these supreme hours on the sea." Later Slocum expressed to Clifton Johnson, a magazine writer, how these shifts affected his written account of his solo voyage. His bouts of solitude had distilled for him the essence of his story: "Everything in connection with the sea would be eminantly respectable and be told in spirituality. No man ever lived to see more of the solemnity of the depths than I have seen and I resent, quickly the hint that a real sea story might be other than religeous. I cannot down my sensitiveness on this point." Throughout *Sailing Alone Around the World* he recounted moments of epiphany and awakening. He wrote to his cousin Joel Slocum about the spiritual connection that is felt on the waters: "Old sailors may have odd ways of showing their religious feeling but there are no infidels at sea."

Any great journey, no matter what instigated it, becomes a journey of the soul. Slocum could not have sailed around the world by himself without being transformed. At every solitary turn, whether battling loneliness, stormy sea or daily routine, he was discovering what made sense to him in the world and what was beautiful and important. He had the skills to meet the challenging power of nature. He tested and stretched his abilities, which were considerable, and in doing so discovered where his limits were to be found. With no one to witness his astonishing feats of seamanship, Slocum took comfort in the knowledge that he had one constant companion at all times, besides the *Spray*. As Slocum told it, "I sailed alone with God."

Captain Slocum was what we may call an uncommon man. He was extremely intelligent, and in his love of roaming and adventure reminded me of the celebrated Moorish traveler, Ibn Batuta, who wandered from Cape Spartel to the Yellow Sea, making friends with white, black and yellow; always observing, making men and manners his study, and living by the gifts of those whose ears he tickled with his tales of travel and adventure. Slocum, like Batuta, was a friend-maker, and everywhere he went the best of the land welcomed him, bid him to the board, and gave attention, while in his inimitable way he spun yarns of his voyages. At Gibraltar he was the guest of the Admiral; at Montevideo the Royal Mail Company repaired his sloop without a charge; in Australia and New Zealand they gave him sails and stores; at Cape Town the Government passed him over its railway lines; and even old Kruger handed him a cup of coffee. From port to port he voyaged everywhere welcomed and entertained . . .

— from Thomas Fleming Day's tribute to
Joshua Slocum in *The Rudder*, January 1911

9

Ports of Call

Though I do not feel oppressively lonely on my solitary voyage, I am always glad to get to port. I am, paradoxical as it may seem, really a sociable man.
— J.S., to a reporter

The hope of landfall sustains a sailor on a long ocean passage. But keen as he is to see it, the appearance of land on the horizon may disappoint more than excite, and bring the realization that the destination may not have been why he first set sail.

The sheer scope of Slocum's voyage meant that he could sail with greater freedom than most sailors: the occasional landfall wouldn't overshadow his broad vistas. The *Spray* was his home, and his address was wherever she happened to be at the time. Circumnavigation was his definite goal, but he felt no hurry. He had no prearranged schedules to live up to, and no one was waiting in port for him. He often sailed as the spirit moved him, even when he had been at sea for extended periods. After sailing for days to make an island in the South Pacific, he changed his plans close to landfall. Most people would have been ready to make port after spending more than a month at sea. Not Slocum, who was caught in the rhythm of a good passage and was reluctant to break it to go ashore. "To be alone forty-three days would seem a long time, but in reality, even here, winged moments flew lightly by, and instead of my hauling in for Nukahiva, which I could have made as well as not, I kept on for Samoa, where I wished to make my next landing. This occupied twenty-nine days more, making seventy-two days in all. I was not distressed in any way at that time."

Aboard the *Spray*, Slocum was a floating citizen of the world. Any port was home for as long as he wished. With each landfall he entered a completely different world. He sailed into scenes that were exquisite in their beauty, and others just as remarkable for their bleakness. He sailed into pristine harbors with sun-bleached cliffs, steep grassy slopes, volcanic rock formations, and white beaches. Although a seasoned world traveler, some of the changes startled him. On sighting the Keeling (Cocos) Islands after twenty-three days at sea, he recalled the excitement of spotting a coconut tree sticking out of the water directly ahead of him: "I expected to see this; still it thrilled me as an electric shock might have done. I slid down the mast, trembling under the strangest sensation; and not able to resist the impulse, I sat on deck and gave way to my emotions. To folks in a parlor on shore this may seem weak indeed, but I am telling the story of a voyage alone."

A sailor of experience and sensitivity knows the signs that land is approaching. Slocum would have noticed the smell of land, often described by people who have made long passages as the scent of vegetation. Or he would have noticed certain seabirds overhead. No matter how prepared, a sailor often feels terribly disconnected on making landfall. There is an exhaustion about getting into port that begins to settle in as soon as the anchor is down. A sailor can feel dulled and overwhelmed once his body registers that it can finally rest. Slocum liked to approach a port on his own terms, to observe it from a distance before getting caught up in the rhythms of life ashore. His pace of adjustment could be slow, as he admitted on casting anchor in Samoa on a summer day around noon: "My vessel being moored, I spread an awning, and instead of going at once on shore I sat under it till late in the evening, listening with delight to the musical voices of the Samoan men and women." This was all the contact he wanted after seventy-two days alone at sea.

When he arrived in Cape Town, he again chose not to hurry: "I preferred to remain for one day alone, in the quiet of a smooth sea, enjoying the retrospect of the passage of two capes." As his trip progressed, he often found that word of his bold endeavors on his seaworthy little boat had arrived before him. Thus, when Slocum sailed in, there was frequently a crowd assembled to greet him. People wanted to meet the "plucky Yankee," as one Australian reporter referred to him, and to cheer him along on his world adventure. At every port that stamped his yacht license, Slocum made quite an impression, and his daring exploits began appearing in the headlines of major papers en route. In Sydney, the *Morning Herald* hailed the captain as "the hero of the solitary voyage around the world," and added that "he was enthusiastically cheered." The enthusiasm over his visit was echoed in Tasmania, where the *North West Post* ran this news item: "So much interest has been attached to the daring voyager and level-headed Yankee skipper, that when it was made known by means of handbills that the *Spray* was to arrive on Sunday, the beaches at Devonport were fairly lined by persons, waiting to catch a glimpse of the tiny boat and its intrepid commander." Slocum was exciting imaginations everywhere. On the small South Atlantic island of St. Helena, the *Spray's* visit was a major event, and the local paper caught the exitement of the moment: "The news of her arrival [caused] a commotion among the members of our apathetic community as is seldom witnessed, and crowds of people have gone to see and visit the vessel in which a feat requiring rare pluck and skill has been so successfully accomplished — a feat which, in its extreme daringness, would appear foolhardiness."

Slocum rose to the challenge of his burgeoning fame

with proper aplomb, seadog charisma and natural flair for making the most of circumstances. The Gibraltar society column for August 23, 1895, reported that "the gallant Captain's miniature galley and 'state room' were inspected with much interest, and tea for a dozen was made at the small stove." By all reports he was a traveling showman and raconteur worth coming out to see. A Tasmanian newspaper ran a feature article entitled "An Intrepid Navigator" that described the sea captain's charm: "Five minutes in his company, and a person feels quite at home, and in drawing out snatches of his history one becomes faced with the fact that for daring this solitary seaman is hard to beat."

Just how real a glimpse his admirers were getting of the captain is hard to know, for Slocum played many roles with ease. He could be Captain Slocum the old seadog, the intellect, the dashing world adventurer, the lone but gregarious traveler, or simply Joshua Slocum the humble, God-fearing sailor. He also knew how to play a crowd, as evidenced in one story out of Melbourne: "During his sojourn . . . he was the means of creating much excitement at St. Kilda by capturing a huge shark, 12 ft. long." He displayed his impressive catch on deck as evidence of yet another spunky deed performed on his voyage.

Traveling from port to port, Slocum could enjoy company for as long as he wished and always on his own terms. When he tired of one place, he had only to pack up and sail away to another, having stayed long enough to

156

be admired, but not long enough to be known intimately. He controlled his own image, and there were certain aspects of Slocum the solitary sailor that he wanted to keep intact. It mattered greatly to him that people appreciated his navigational skills. His adamant response to a newspaper story that questioned his ability and integrity may have given people a true indication of just how ornery and insecure he could be: "By the way, some one in Melbourne started a rumor that I could not possibly handle the vessel by myself, and that I had two men with me who were stowed away on arriving at a port. This is quite untrue, and I wish you to state that anyone is at perfect liberty to fumigate, search, or turn steam into the vessel, and I'll guarantee that nothing will be found."

Other misconceptions along the way must have given Slocum reason to chuckle to himself. Some of the situations he sailed into were downright ludicrous. His arrival off the island of Rodriguez, in the Indian Ocean east of Mauritius, coincided with the biblical teachings of the local abbé. The islanders were contemplating the coming of the Antichrist when the *Spray* sailed into their harbor like a white apparition, her sails taut before a strong wind. The good folk of Rodriguez scrambled from shore, certain that the Antichrist had arrived. To prove he wasn't the Evil One, Slocum set about introducing himself, hoping to calm the commotion. Convincing as the old salt could be, fear of the ancient prophecy had a powerful grip on a few souls. He later recollected that one elderly woman "when she heard of my advent, made for her house and locked herself in. When she heard that I was actually coming up the street she barricaded her doors, and did not come out while I was on the island, a period of eight days." The governor of the island was entertaining that evening and invited the "destroyer of the world" — as Slocum now jokingly referred to himself — to share some of his adventures.

In Samoa he received another unlikely greeting. Three young women paddled their canoe up to his boat for closer inspection. They did not believe he had sailed the world alone. That he was alone at that point could only mean that he had eaten his companions. When he arrived at the Keeling (Cocos) Islands, his every move was monitored by children. It turned out that an island man had disappeared some years before, and the youngsters were trying to determine whether Slocum was the lost man with a change in skin color. There was further confusion as the captain was busy at work spreading a goopy mixture of coal tar on the *Spray*. Curious little eyes watched in amazement as he ate a lunch of sea biscuits topped with blackberry jam. Slocum heard them shouting, "The captain is eating coal-tar! The captain is eating coal-tar!" as they ran into the village to spread the wild news.

It is hard today to imagine the world through which Slocum was sailing. Nineteenth-century sailors stayed out of certain waterways for fear of piracy, avoided areas inhabited by cannibals, and were often greeted as the

first strangers ever to visit a locale. Unlike the missionaries, who often found their way to remote spots, Slocum
had no desire to change how the native people thought;
on the contrary, he expressed his disdain of proselytiz-
ing in a letter to a friend from the Keeling Islands: "The
heart of a missionary is all on fire to reconstruct the reli-
gion of this people. If ever one sets foot on this peaceful
land, I hope he will not be of the soul-destroying sort
that spoiled my early days." Years later, Slocum's son
Ben Aymar described what his father thought of the missionary spirit: "He didn't want your ignorance (on religious matters) crammed down his throat." Slocum
himself wrote in a letter that "I myself do not care much
for your longfaced tyrannical Christians" and that he
"never cared much for the devil after I grew up and got
away to sea."

Notwithstanding his somewhat irreligious attitude,
Slocum had some personal pilgrimages to make along the
way. While in Montevideo he made a short excursion up
the River Plate with an old acquaintance from Cape Cod.
Later he would give no reason for this trip, which he
acknowledged was made "instead of proceeding at once
on [the] voyage," but he may well have wanted to sail past
the cemetery where Virginia was buried. In Cooktown,
Australia, he moored the *Spray* near the monument to
Captain Cook. Here, Slocum did go ashore "to feast [his]
eyes on the very stones the great navigator had seen, for
I was now on a seaman's consecrated ground." His love

of literature enticed him to stay for over a week on the island where a Scottish sailor, Alexander Selkirk, had asked to be marooned after a violent argument with his ship's captain. Daniel Defoe had based his novel *Robinson Crusoe* on Selkirk's adventures, and Slocum "of course made a pilgrimage to the old lookout place at the top of the mountain where Selkirk spent many days peering into the distance for the ship which came at last." According to the inscribed rock tablet at the lookout, Selkirk lived in isolation on Juan Fernández for four years and four months. Slocum was so enchanted by the "blessed island" that he could only wonder, "Why Alexander Selkirk ever left you was more than I could make out." Later, he would remember his final day on the island as quite possibly "the pleasantest on my whole voyage." He spent his time with the children, who begged him to tell them the English names of objects, repeating them after him in sounds that "made the hills ring with mirth." It was also on Juan Fernández that Slocum visited the graves, marked with rough lava rocks, of seamen "landed here to end days of sickness and get into a sailors' heaven." From Juan Fernández, Slocum left for Samoa on another literary pilgrimage. This time he met Fanny Stevenson, widow of Robert Louis Stevenson. In her he found a kindred spirit: "She told me that, along with her husband, she had voyaged in all manner of rickety craft among the islands of the Pacific, reflectively adding, 'Our tastes were similar.'" Slocum was honored when she presented him with four volumes of her husband's sailing directories of the Mediterranean, inscribing the first of them:

> To Captain Slocum.
> These volumes have been read and reread many times by my husband, and I am very sure that he would be pleased that they should be passed on to the sort of seafaring man that he liked above all others.
> Fanny V. de G. Stevenson.

Slocum relished his travels to these remote ports. He was curious about other cultures and for the most part left his Western sensibilities aboard the *Spray* when he was invited to take part in local celebrations and ceremonies. On Thursday Island he watched dancers dressed and painted as island birds and animals perform amazing leaps over open fires. Slocum was intrigued by the wood and bone musical instruments that accompanied the dancers, but thought their performance was "at once amusing, spectacular and hideous." He was repulsed, he said, by the aborigines' facial features. But in Samoa, Slocum "saw nothing to shake one's faith in native virtue," although one of their gatherings caused the captain a degree of culinary distress, as he later recalled in a feature article in *Good Housekeeping*: "I had a curious experience in Samoa. I gave a party of natives some of my salt horse — beef, you know — and they were so highly pleased with the delicacy that they invited me to a feast at their village where they roasted pig in my honor. They roasted the pig whole by putting it on a bed of hot stones and piling hot stones over it. The flesh was crisp outside, but the roasting process was incomplete and no salt was provided. I found the pork under the circumstances rather unpalatable and the next time I was invited to the village I carried along some salt in my pocket, but they failed to have roast pig that time."

In out-of-the-way ports, the natives were often highly superstitious. On Juan Fernández, the locals told Slocum he would not be allowed to climb on the rocks unless he had eaten goat meat. Apparently it would guarantee his surefootedness and keep him out of harm's way generally. In Samoa, tradition required him to partake of ava — that is, to drink from a shared coconut-shell bowl, then toss some of the drink over his shoulder, salute the gods, and twirl it across a mat to his hosts. Slocum later allowed that "to the unconventional mind the punctilious etiquette of Samoa is perhaps a little painful."

It wasn't only in out-of-the-way settlements that Slocum encountered ideas that defied rational modern thought. In Pretoria he was introduced to President Paul Kruger of the Transvaal, known affectionly as "Oom Paul." The introduction went sour when Slocum was referred to as the sailor who was on a voyage "around the world." Kruger became prickly at the notion of such an excursion, proclaiming it impossible. The president believed firmly that the earth was flat: "You don't mean *round* the world, it is impossible! You mean *in* the world." For Slocum such fiery passion was more enjoyable to watch than the social niceties that surrounded most formal occasions. He had gotten wind of the fanatical "flat-earthers" at an earlier stop in Durban; a small group came up from Pretoria to collect data from him to confirm their flat earth research. He met with "one of the party in a clergyman's garb, carrying a large Bible." When Slocum said he could not help them prove their theory by his sailing experience, the clergyman became indignant and started "losing himself in a passion, and making as if he would run me through with an assagai." Slocum recalled his final showdown with the man: "The next day, seeing him across the street, I bowed and made curves with my hands. He responded with a level, swimming movement of his hands, meaning 'the world is flat'." The "good, but misguided fanatic," as Slocum came to see him, got one last word in by post. Before leaving South Africa, Slocum opened his mail to find a flat-earth pamphlet from the Transvaal geographers.

Slocum often found himself in the company of important people. He dined with governors "in the land of napkins and cut glass." These elegant dinners caused him to reflect on how he lived aboard the *Spray*, and he was, as he put it, visited by "the ghosts of hempen towels and of mugs without handles." On those occasions when he was feted this way, Slocum enjoyed the company, the exchange of wit, and most definitely the honors bestowed.

While in South Africa he met the famous explorer Henry Morton Stanley, who questioned Slocum about the *Spray*'s seaworthiness and then acknowledged the challenges of his circumnavigation with a matter-of-fact comment, "What an example of patience." On Thursday Island he sailed into harbor as part of Queen Victoria's Diamond Jubilee celebrations. And on the island of Mauritius he visited a horticultural conservatory, where the chief botanist named a newly discovered plant "Slocum" in the skipper's honor. Another scientist, the astronomer David Gill, impressed Slocum with his discoveries in stellar photography. The two pioneers exchanged ideas concerning time: "He showed me the great astronomical clock of the observatory and I showed him the tin clock on the *Spray*." Slocum had the privilege of sharing an evening lecture with Dr. Gill. This recognition guaranteed Slocum a full house and enough money for the rest of his voyage.

The captain had given his first public lecture during his summer cruising around Tasmania. He admitted to being nervous about that event and was offered some pointers by a local public speaker: "Man, man, great nervousness is only the sign of a good brain." It was an entertaining evening, and Slocum saw the money-making potential of these lectures. He realized that he "had to do something for the expenses of the voyage, other captains might draw bottomary bonds but I lectured the *Spray* around the world." His second lecture, in Bowen, Australia, was advertised in the local newspapers, and was also proclaimed by a bell ringer, who cried out about the significance of the voyager sailing from "Boston to Bowen, the two hubs in the cartwheels of creation." This lecture was illustrated by stereopticon slides. During other lectures he showed lantern slides of some three hundred scenes, and at the Cape Town Normal College he traced out his sea route on a large map of the world. It was reported that he "proceeded to exhibit a large number of excellent Lantern Slides. The large audience was thoroughly appreciative and as heartily cheered the successive views and the Captain's descriptions — at once humorous, caustic, and racy." The paper also noted that in the full house in Cape Town, a large number of women were in the audience. The captain was a great success and received enthusiastic reviews. His circumnavigation had become a strong draw on the lecture circuit; evenings with Captain Slocum were billed as "accounts of perilous travels round the world. Instructive and amusing."

There was trouble in one port along his route. When Slocum arrived in Newcastle, New South Wales, early in the fall of 1896, he received a hero's welcome. Australians embraced the Canadian-born sailor, whose first wife's relatives, the Walkers, still lived in Sydney. Slocum decided he would venture on to wait out some of the season in Sydney visiting Virginia's family and giving tours of the *Spray* and newspaper interviews. The limelight brought him to the attention of an old enemy, Henry Slater, the bullyman he had disciplined severely thirteen years before on the *Northern Light*. Slater, who was now living in Sydney, decided to destroy the captain's credibility by embroiling him in an old controversy. He went to the newspapers and the unsavory affair was aired again in great detail. Slater's account of the cruelty he allegedly suffered was damning, as this quote from the Sydney *Daily Telegraph* on October 9, 1896 illustrates:

When I got out on deck I was seized from behind, knocked down, and two pairs of handcuffs were put on my wrists. I was then dragged after to the poop, where shackles were put on my ankles. A chain was then placed round my throat, crossed behind my neck, wound round my body and on through my legs, then up to the back of my neck and made fast. Then a length of chain was made fast to shackles on my ankles, and the whole lot of chain rivetted together, I had then eighty pounds of chain on my body.

Slater went on to describe the extent of his misery: "At first my daily fare was one ship's biscuit and half a pint of water. That did not kill me, so the same amount of biscuit and about three or four tablespoons of water was tried. Still I did not die. For the first three weeks in this 'box' I suffered the tortures of the damned, my hunger and thirst were intolerable. I begged Captain Slocum to give me water and food, but in vain." The account continued with descriptions of unimaginable horrors. Slater claimed that he was strung up in the air for days by his limbs, that Slocum covered him in melted butter to attract rats, and that at one desperate moment Slater actually squeezed the life out of a rodent and ate it.

Slater noted that he had been arrested and tried for mutiny and been honorably acquitted. Then he put out a challenge to the people of Sydney: "I ask the public before making a god of this man to wait until I am placed face to face with him. I do not make these statements to gain notoriety, or even sympathy, but simply to show my fellow-citizens what kind of a man they are dealing with in Captain Joshua Slocum."

Slocum had a chance to respond to the fracas while still in New South Wales. The reporter who interviewed the captain wrote that "Captain Slocum declined to make any set statement in reply to the allegations of Slater, but he placed at the disposal of your reporter a book containing a number of clippings from American papers referring to the case of the *Northern Light*." The day after Slocum learned of what was brewing, he set sail for Sydney to confront his accuser. The harbor police were waiting and gave him "a pluck into anchorage." Slocum's written accounts of what happened next are sparse and cryptic. There is no mention of the Slater affair, only that the police "gathered data from an old scrap-book of mine . . . Some one said they came to arrest me, and — well, let it go at that." Newspapers printed accounts of Slocum's defense made from old stories and clippings kept in his scrapbook. He didn't deny imprisoning Slater, but told the press he was "disgusted" by Slater's malicious attack. Slocum made a smart and unexpected first move. He had Slater summoned before a magistrate, before whom Slocum testified that Slater was capable of violence. He pointed out that Slater had once threatened, "This Captain Slocum, God help him when we meet. I'll not be responsible for my actions. This man you are making an angel of, I'll make an angel of him when I get hold of him."

This immediately put Slater on the defensive, as the records of his cross-examination of Slocum illustrate:

Slater: You have been here for ten days, and have I done you any harm?

Mr. Addison: What's the use of asking such a question?

Slater: Is this not the first time you have seen me for about thirteen years?

Captain Slocum: I have not seen you for about that time.

Slater: Are you afraid of me?

Captain Slocum: Well, you are a most excitable man, and from the language you have used, you might possibly do me an injury. I certainly am, to a certain extent, afraid of you.

Slater: You ought to be at least morally afraid of me.

The magistrate ruled that Slater must pay eighty pounds as security that he would keep the peace for six months.

Slater continued the challenge, begging some kind of public debate and forum where he could show the assembled crowds how he had been bound and shackled years ago. It took well over a month for the rotten affair to be cleared up for Slocum, but as the tension faded and talk died down, he was able to enjoy touring about. He set sail in early December after a stay of almost two months in Sydney and worked his way down the Australian coast to Melbourne. Off Cape Bundaroo, people on shore shouted out their Christmas greetings to the passing *Spray*. He exchanged signals with the lighthouse keepers and continued south for Melbourne, then on for Tasmania.

Generally, Slocum was well cared for wherever he went. People showed respect for his mission with their kind support and monetary gifts, though money was not as important, especially when he moved away from main ports. "As I sailed farther and farther away from the center of civilization, I heard less and less of what would and would not pay," he wrote of his sojourn in Samoa. Slocum was experiencing the generosity of a give and take, barter and trade world. On Juan Fernández he taught the islanders how to make doughnuts and fried them in the salvaged tallow the *Spray* was carrying. In payment, Slocum was given ancient coins from the wreck of an old galleon.

Slocum was introduced to such generosity on his arrival in Gibraltar early in the voyage. The Gibraltar

Chronicle noted that the *Spray* had "received a new coat of paint, sadly needed after more than a month's knocking about in the Atlantic, and now looks quite smart." Shipyard reports note that the "repairs to hull and sails of the *Spray* must have been done unofficially by the Sailors from the Fleet and there is therefore no record." The *Spray* was refitted in Cape Town, and Slocum was given a railway pass to travel free throughout South Africa. He was treated royally at every port on his voyage. In Sydney he was presented with a telescope and a badge during a congratulatory address. Also in Sydney he was given a new suit of sails by the yacht club commodore, Mark Foy. Women gave him stores of jams and jellies. He sailed away with clothes, bottles of raspberry wine, fresh fruit and vegetables, cakes, gifts of money and a new stove. One critic felt that the old captain was nothing more than a hustler and called him an "intrepid water tramp." That may have been true, but he was a charming one. If people wanted to shower him with goods and kindness, he wasn't going to refuse.

One gift he came to wish he had refused was given to him in St. Helena. As the local *Guardian* newspaper reported his departure from the island in April 1898, "Captain Slocum left us in his little yacht *Spray* on Wednesday evening last about 6 o'clock. He took with him a kid and a lamb, but the latter jumped overboard just when leaving the harbour and was unfortunately drown." Slocum must have wished the goat had met the same fate: it was a complete menace on board. In a humorous passage in *Sailing Alone Around the World*, he remembered the gift as given "in an evil moment" and recounted the chaos it unleashed:

> I soon found that my sailing-companion, this sort of dog with horns, had to be tied up entirely. The mistake I made was that I did not chain him to the mast instead of tying him with grass ropes less securely, and this I learned to my cost. Except for the first day, before the beast got his sea-legs on, I had no peace of mind. After that, actuated by a spirit born, maybe, of his pasturage, this incarnation of evil threatened to devour everything from flying-jib to stern-davits. He was the worst pirate I met on the whole voyage. He began depredations by eating my chart of the West Indies, in the cabin, one day, while I was about my work for'ard, thinking that the critter was securely tied on deck by the pumps. Alas! there was not a rope in the sloop proof against that goat's awful teeth.

The ravenous goat ate the captain's sea charts and his straw hat. According to Slocum, it was the latter misdemeanor that decided the creature's fate. On the volcanic rock formed island of Ascension, he marooned the hapless creature to fend for itself.

Besides the goat, he brought the people of Ascension their mail from St. Helena. Slocum had neglected his own correspondence. He had lost touch with his home port and with the lives of his wife and four children. For Hettie, Ben, Victor, Garfield and Jessie, a long time between letters was not taken as a good sign. On August 24, 1897, the following report ran in the Providence *Journal*. It read like a death notice, even though the captain's first name was given incorrectly.

PROBABLY LOST
Family of Capt. Josiah Slocum Relinquish all Hope
Captain Josiah Slocum, who sailed from Boston April 24, 1895, with the intent of circumnavigating the globe in a cockle-shell, is probably lost. His daughter, who lives in Attleboro, has heard nothing from him for some time, and it is believed that his little boat *Spray* has been overcome in an ocean storm. Captain Slocum kept those at home posted as to his movements and when the weeks and then months passed without word of any kind from him the fear became the belief that he was no more.

The story then advanced the idea that Captain Slocum was drowned during one of the terrible storms "for which the Southern seas are noted."

At the time of this report, Slocum was moseying carefully around the South Seas, where he was charmed by the idyllic lifestyle and mused, "If there was a moment in my voyage when I could have given it up, it was there and then; but no vacancies for a better post being open, I weighed anchor April 16, 1897 and again put out to sea."

Slocum had no idea he had been presumed dead and felt no homesickness for New England. His home was the *Spray* and he changed his course and his mind with the winds. As he told one newspaper reporter near the end of his voyage, "I have not yet decided whether to go west round Cape Leeuwin, or east through Torres Straits. In any case the course will probably be laid round the Cape of Good Hope, and home to Boston."

Differing in many respects from the average deep-water sailor, the master of the Spray *has an individuality all his own, born, perhaps of silent communion with nature, in the vast solitudes of the sea . . .*

Tall, slight of build, with a deep-blue eye, so often characteristic of those who go down to the sea in ships; criss-cross wrinkles encompassing them, as though decades of steady gazing into the faces of [the] suns had puckered the skin about the deep-set eye-sockets like well-tanned alligator hide; thin of face, with high brow rounding off into a head unencumbered by any burden of hair beyond a thin fringe about the edge of the dome, like a growth of sparse underbrush on the edge of the snow line of some lofty pinnacle; grayish brown beard, kept tolerably close cropped — for the captain is something of a stickler for his personal appearance under all conditions — these are physical characteristics that strike one at first glance.

— A reporter's description of Captain
Slocum after his return

10

Booming Along
Joyously for Home

I had a desire to return to the place of the very beginning.
— J.S., Sailing Alone

Christmas of 1897 found the *Spray* rounding the Cape of
Good Hope. Slocum now had his mind set on the final
leg of the voyage. He had been at sea for close to three
years. There had been drama and adventure at many
turns, and the six months of this final passage were to be
every bit as eventful. In many ways this homeward leg
was like the last movement of a symphony. Composer
Igor Stravinsky described a symphonic finale as "a succession of impulses that converge toward a definite point
of repose." Slocum's world voyage was moving steadily
toward that point.

After returning from the Transvaal in mid-December,

Slocum caught "a morning land-wind," cleared the bar and headed straight for the next salient point of land, the Cape of Good Hope. Anticipating a rough sea, he reflected on the early Portuguese navigators who had faced the "Cape of Storms" before him, and who had struggled for sixty-nine years to sail around it. Slocum was philosophical about the conditions on that part of the ocean: "One gale was much the same as another, with no more serious result than to blow the *Spray* along on her course, when it was fair, or to blow her back somewhat when it was ahead." It was in this same reticent tone that he related what happened to the *Spray* in those waters on Christmas Day: "The *Spray* was trying to stand on her head, and she gave me every reason to believe she might accomplish the feat before night." Slocum had something of a baptism in these waters, being dunked three times while standing at the end of the bowsprit. He wasn't pleased with his Christmas soaking. He kept company along part of the coastline with a steamer ship. He sailed past Cape Agulhas, into Simons Bay and around the Cape. Again his mind turned to sea lore, and he remembered that the Flying Dutchman was still thought to be sailing somewhere off the rugged coasts of the Cape.

Having rounded the Cape, Slocum was feeling optimistic: "The voyage then seemed as good as finished; from this time on I knew that all, or nearly all, would be plain sailing." Slocum also saw this point as "the dividing-line of the weather": "clear and settled" to the north, "humid and squally" below to the south. He rested in the calm under Table Mountain and waited for a breeze. Once into Cape Town, just round the bend of the cape, he decided to put the *Spray* into dry dock for a three-month rest; this allowed him a lengthy interval for traveling in the African countryside. This detour — with a free railroad pass — gave the captain a last taste of international fame, and he spent much of his time lecturing and hobnobbing with the governmental and scientific elite. After returning from Pretoria through hundreds of miles of barren African plains, Slocum found his sloop ready for the thousands of miles of ocean still ahead. On March 26 he set off from "the land of distances and pure air," and soon he was in swelling seas off the peaks of the Cape. Once again he was reminded of the history connected with this grand passage, and of the awe this sight had inspired in other navigators. He believed it was Sir Francis Drake who had observed, " 'Tis the fairest thing and the grandest cape I've seen in the whole circumference of the earth." Somewhere in the power of the moment, Slocum felt a shift in his own voyage occur: "The *Spray* soon sailed the highest peaks of the mountains out of sight, and the world changed from a mere panoramic view to the light of a homeward-bound voyage."

Away from the boisterous gales off the Cape, the *Spray* "ran along steadily at her best speed," the tempo of the voyage picking up to a light-hearted *vivace*. Slocum's mood seemed to take off with the wind, and he plunged into the new books he had received in South Africa. He was remarkably light of heart, musing about the flying fish he saw, which he likened to arrows shooting from the sea. The play of the waves captivated him, and he noted how the *Spray* was "just leaping along among the white horses, a thousand gamboling porpoises keeping her company on all sides." Before he made landfall at St. Helena, he drank some port wine in a toast to the health of his invisible friend and guardian, the pilot of the *Pinta*, with whose spirit Slocum had been conversing since early in the voyage. The jaunty passage had been a delight to the old sailor, who was moved to reflect, "One could not be lonely in a sea like this."

On St. Helena, Slocum was again welcomed cordially, and was asked to give two of his now famous lectures. The audience was delighted by the wry captain, who was jokingly introduced as a Yankee sea serpent. He was treated royally and was invited to stay at the governor's mansion, Plantation House. The mansion was said to be haunted, and on hearing this, he stayed awake in the hope of communing with another spirit from the pages of history, that of the exiled Napoleon Buonaparte. Wherever he had sailed during his circumnavigation, Slocum was alert to his place in the historical scheme of things. Here, his mind turned not only to the Corsican emperor, who ended his days on the island, but to stories of witch burnings on this "island of tragedies." When he left, he took a fruitcake aboard the *Spray*, a gift from the governor's wife.

179

He had begun the voyage with his sister's fruitcake, which had lasted him forty-two days out of Brier Island. It seemed somehow fitting to near the end with another cake, "a great high-decker" that would last him into early June.

Just off the island of Ascension, where he marooned the rambunctious goat, Slocum invited a mid-ocean inspection of the *Spray*. He asked that the sloop be thoroughly investigated and fumigated, and certified to be commanded by a one-man crew. This would turn out to be a wise request. As he made sail, he declared confidently, "Let what will happen, the voyage is now on record."

On May 8, 1898, the *Spray* crossed the sea path she had first sailed on October 2, 1895, en route to Brazil. In doing so, she had completed a circle. However, Slocum still had four thousand miles to go before he could claim to be back to his starting point, and those miles were not to be easy ones. Soon after, the *Spray* entered the zone of the trade winds, where "strange and forgotten current ripples pattered against the sloop's sides in grateful music." Slocum found this sound enchanting, but he still made good time, sailing "the handsome day's work of one hundred and eighty miles on several consecutive days."

Then he heard some startling news. He had had no idea, until he moved north of the equator in mid-May, that America had declared war on Spain. He met up with the U.S. battleship *Oregon* flying the signal flags C B T, which Slocum knew to mean, "Are there any men-of-war about?" He hoisted an immediate reply: NO. (He hadn't, of course, thought to watch for any.) He then sent another signal to the *Oregon*: "Let us keep together for mutual protection." While he waited for a reply, the *Oregon* — which was roughly one thousand times *Spray*'s size — sailed on. Slocum assumed that her captain didn't regard his proposal as worthwhile. As the *Oregon* sailed out of sight, Slocum was left to consider the consequences of the war for him alone in his small boat. He could have been taken prisoner at any point in the weeks before, not even knowing that a war had been declared (although he had been warned in Cape Town that the conflict was escalating). The idea of war unsettled Slocum, who "pondered long that night over the probability of a war risk now coming upon the *Spray* after she had cleared all, or nearly all, the dangers of the sea."

Slocum continued sailing peacefully along. On May 18, he felt ecstatic when Polaris appeared in the heavens: for close to three years he had been sailing without its guidance. Sighting Tobago on May 20, the captain reflected on how near to home he was; but that night he "was startled by the sudden flash of breakers" and decided there had to be a coral reef ahead — and a dangerous one. He worried about other lurking reefs and where the current might take him. He considered how likely shipwreck was in such waters, especially without a chart. "I taxed my memory of sea lore, of wrecks on sunken reefs, and of pirates harbored among coral reefs where other ships might not come, but nothing that I could think of applied to the island of

Tobago . . ." He turned his mind to descriptions in *Robinson Crusoe*, but could conjure up no more information about reefs. He held firm in his memory, though, the dangers lurking below the water's surface, and tacked off and on until morning light, trying to stay clear of what he called "imaginary reefs." He missed his charts badly, and his only satisfaction came in contemplating revenge: "I could have nailed the St. Helena goat's pelt to the deck."

Still in uncertain waters, he made his way north for Grenada. He gave a public lecture and then sailed north again, for Antigua. Another lecture and Slocum was on his way back home. He set sail on June 5 from the West Indies. His next landfall would be the United States. Excitement was mounting, and Slocum wrote of the climactic spirit of this final stretch, "The *Spray* was booming along joyously for home." His reverie was brought to an abrupt halt: he had sailed smack into the horse latitudes and a dead calm. After an eight-day spell of becalming, the *Spray* made headway once again, and sailed into the Gulf Stream on June 18. Slocum described the scene as turbulent, noting that the *Spray* "was jumping like a porpoise over the uneasy waves." This was merely a hint of what was blowing Slocum's way. By June 20 there was not only another gale but a great cross-sea that made for treacherous sailing. For the second time in two days he had to repair the rigging. This time the *Spray*'s jibstay had broken right at the masthead, and jib and all had fallen into the ocean. Slocum, now fifty-four years old, once more resorted to pure seamanship: "The great King Neptune tested me severely at this time, for the stay being gone, the mast itself switched about like a reed." Nevertheless, he succeeded in climbing the mast and making the necessary repairs. This feat required agility and stamina, and although he still had plenty of both, Slocum was ready to bring the voyage to its conclusion. By June 23 he had lost the psychological edge he had maintained for more than three years and was ready to put down anchor: "I was tired, tired of baffling squalls and fretful cobble-seas." This last leg was marked by the constant eerie whistling of wind through the *Spray*'s rigging, and by the sound of seawater slopping up against the boat's sides.

Slocum was now sailing triumphantly for New York harbor, but on June 25, just off Fire Island, he sailed into the "climax storm of the voyage." The *Spray* found itself caught in the clutches of a tornado that had pummeled New York City only an hour earlier. Again Slocum displayed his remarkable skills and foresight. He knew all the signs of treacherous weather ahead and had already prepared *Spray* to receive it. Its impact still shook the *Spray* hard, and Slocum abandoned his plans to sail into New York, choosing instead to pull into a quiet harbor where he could mull things over. He headed into Newport, Rhode Island, never considering that the harbor would be mined as a defense against wartime attack. It was, and his little sloop "hugged the rocks along where

neither friend nor foe could come if drawing much water."
The guardship *Dexter* called "Ahoy," and at one o'clock in
the morning of June 27, the *Spray* anchored. It was a quiet
return "after the cruise of more than forty-six thousand
miles round the world, during an absence of three years
and two months, with two days over coming out."

Applause was slow to come, and when it did it was a
reserved trickle. Slocum's sailing feats had been hailed
in foreign ports all along the way; in his own land he had
to explain the significance of his voyage. His homecoming
was poorly timed, in that so much attention was being
paid to the war. There was little newspaper coverage of
the old sailor and his gallant little boat. The local Newport
Herald did cover his return, but ran it on page 3, reporting
that "early yesterday morning a staunch-looking little
craft swung lazily into the harbor . . . She was a stranger
in these waters and her rig . . . attracted the attention of
the early risers." Slocum was portrayed as not appearing
overly concerned with the impression he was making:
"The solitary occupant of the boat busied himself in making everything neat and tidy aboard ship and appeared
to be totally oblivious of the curiosity he was arousing.
When the master of the craft had prepared everything to
his satisfaction he jumped into a dory and sculled ashore."

For three years Slocum had been welcomed around the
world as a seafaring celebrity, but in this American port he
was listened to skeptically. Many thought the old seadog
could spin a pretty convincing tall tale, and Slocum was

glad to have a stamped yacht license to prove his amazing achievement. To make matters worse, some people thought it was all a ruse to cover his real reason for sailing foreign waters: diamond smuggling. But there was one who had always considered Slocum a gallant captain, and she headed straight for Newport on news of his return. It wasn't Slocum's wife, Hettie, but rather Mabel Wagnalls whose welcome home touched the captain: "The first name on the *Spray*'s visitors' book in the home port was written by the one who always said, 'The *Spray* will come back.'" Slocum returned the "musical story" she had given him with an inscription about the wild adventures the book had had on the *Spray*: "A thousand thanks! Good wishes are prayers, heard by the angels. And so on June 28 1898 the little book, after making the circuit of the earth in the single handed *Spray* returns in good order and condition."

Recognition of Slocum's unique achievement gradually spread, and the *Spray* began to attract attention and visitors. As for Slocum, he was feeling chipper and pleased with himself. The voyage had changed him, and he made it known that he had returned a new man: "Was the crew well? Was I not? I had profited in many ways by the voyage, I had even gained flesh, and actually weighed a pound more than when I sailed from Boston. As for aging, why, the dial of my life was turned back till my friends all said, 'Slocum is young again.' And so I was, at least ten years younger than the day I felled the first tree for the construction of the *Spray*."

In buoyant spirits, Slocum set out to bring his voyage to a symbolic end. He decided he must "return to the very beginning," where he had given the *Spray* new life. On July 3 the *Spray* sailed into Fairhaven on a fair wind and there Slocum brought her to her point of repose, and his voyage to full circle: "I secured her to the cedar spile driven in the bank to hold her when she was launched. I could bring her no nearer home."

Occasionally lapsing into the lingo of the sea, but often varying his speech with words of sonorous sound and length that seem to argue an earnest and painstaking study of either the chef d'oeuvre of one Webster, or an intimate acquaintance with the best writers of history, the mariner's flow of language is of a sort to impress, and at the same time affords an admirable vehicle for the tales of solitary ocean travel, which make him an A 1 entertainer, and which give to his lectures on his voyage round the world a unique charm.

— a reporter's description of Joshua
Slocum after his return

11

That Intrepid
Water Tramp

I am longing to be useful.

> — J.S. in a letter to the New Bedford
> *Standard*, July 3, 1898

Slocum had been back all of five days when he wrote a ranting letter to the New Bedford *Evening Standard* expressing a fervent desire to defend and fight for his country: "I want to give your people an earache. I'm not coming to say, 'Oh! I've played the deuce, listen while I tell'; life is too short and there is too much to be done for that. I burn to be of some use now of all times. I spent the best of my life in the Philippine islands, China and Japan, but there is some life still in the old man . . . I am not fanatically suffering for a fight, but I am longing to be useful. Does Mr. McKinley want pilots for the Philippines

and Guam? If more fighting men were wanted I would
be nothing loth."

So he continued for over a dozen more lengthy sentences, before concluding with a gush of patriotism:
"But my heart is too full to write. I only blurr the paper.
America is all right! After seeing much of the world this
choice part of it is good enough for me! I'll fight for it!
But it is peace we want, not war! And peace we're going
to have, if we have to lick all creation to get it!"

Whenever Slocum was at loose ends, he looked to
create purpose in his life. After taking on a trip around
the world, he tended to think big. Four months later he
unveiled the latest Slocum scheme to an audience in
Carnegie Hall. His idea was to train young men in the
science of navigation aboard a college ship. However, not
just any ship would do. He wanted to build a vessel based
on the most glorious of American clipper ships, with
modifications to accommodate the three hundred stu-
dents who would be making this two-year study voyage
around the world. He hoped to attract educated young
men who were already at college, rather than apprentice
sailors. Perhaps courses in astronomy and literature
could also be given aboard ship. He did not see the trip
as *all* work, and mentioned to the Boston *Sun*: "the time
to be spent in steady, practical work and the desirable
recreation that visits to Oceanica [*sic*] and the Orient
would supply." His goal, he added, was "to equip [his stu-
dents] as navigators, capable of handling and directing

189

sailing and steam ships, including men of war." He envisioned a college ship that would "induce people not primarily out for instruction in navigation to go on its cruises." Slocum felt strongly that women should also be given the opportunity to sail, and made this curious admission, paraphrased by the reporter: "In fact, just as once on his voyage in the *Spray* he refused to stop at an island he might have made, although then 43 days out, because they wouldn't have women there [Slocum passed Nukahiva of the Marquesas Islands preferring to stop at Samoa, another twenty-nine days away], so he says, he wouldn't have anything to do with the scheme he has originated if women could not be included in its benefits."

Nothing came of this grand dream, and Slocum responded as might be expected — by dreaming harder. He had always been an entrepreneur, and sometimes an outright huckster. And just as often he had nothing financially to show for it. He boldly told audiences everywhere, "I am not ashamed to say that when I started my enterprise [I had] $1.50 to my name . . ." Anyone who had known him long must have wondered what harebrained scheme the old skipper would come up with next. And they would have remembered him in the early days, as a merchantman hustling codfish. Then he had placed an ad in the *Morning Oregonian* proclaiming his codfish to be "pure." Slocum knew how to put a spin on things, and marketed the ugly white fish as a kind of wonder food. It wasn't technically a hoax, but all the word "pure" really meant was that Slocum hadn't processed the cod. Without realizing it, he had become one of the first purveyors of natural foods.

The captain had the freelancer's shrewd knack for turning everything to some good. His son Victor wrote years later that his father's skill in trading came from acting on intuition and general impressions. But he recalled one unfortunate deal involving ostrich feathers that Slocum had brought from Cape Town to New York City. The captain arrived in the American city to learn that a new law forbade decorating hats with bird feathers, and he was forced to store them. Throughout his career he was a tinker, always ready to fix or trade anything. He salvaged goods from shipwrecks to sell or barter at ports wherever he stopped. Slocum claimed that he had arrived home from his circumnavigation with "several tons of freight on ship's account, which will pay me ship master's wages and more for the whole voyage." In an article of June 12, 1898, a reporter for the New York *Herald* who boarded the *Spray* noted the treasures he saw in the sloop's cabin: "Curiosities of all sorts and from distant parts of the world hung on the walls, books and papers in profusion lay on all sides, besides many other objects, which at once impressed the fact on my mind that Cpt. Slocum is no mere foolhardy adventurer . . ." Slocum had always had a flexible mind and could readily adapt whatever was at hand to meet the needs of the situation. In the Grand Caymans he saw conch shells that he wanted to add to his collection of well over a thousand. The shells were difficult to collect, and he turned his mind to a solution. Recalling the quahog rakes that were used in New England to harvest clams, he made his own rake from stiff wire from aboard the *Spray*. Not only did he have the desired shells but he also had a good story.

For Slocum was a brilliant storyteller. He even looked the part. The *New York Times* summed up his appearance: "Captain Slocum is fifty-four years old and is a perfect type of the weather-beaten, knockabout sailor." Slocum knew he was on to something that could make him money. He had tested out his storytelling along the way, and summed up his successes in that department in a letter to the *Times of London* toward the end of the *Spray*'s circumnavigation: "It is not 'the greatest-show-on-earth' sort of scheme, neither am I a dime-museum navigator. If I can stand up and interest intelligent people by speaking to them of the world as I have seen it, I will be satisfied. I have already given many lectures in the places I have put into and while I have not made a fortune out of my voyage, I made more money than I did when I was sole owner and commander of a little bark." He made this same point repeatedly in interviews upon his return. Now back in America, Slocum seemed destined for the role of raconteur cum lecturer.

Slocum had arrived home with an impressive array of clippings from newspapers around the world. He compiled some of the most complimentary and intriguing of these in a publicity flyer, "Press Comments — Captain Slocum's Lectures." Slocum must have felt it sounded a bit formal and crossed out the word "lectures," scribbling instead "Talks — 100 slides of places visited and of peoples met on the voyage, savage and otherwise." By most accounts, the skipper was an act worth catching: "The Captain has a droll, quaint humor and a characteristic Yankee turn of phrase which will add interest to a story intrinsically entrancing and well worth listening to," reported the Natal *Mercury* during his November 1897 stay in South Africa.

The publicity worked. Slocum didn't stop to rest from the trip before he began lecturing again. He gave his first talk just days after arriving back in Fairhaven, at the New Bedford City Hall. His show was illustrated by some three hundred lantern slides, most probably made from photos people had given him along the way. Slocum stood by his product, saying that his best slides would be "called first class in New York or London." New Bedford's *Standard* must have agreed. It commented on his lecture, "The views were very fine, equal to anything ever before presented in this city."

By all reports, an evening with the captain was guaranteed to be entertaining. His manner may have been dry, but he knew instinctively how to tell a good yarn and keep an audience laughing: "I soon found that people wanted to help me. They wanted to laugh — not cry. I managed invariably to keep my audiences from falling asleep." Slocum was being modest — in fact, he knew how to hold them in the palm of his hand. He described the winds in the Strait of Magellan as strong enough to "blow the hair off a dog's back." Then, with superb timing, he added as an afterthought, "I left my hat there," and rubbed his bald head. Audiences loved his tales of adventures, and word of his comedic gifts spread. One newspaper account related what Slocum ingenuously claimed to be the real reason he sailed alone. It was "because 'her' [Hettie] he wanted to come wouldn't come, and those who were willing to come with him he didn't want," and also "because he could not get a captain to suit him."

Slocum had kept logs throughout his voyage, and on arriving back in Massachusetts he began corresponding with an editor at *Century Illustrated Monthly Magazine*. The captain had received a telegram from its editor, Richard Watson Gilder, asking him whether he would consider writing his story for the magazine. Gilder and his brother Joseph had a fast reply from the captain: an enthusiastic letter addressed to "Mr. Editor, Century Magazine." "I have a fund of matter to be sure," Slocum wrote, "but have not myself, had experience in writing magazine articles — I have very decided literary tastes and could enter into such parts as I am able to do with a great deal of energy." He told them he was tired of feeling misunderstood and being misquoted by the newspapers, and added that he was certain his were tales worth telling: "Without say Slocum Slocum all the time — that I do

Following completion of his world voyage, Slocum wrote the best-seller *Sailing Alone Around the World*. He is photographed here in East Boston by his son, Ben Aymar. (1898)

A classic "cabinet card" photograph of Slocum dating from 1898. At the time, he was promoting himself as a lecturer and adventurer. Martin H. Frommell (circa 1898)

Slocum photographed in 1902 aboard the *Spray*. He had returned from his world-wide lecturing and book-peddling junket. Clifton Johnson (1902)

Slocum and Hettie aboard the *Spray,* which he sailed to the Cayman Islands every winter after his return to America in June 1898. Clifton Johnson (1902)

Slocum and Hettie at their farmhouse in West Tisbury, Massachusetts.
He bought the small house on Martha's Vineyard for $305. Clifton Johnson (1902)

Working in the garden at West Tisbury. Slocum told the newspapers that he was
going to give this "land living" a try. Clifton Johnson (1902)

A portrait photograph of Slocum taken at Marion, Massachusetts. His family and neighbors were beginning to see his true eccentricity. Unknown photographer (1903)

Back on the water, Slocum moors the *Spray* at Port Antonio, Jamaica. Edward Brooks (1907)

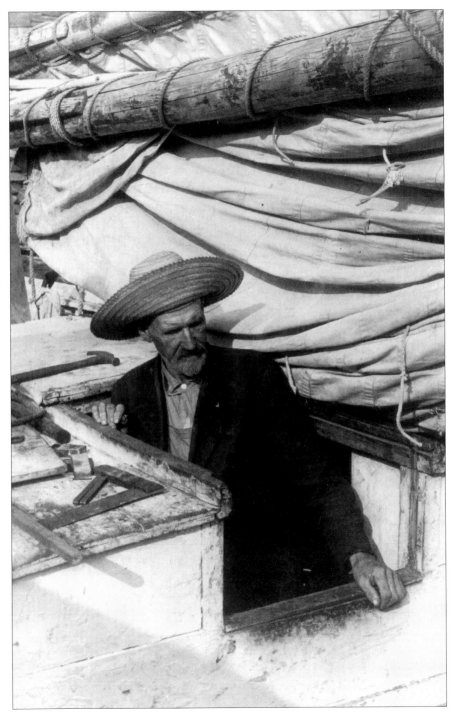
Slocum emerges from the companionway of the *Spray* while moored in Washington. D.C. Winfield Scott Clime (1907)

While in Washington, Slocum regaled school children with stories of his adventures on the high seas. Unknown photographer (1907)

not care for I know the whole story will be hard to beat." In this same letter Slocum made it clear that he intended to write a book.

While the captain's letter was still en route to *Century*, Richard Watson Gilder wrote Slocum a quick note asking which parts of the circumnavigation story had already appeared in print, and whether there was any truth to the rumors that there were diamonds on board the *Spray*. Slocum replied promptly in a letter dated July 1, 1898. He acknowledged that "one or two short letters" had appeared in New York *World*, but did not mention his letters home to the Boston *Globe*. He also glossed over that the syndicate had given up on him as a correspondent. Instead he told Gilder, "These I discontinued for my own reasons long ago." As for the diamonds, Slocum set the record straight: "If my countrymen have hinted at diamonds coming in on the *Spray*, it is hardly fare of them to do that I had but $1.50 when I began to build my ship I hadnnt much to trade one or even for luxuries for the cabin for a long time." He admitted that he had considered bringing one diamond back, but had instead brought home enough gold from Johannesburg to pay his old debts. He assured Gilder that the "vessel has in a cargo, tobesure, but clean open and above board." One thing would have been clear to Gilder from Slocum's passionate defense: while the old captain could certainly get his ideas across, spelling and punctuation were not his strong points. Slocum knew his literary limitations, and confided to Gilder, "There were indeed features of my trip striking enough to interest anybody. It would take the pen of a poet to tell some of the voyage — That of course is beyond me!"

Slocum and Hettie had spent most of the autumn in New York, taking rooms on the Lower West Side. With nothing to keep them there, they moved back to East Boston to find cheaper lodging with one of Hettie's sisters. Over the winter, Slocum began writing for the *Century*. He was reliving the adventure, and by January 1899 he could inform the assitant editor, C.C. Buel, "My 'type-writer' and I are working along around Cape Horn now and will soon have some work ready to submit." Having long ago survived those tempestuous waters, Slocum was now battling storms of syntax and grammar and trying to stay afloat as a writer. Slocum was taken out of school at age ten and had never learned proper spelling and punctuation. He continued writing while on the move. He sailed back to New York that spring, mooring the *Spray* in South Brooklyn. After delivering his manuscript to the *Century* he sailed up to Cape Cod to visit relatives on Martha's Vineyard, where he marked his letters "*Spray*, Cottage City, Mass."

It is obvious from a letter he wrote to an associate at the *Century* that he found the editing process exacting and the whole project a trifle worrisome: "Mr. Johnson I dare say has slaughtered, judiously and liberally . . . I am most anxious to see a clear story appear in both Magazine and book with no superfluous matter . . . I have tried the editors patience, I dare say . . . Magazine work, as you know is intirely new to me, the great Century being the first I ever tackled . . . be patient with me still." His insecurities concerning his writing were echoed in his desire to add enough touches so as to "make it not the worst marine story in the world."

The magazine editors allayed his fears, encouraging the reluctant captain to supply them with more details. On one occasion, Slocum jotted down the answers to their nautical questions about the *Spray*'s alterations on their letter as he read it. His notes included these: Yes, he had shortened the mast by seven feet, and the mast by five feet at Buenos Aires. Yes, he also shortened the boom inboard four feet at Pernambuco and the outboard had lost four feet at Port Angosto. His editors wanted him actively involved, and were concerned with accuracy, pointing out to the captain, "When you see an error in a picture we want you to speak up."

Years later, the publisher's daughter, Constance Buel Burnett, claimed that her father had taken "a prominent part in the publication of . . . Joshua Slocum's own account of his solitary cruise" and recalled that the *Spray* had spent a good deal of the summer of 1899 moored in front of their summer home. By mid-August, with the pressure mounting, Slocum was on the move. This time he wrote from Woods Hole, Massachusetts: "I write to assure you that I am not neglecting this interest . . . I can do the work better away where it is quiet." It must not have been quiet enough, for two days later Slocum wrote his editor from Fairhaven to confess, "I find it rather difficult to condense the variety of experiences while sailing free over the smooth sea from Good Hope. It was all ripple ripple. However the editor will know how to slaughter my pet."

In September 1899 the *Century* published the first installment of "Sailing Alone Around the World." The captain's story ran through to March 1900, with illustrations by Thomas Fogarty and George Varian. Slocum was moved to write Buel concerning the publication, " I congratulate the Century and myself." Then he was on to other projects. He had moved out of the lodgings that he and Hettie had been sharing with another of her East Boston sisters and was living quietly by himself in a New York hotel. There he put the finishing touches on the book-length account of his voyage. *Sailing Alone Around the World* was launched on March 24, 1900; the first edition was attractively bound in heavy navy-blue cloth embossed with two seahorses on either side of an anchor. Inside was the dedication, "To the one who said: 'The *Spray* will come back'." In later years, Hettie told biographer Walter Teller that the dedication was for her, but Mabel Wagnalls's copy, given to her by Slocum, was inscribed, "To Mabel Wagnalls who said, 'The *Spray* will come back' and who first read the manuscript of the Voyage. With sincere good wishes. Joshua Slocum New York April 8, 1900."

Slocum was still questioning his worth as an author and worried about how the book would be received. Anxiously, he waited for the reviews. He expressed his insecurities in a letter to Buel: "I have heard nothing from the critics about my 'fine writing' and hope to hear nothing . . . If they'll only pass me this time I'll steer clear of like shallows in the future . . . I was considerably interested in the story at the time of telling it and didn't see the enormous sunken ledges that I see now."

The reviews were soon in, and Slocum could breathe a sigh of relief: the critics loved *Sailing Alone*. *Bookseller* magazine proclaimed it to be "one of the most remarkable narratives of actual adventure ever penned." Some compared his account to sea classics like *Robinson Crusoe* and *Treasure Island*. It was proclaimed "a nautical equivalent of Thoreau's account of his life in the hut at Walden." Sir Edwin Arnold was moved by Slocum's honest accounts: "The tale is true from first to last, written in a style plain as a marlin-spike, and yet full of touches which show what hidden poetry and passionate love of Nature were in the soul of this 'bluenose' skipper." Some suspected that the captain's poetic style may have been improved considerably by his editors; however, the reviewer for the New York *Evening Post* acknowledged that the voice of the sailor was clearly audible: "Absence of literary finish and florid word-painting sinks into insignificance compared with the overwhelming impression his story conveys of dominant courage and placid self-reliance." The reviews were more than a celebration of a book — they were a recognition of a great voyage. The *Nautical Gazette* considered the captain's place in history: "There is no question as to his name being handed down to posterity as one of the most intrepid of navigators."

The praise and recognition he had earned for his writing gave Slocum the confidence to dream about new possibilities for a man of his skills. He was flattered by an introduction given by his cousin Joel Slocum to a lecture he delivered in Concord, New Hampshire, and later wrote to his admiring relative, "You see I had, with my many accomplishments (excuse me) forgotten that I was a poet . . . and the words came up new and crisp. You said 'prophetic' and you were entirely right." The same month his book came out, Slocum was considering some kind of submarine adventure. He wrote to C.C. Buel, "I hope that the *Century* will not forget me and my Iceland trip! It may not be of absorbing interest — but I have a voyage in mind that will fasten itself upon all classes of readers and to realize that voyage I am looking to the disposal, first, of the *Spray*; people buy things rare in history someone may buy my old boat and so help me into my submarine explorer."

Once again, nothing came of his plan, and Slocum grew increasingly restless. He and Hettie again took rooms in New York, where he paced and tried to arrive at a new plan. One scheme was outlandish even for Slocum: he thought he might try his hand at aviation, and sent a naive letter of inquiry to Professor Otis Mason at the Smithsonian Institution. "I am not the old fossil that some take me for," he asserted, "and I am not for old ideas when new are better." Mason was a colleague of aviation pioneer Samuel Pierpont Langley, who had gained worldwide attention with his unmanned free flights. Slocum saw himself as holding a second mate's position on a flying ship, and pointed out his qualifications: "I consider the human mind above all else that we know of in this world. You will see that at any rate I could trust even my own poor head to find my way about independent of the machine we call chronometer. I sailed scientifically, too." What Professor Mason made of Slocum's proposal isn't known.

Son Garfield, who was living on the *Spray* during the winter of 1901, believed that his father needed to be alone, away from Hettie. He summed up the matter simply: "I assume that he and Hettie did not pull on the same rope." Finally, Slocum came up with a plan: he would take the *Spray* to Buffalo to exhibit at the Pan-American Exposition. The *Spray* had always been an attraction, and at every stop on his circumnavigation Slocum had picked up curios to display. A New York *Post* reporter marveled at the treasures he had found aboard: "The cabins of the *Spray* are now an instructive museum. He shows you a piece of rock which was taken from Robinson Crusoe's cave, native weapons, mats from the several islands he has visited, and also a fair-sized canoe hewn out of the solid wood. He has marine curiosities in abundance, the collection of coral being especially good." Another reporter remarked on "a hold full of curiosities, shells, sea fans, canoes, bamboo sticks . . . He has several books full of newspaper clippings." Others recalled seeing a Hammond typewriter, an Australian boomerang and a Zulu spear. Some remembered how Slocum welcomed visitors and showed them around the *Spray* for the price of an autograph in her visitors' book. But not always — others recalled paying ten cents to board and that Slocum later upped the entry fee to a quarter.

Slocum exhibited the *Spray* in Buffalo from May to November 1901. Traveling there and back was complicated. He purchased a lifeboat, and a small engine to power it, to tow the sloop up the Hudson River as far as Troy; there it entered the Erie Canal with its mast unstepped and secured to the deck. In Buffalo the *Spray* was hauled out, raised in a sling and loaded onto a dray to be pulled by horses to the exposition's lakeside site. The *Spray* was moored in one of the fairground lagoons, just past the Electric Tower and the performance stadium. A sideshow atmosphere prevailed. Slocum shared the limelight with Chiquita the Human Doll, an infant incubator, a hula dancer, and Eskimos (as they were then billed) exhibited in imitation snow igloos. The "Bennett Illustrated Souvenir Guide Pan-American Exposition, 1901" advertised Slocum as "A Daring New England Yankee." As for why one would want to visit him, the brochure explained,

"The captain made ports where none were ever made before and picked up numberless curios which constituted the cargo of the 'Spray' when he once more hove to in Boston harbor. This curio collection, as well as his vessel, he has brought with him to the Exposition, and it will be to the profit of every visitor to shake hands with the gallant captain, a man of stout heart and steady nerve, a veteran of the salt sea, and a man of mighty mould and character." After paying an admission fee, fair-goers were rowed out in the *Spray*'s dory to meet the captain, who regaled them with tales from his travels, the "carpet tacks on the deck" yarn being a big crowd pleaser.

Always eager to make a buck, Slocum came up with an ingenious bit of marketing. He had saved the old sail that had taken the *Spray* as far as Australia. He cut it up and inserted small pieces of it — "A piece of her original mainsail, which was torn, beyond repair, in the gale off Cape Horn, 4th to 8th of March, 1896 — a fierce tempest!" — inside the booklet he sold. Thus, the real reason for buying the booklet was to acquire the little "Sloop *Spray*" souvenir that accompanied it. For some admirers this was like buying a piece of the true cross.

By the end of the exposition, Slocum had squirreled away enough money to buy his first house and some land. The *Spray* was a poignant sight as she headed down the Erie Canal with, as the local paper noted, "an old work horse for a sail." When asked if he had had the horse sharp shod, a Buffalo newspaper reported Slocum's answer:

203

"'You see', explained the captain, 'it don't make much difference which way the wind blows, we get there just the same. No, I didn't have the horse sharp shod. The canal don't go over many hills between here and the Hudson'"

The man who had not had a permanent address since childhood was now going home to a family farm in the Cape Cod village of West Tisbury. And the Buffalo paper didn't miss the significance of the moment: "The horse that furnished the motive power to run the sloop down the canal will furnish the power to run a plow on the captain's farm in Martha's Vineyard. The hand that steered the tiller of the *Spray* will steer the plow; the hand that refused to allow a woman to accompany him across the Atlantic will say 'gee-up' to the horse, when it comes plowin' time."

But he was one of that rare breed that is alive only at sea. When we first went aboard, he had been sitting, or perhaps slumped is the better word, by the wheel in an attitude that betokened complete dejection. There was an air about him of abstraction and disinterest that was so deep it was as though he was living in a private dream world.

But the minute the lines were off and the Spray *gathered way, he had turned into quite another man. He moved precisely, firmly, quickly but not hastily, about the ship's business, and he had the* Spray *in hand about as effortlessly as anyone could. There was, I do believe, a sparkle in his eye, and there was little aboard that he didn't notice. He didn't say much, but you knew that he was a ship's captain, if from nothing else, from his confident bearing, and from the quiet preciseness of his commands.*

— H.S. Smith in *The Skipper*, March 1968

12

Swallowing the Anchor?

Ports are no good . . . ships rot . . . men go to the devil.
— Joseph Conrad, *The Mirror of the Sea*

On land sailors are square pegs, and it quickly became obvious to the people of Martha's Vineyard that their famous captain was an eccentric, to put it kindly. Living aboard boats most of his life had made Slocum an outsider to polite society. But he had decided to give this "land living" a try, or so he told the papers on his way home from Buffalo.

Martha's Vineyard offered Hettie her first home as a married woman. For sixteen years she had been forced to move back and forth between relatives, to make do and live with whoever would have her. In effect, she had been abandoned financially and emotionally by her husband, left behind to care for his children. But that was about to change, or so it seemed; her husband was on his way home and intending to stay ashore. The small house on Martha's Vineyard had cost Slocum $305 — money he had made from his world lecturing and book peddling. The June 26, 1902 edition of the Vineyard *Gazette* noted that "Capt. and Mrs. Slocum arrived Saturday and occupied their newly purchased house on the Sabbath."

The village of West Tisbury was the agricultural heart of the island. Slocum had decided he would become a farmer; the *Spray* would be moored nearby and taken out only for short business trips. Slocum was "swallowing the anchor" — at least, that was the impression given in an article by Clifton Johnson in the October 1902 issue of *Outing* magazine: "Of late the captain has become a thoroughgoing landsman and has cast anchor on a little Martha's Vineyard farm, where he lives on the outskirts of a rural village with several old sea captains for neighbors. His house is one of the most ancient on the island — an oak-ribbed ark of a dwelling with warped floors and tiny window panes and open fireplaces. Its aspect is at present rather forlorn and naked, but the captain knows how to wield the hammer and the saw, and will soon make it snug."

The hammering and sawing resulted in a small boxed porch on the front of the house. Other additions were not quite so conventional. Slocum had designed the *Liberdade* with a mind to dories, sampans and native canoes, and the same eclectic touch was evident in his land home.

He created overhanging eaves, influenced by the houses in the South Pacific, where such eaves were necessary for shade. One of his West Tisbury neighbors complained that Slocum showed no regard for architectural unity when he added a Japanese-style roof over the front of the house. However, a local newspaper was impressed, declaring that "it was his own taste which transformed it into one of the most attractive places on the island." In a letter to Walter Teller, Garfield remembered that his father had liked the house because of the large timbers and because the knees put him in mind of a ship's hold. Another neighbor recalled the house as having a "marine flavor." Beside the front door the captain arranged shells and coral. Throughout Fag End, as Slocum named the old house, there was more evidence of a seafaring man's touch: starfish, sea fans, brain coral and some old scallop shells. One relative relieved him of a large clam shell with fluted edges, to use for a birdbath in her garden. Slocum held on to the most enormous shells, as they were perfect for ballasting the *Spray*.

Slocum had plans for making the most of the land at Fag End, or Rudder Ranch as he jokingly referred to his property in a letter to Clifton Johnson. And Johnson in his article for *Outing* was impressed by how quickly the old seadog seemed to be getting his land legs: "In a single season he has become an enthusiastic agriculturist, is proud of his flourishing garden and would like to own and make fruitful all the land about. He delights to point out the beauties of the sturdy oak woods which over-spread much of the region, the promising condition of the abounding huckleberry bushes, the possibilities of the wet hollows for cranberry culture and of the protected slopes for fruit trees."

What didn't appear in the article were Johnson's impressions of Slocum's character. The journalist's scrib-bled notes offer insights that would have annoyed Slocum. He observed that the captain "has a temper and explodes like a firecracker when he is affronted . . . Likes to relate his experiences and observations . . . Wags his head and gestures and sometimes acts out bits." He summed up Slocum as "lithe, nervous, energetic . . . He looks 10 years younger than he really is." Although it is not known what evidence Johnson had for the following remark, he also cited a quality that would have been essential to Slocum at sea: "Never loses his head in an emergency."

Now that Slocum was landlocked, people were finally getting to know him, warts and all. His temper was some-thing he could no longer hide away and take for a sail. One of Slocum's cousins, Grace Murray Brown, remembered him as "capable of letting his irascible side show up if sufficient provocation was given or was suspected. One could not hide anything from a mind like his . . . slights would never be forgotten or forgiven." She felt that her uncle (as she called Slocum) had a capacity for caring for people of like sympathies, but was also too impatient when he could not "be as independent as his nature demanded." Perhaps she summed him up best when she pointed out in a letter to Teller, "I can not be too emphatic in saying Uncle Josh did not suffer fools gladly . . . that may be hackneyed but he never bothered with anything or anyone who did not measure up. But was so appreciative when he found them acceptable."

Slocum was often testy with his brother Ornan, who lived on the island and ran a shoe shop in Vineyard Haven. Ornan did not have his brother's strong constitution, and Joshua had little patience for him. When the kindly but slower-moving younger brother came to help Joshua plant fruit trees at the West Tisbury farm, the two ended up bickering, as they always did. Slocum was outraged at Ornan, whom he accused of running the cultivator or the horse up against his precious trees. Grace Brown remembers it as "a terrible row . . . the Captain said Ornan was trying to ruin his beautiful little trees out of pure cussedness." The family folklore as related by Grace Brown is that after the explosion, they refused to speak to each other "until one day they ran afoul of one another on a narrow path. Ornan, goodhearted soul, thought what two jackasses they were, so as they were about to pass eyes straight ahead, Ornan gave Josh the shoulder spinning him around. Luckily Josh had his sealegs on or this tale might have ended differently. Ornan with a wide grin greeted him with a 'Good morning Captain'. Josh relented by gripping his brother's hand in a lusty shake and a cry, 'How are you Ornan?' So ended that bit." Ornan never did return to work the cultivator. In fact, Joshua's days with the cultivator were drawing to a close. He was wearying of land life. He tried growing hops the second season on the Vineyard, but was not successful.

It was becoming obvious to the islanders that their famous captain was having trouble adapting to land life. Joseph Chase Allen was a boy of about eight when he knew Slocum on Martha's Vineyard. He described the captain this way: "very quick in his movements, spoke rapidly, clipped off his sentences, inclined to be snappy in his speech as men will be who are accustomed to give orders, and not the kind of man one would be tempted to take liberties with." Islanders long remembered Slocum giving one young man a cutting lecture on the proper way to come up alongside a boat without smashing into it.

Allen also remembered some of Slocum's eccentricities, which were the outcome of a long, solitary life. On one occasion he and Slocum joined a small coach of travelers coming home from the island ferry. One of the passengers was a well-dressed lady. "I was on the front seat," Allen recalled, "when I heard a hell of a rustle of paper. The man leans forward and says to the woman, 'I hope you don't object to the smell of salt codfish.' I looked round and he had the biggest jack-knife I ever saw in my life and was hewing chunks off the fish and eating it and he ate a good deal of it the way to West Tisbury. That was Slocum in 1904."

There was no missing the fact that Slocum was an old

seadog. Even his relatives didn't know what to expect next. According to Grace Brown, her whole family knew that Slocum had a gift for the dramatic, but he still could surprise them. In everyday conversation, her Uncle Josh would just start shouting poetry by Robert Burns that he had memorized. Another day, "he burst upon our view by way of the kitchen with an enormous salt cod tucked under his wing with just a paper around its middle but the tail sticking out and part of the other end where the head was happily off. Mother laughed so at the sight that father and the rest of us came in from our share of the jobs. Captain had been up and down Atlantic Avenue renewing friendships along the wharves where one of the old salts gave him the cod."

Slocum still had his sea captain friends, but wasn't a popular man with other contemporaries. He made small efforts to contribute to island life with his famous stereopticon lectures. The *West Tisbury News* advertised "an account of his voyage around the world, at Agricultural Hall, Thanksgiving evening, November 27th. Capt. Slocum has kindly offered to donate the proceeds of his lecture to the Congregational Church." But one islander who heard him lecture about his sea adventures felt that Slocum had become "a little alienated to social joys"; "I daresay the local gossip of West Tisbury had become a little tame to one who had spread tacks on the deck of his boat in Tierra del Fuego," he speculated. In his short time on land Slocum had gained a reputation for being opinionated, acerbic and difficult to befriend. As Hettie put it with subtle irony, "It did not hurt his feelings to let you know what he was thinking." She joked that she referred to him as "Josh, Joshua, or Captain if I thought he needed the honor."

Grace Brown expressed some sympathy for Slocum's growing uneasiness. "A winter would be unthinkable for a man of his volatile nature holed up in a small house in a small village," she opined. "It might have been manageable if Hettie had had a different makeup but even a siren would have a hard time of it . . . to keep his wings clipped." More and more often, Slocum was seen aboard the *Spray*. During some of that time, Garfield sailed around the island with his father. He noticed how Slocum paced the deck, stared out to the horizon, and then simply went below with his books. Garfield was worried about his father's growing agitation: "Father was a changed man when he returned from his lone voyage. He acted to me like he wanted to be alone. That voyage was a terrible strain on him. Father was so different when he returned from sailing alone, he did not talk to me much. He appeared to be deep in thought." It was obvious to all who knew him that it was time for him to be alone again — to return to life aboard the only home that made sense to him, the *Spray*.

Though Slocum had added his eccentric touches to the farmhouse, his boat was the true reflection of who he was and what his life was about. Joseph Chase Allen visited the *Spray* around 1904 and remembered how

213

exotic it appeared to the eyes of an eight-year-old. Slocum "carried a small round bottom boat in the alleyway and it was chock full of all kinds of junk. A beautiful Chinese gong hung alongside the companionway, black with gold and red figures and hanging beside it on a silk rope was a wood hammer. It made a beautiful sound. I remember, too, his topping lift was a native grass rope. Looked as though it were made out of leaves. A coil of the same stuff was on top of one of the houses and looked as though it were used for a heaving line. It was whiter than flax bottom chairs . . . Captain Slocum had a panful of wild cherries on the transom. I remember him saying if he could get one more panful he'd be ready for a trip."

Slocum must have picked that "one more panful" quite soon afterwards, because his life was more and more on the waters. He had been "hustling a dollar," as he saw his business of receiving visitors aboard his boat, taking parties out for day trips, selling books and giving lectures. The boat itself was a floating story. Pictures and autographed books from that time have since turned up in harbors all along the New England coast. His world trip stayed alive in his mind as long as he kept telling the story. The books continued to sell, but interest in the lectures was dropping off. A local paper reported that the captain "lectured to a small but appreciative audience at the Theatre on Saturday night on his adventurous voyage around the world in his little boat alone." Later, the New Bedford *Standard* noted that "the audience was miserably small and was composed entirely of tourists and a few members of the local yachting clubs." The decline in interest was explained by Major James B. Pond in his book *Eccentricities of Genius*. Pond had been Slocum's booking agent for a short time and felt that Slocum's story was being told too late: "Had all this occurred twenty years ago, it would have meant a fortune for Captain Slocum, and a stimulant for the Lyceum." Pond regretted the changes taking place in lecture circuits, the result of agents who presented lecture courses as package deals to communities and did not make allowances for independent ventures such as the captain's. Pond felt that Slocum "absolutely charms and fascinates his hearers as few ever did or ever could do . . . I have listened for hours to these seeming tournaments in navigator's skill, and never yet did the captain hesitate for an instant for a reply that went straight to the mark like a bullet."

If this was all a disappointment to Pond, one can only imagine how Slocum was feeling at age sixty. His stories were uniquely courageous accounts of great navigational skill, but few ears were still willing to listen. Children who stopped by to see him on the *Spray* were told the stories, often learning them to retell while helping the captain sell his tropical shells, sponges and curios. Carol W. Saley was one of the children who helped Slocum out, and she and her friend were spellbound by his stories. The captain taught them the tales behind each object they helped sell and "how to blow the shells for customers as the captain did when he needed a foghorn. We did well and he was much pleased with our work, paid us well for youngsters and was kind to us always."

Slocum was fast losing his sense of purpose, and there was another Cape Cod reality that was driving him back to sea. From West Tisbury he wrote to his friend William Tripp on March 18, 1904, "I became so interested in trying to keep warm these winter days that I forgot all, except the woodpile. I have an oak grove, fortunately, near my house." Slocum started going south in the cold months. A local paper reported, "He is now on a cruise of the Caribbean for the benefit of his health. After touring the world he settled down to farming; but having lost money in growing hops, he 'chucked' it."

On October 15, 1905, the Providence *Journal* reported that Captain Slocum "was bound west to pick up Mrs. Slocum for a winter in southern waters, and then sailed away again, after renewing his license as a master mariner. His boat is his house and he spends most of his time in her." The statement was true, except for Hettie coming along. That never was to happen. The pattern was set: the *Spray* was once again his solitary home. Every winter he sailed south to Miami, then to the Bahamas, Grand Cayman, Jamaica or somewhere else in the West Indies to stock up with tropical shells and coral, which he returned in the late spring to sell. The West Tisbury "Miscellanies" and the island social columns from 1905 to 1908 are a sad comment on Hettie and the captain's life together. Their comings and goings tell the story of a couple seldom in the same place at the same time:

August 31, 1905 — "Capt. Joshua Slocum has returned home after an absence of about six months."

October 5, 1905 — "Capt. Joshua Slocum has gone to Boston."

October 12, 1905 — "Capt. Joshua Slocum was among the arrivals on Monday's boat."

October 26, 1905 — "Mrs. Joshua Slocum has returned from her trip to Boston."

November 9, 1905 — "Mrs. Joshua Slocum has gone to Boston and expects to remain there most of the winter."

January 11, 1906 — "Captain Joshua Slocum is cruising among the West Indies."

After the 1906 winter trip, Slocum's life took a troubled turn. He left the Cayman Islands with his usual load of seashells and coral for resale as souvenirs. But that spring he had a cargo some of whose unusual contents excited him: a specimen of the lace tree and some rare forest orchids. He had half a dozen of these exotic plants, and he decided to present them to President Theodore Roosevelt. On his way to Sagamore Hill, he stopped as a guest at the Riverton Yacht Club in New Jersey. As was his usual routine, he presented a lecture, and friends arranged for a social event afterwards in his honor.

Slocum, as always, extended an open invitation to look around the *Spray*. A twelve-year-old girl, Elsie Wright, came aboard the next day with a young male companion. Slocum was bewildered by the story she told her parents when she got home. Within hours Slocum was arrested on a charge of rape, and the next day the whole town of Riverton heard the story. The scandal was front page news in the Riverton *New Era:*

CAPT. SLOCUM IN TROUBLE
Accused of Maltreating a Girl on His Famous Yacht, the Spray

Riverton, N.J. May 26 — Capt. Joshua Slocum, formerly a commander of clippers, who has been in trouble several times for alleged ill treatment of his crews, and who for several years has been living off the glory and the story of sailing around the world alone in the little sloop *Spray*, was sent to jail here this morning on a charge of maltreating twelve-year-old Elsie Wright, daughter of Charles D. Wright . . . When Elsie got home she told her parents and they called in Dr. C.S. Mills, who said that she was not much injured, but was suffering from shock. Capt. Slocum had left Philadelphia, which is about eight miles from this place, and was arrested on his return last night as he stepped off a trolley car. Captain Slocum asked that nothing should be said about his arrest. He said tonight in his defence that he was suffering from mental aberration.

The friend that Slocum had been visiting in Philadelphia prior to the arrest thought at the time that Slocum was "lean and hungry looking and gaunt. But he looked as though he could take care of himself. I never was disappointed in his appearance or behavior, though I am quite sure he was a little cracked." He also described him as "a little dippy." The pitiful-looking sixty-two-year-old captain with his boatload of orchids seemed confused by the charge. All he could say was that he did not remember the incident occurring; perhaps it was one of his "mental lapses" was his sole attempt at an explanation. He claimed that he had suffered from these since one day in Newcastle, New South Wales, on his round-the-world trip. His story was that a heaving line had swung around and struck him on the side of the head. One newspaper implied that Slocum's word might not always be trusted, noting that the captain was "a good hand at spinning a yarn." Press accounts portrayed Slocum as protesting his innocence. The local newspaper reported, "The old sailor was indignant at his arrest. He ridiculed the charge against him and when being taken to the jail said he would be vindicated." Bail was set at one thousand dollars, and Slocum was jailed in Mount Holly to await trial.

Elsie Wright was examined by a doctor, who determined — much to her family's relief — that there could be no charge of rape. Even so, his daughter had suffered, and Mr. Wright wanted him held publicly accountable. The father wrote to the Riverton weekly paper, "There was no attempt at rape for the child is not physically injured although greatly agitated by the indecent action and exposure of this creature now posing in the limelight of cheap notoriety." He added that he and his wife "regret exceedingly the necessity of publicity for the child's sake but feel assured that the exposure of such a fiend will be regarded as a service rendered the public."

The girl's father may have suspected the offense was not as serious as first thought, and made it known that he did not wish to see an old man punished severely. While Slocum awaited trial, he was placed in a small cell with a fireplace, a narrow window at eye level and access to an enclosed exercise yard. After forty-two days in the Mount Holly jail, Slocum had his day in court. The Burlington County Prison Register for 1904–1906 has the following entry:

Name: Capt. Joshua Slocum
Charge: rape
When received: May 26–06
When discharged: dis July–06
Name of committing officer: Silas J. Coddington
Number of days: 42

The charge of rape was reduced to indecent assault, and Wright recommended leniency. The *Mount Holly News* for Tuesday, July 10, 1906, reported on the captain's day in court. It noted that Slocum had signed a waiver allowing for his case to be heard without a jury, and stated, "Senator John G. Horner, private counsel for Mr. Wright, with permission of Prosecutor Atkinson, said there had been considerable exaggeration both in the newspapers and the community as to what actually took place on the boat. Slocum was a seafaring man with no home . . . The captain was certainly guilty of great indiscretion. He did not violate the person of the child acquainted with matters unknown to one of her tender years. Slocum had been struck by a boom which brought on occasional aberrations of mind, and he has no recollection of the crime. The Senator asked the court to be lenient. There was no desire to have him harshly dealt with. He had been in jail six weeks and that was probably punishment enough . . . The family wanted his absence more than his retention in prison."

Slocum pleaded "non vult contendre," meaning "I will not contest," which in the state of New Jersey at the turn of the century was the same as a guilty plea but did not invoke the mandatory penalties. His counsel, Samuel W. Shinn, noted the captain's "enviable reputation" from his famous circumnavigation and let the court know there had been no intention to do bodily harm to the person of the girl. Presiding Judge Gaskill brought the matter to a close with these words to the old sailor: "I am very sorry to be obliged to administer reproof to a man of your experience and years, and I am glad, and no doubt you are, too, that in this case there was no attempt made to injure the person of the girl. Upon request of the family I can deal leniently with you. You must never return to Riverton either by rail or water. By payment of all costs you are discharged."

What happened to Elsie Wright cannot be known. We do know that the episode marked the low point in Slocum's steady descent. One theory about what actually happened was based on Slocum's pitiful and bewildered behavior after the arrest. It was supposed that the only crime the old man had committed was exposing himself, and then probably not on purpose. It may have been that he had left his trousers negligently unbuttoned and, having lived in solitude aboard for so long, was unfamiliar with the advisability of always wearing underwear. Perhaps what had made the young adolescent so distraught was merely getting an unexpected peek at Slocum's private parts.

When Walter Teller was researching this part of the captain's story in the 1950s, he interviewed a woman who had met up with Slocum around the time of the incident. She had been fifteen at the time and had been delivering a pail of milk from her father's farm to the captain, who was living aboard the *Spray* in Menemsha. She claimed that the captain had not only taken the milk but had grabbed her by the arm. Teller wrote that she had been "scared to death of the old codger because he was so fresh with the girls." But Teller did not use this anecdote in the biography "because on further investigation I found out that my informant in her younger years had not a very good reputation. I wondered if she might not have been one of those provocative adolescents who can do so much mischief among unhappy old men? Wasn't sure of her trustworthiness, neither was I sure there was nothing to what she said." He agreed with a friend that there may have been a hint of the Salem Witch Trials about young Elsie Wright's hysteria. In the end, Teller concluded that the "pitiful" affair rendered Slocum's life "almost a Greek tragedy."

The Riverton affair was Slocum's third serious tangle with the law. He boarded the *Spray* a confused, tired and disgraced old man. His days of glory seemed long ago. But true to his nature, he had a plan that was keeping him afloat for the present moment. All of the orchids but one had died while Slocum was behind bars. Fresh out of jail, he sailed away to Oyster Bay to give the lone survivor to President Roosevelt.

He looked like the typical beachcomber — wore a battered old felt hat — originally a black hat bleached out irregularly from sun and rain, a collarless shirt open at the neck, a vest, unbuttoned trousers that would disgrace a clamdigger and a pair of high lace-up shoes badly in need of a polish . . . . Spray *was dirty — not just a little dirty but very very dirty.*

— H.S. Smith, in *The Rudder*, March 1968

13

Seaworthy for the Last Time

I can patch up the Spray, *but who will patch up Captain Slocum?*

> — J.S., comment to reporter Louise Ward, 1907

The old captain was to have one last moment of glory. He sailed into Oyster Bay, Long Island, early in August 1906 with the one surviving orchid, planning to send the plant ashore to Sagamore Hill with a note attached for the president's secretary. But the messenger that day on the docks was none other than Archie Roosevelt, the young son of the president, who, recognizing the *Spray*, immediately jumped aboard. Archie shook the captain's hand and told him his father wanted to meet him. So Slocum, barely cleaned up from over a month in jail, was on his way to meet the President of the United States. That meeting led to a poignant friendship between a young boy and an old sailor. Roosevelt asked Slocum to take Archie sailing. On August 6, 1906, the president wrote to Henry Cabot Lodge, "Archie is off for a week's cruise with Captain Joshua Slocum — that man who takes his little boat, without any crew but himself, all around the world." Over five days, Slocum and Archie sailed from Oyster Bay to Newport.

That voyage was the start of Archie's apprenticeship with a master navigator. According to a local newspaper, Slocum complimented the lad, declaring him to be "the best young sailor who had ever stepped aboard his craft." He added that if the *Spray* ever needed a mate, Archie would be given the berth: "Archie is one of the cleverest boys I have ever known. He has learned to sail the *Spray* almost as well as I can myself. I like him because he always does what I tell him to. You wouldn't believe, but he knows how to set the sails at their proper balance and to lash the helm so that it skims along by itself. That is a trick which excites admiration wherever I go, and which few sailors understand. Archie learned the trick last year, and he did wonders with the boat." Archie later recalled their relationship as one of mutual admiration, noting the great skills of the old navigator: "Of course we [Archie and Obie, a sailor on the presidential yacht, the *Sylph*] saw the famous alarm clock, which had to be boiled before it would run. Beyond my comprehension were his sheets of calculations for the lunar observations he had made single-handedly — a feat, I believe which is supposed to require three people to work out."

Slocum also showed Archie the finer points of nautical salesmanship. He showed the boy how to file the points off shells to make foghorns. And he showed him how to sell finished goods, be they foghorns, coral or books. The boy was eager to learn, and during their time together Slocum must have gained back the hope and courage to pull himself up after a devastating debacle. His skills were appreciated once more, and by none other than the president himself. That Roosevelt had entrusted his son to the old captain could only have felt like a pardon — a second chance for respectability after disgrace. The president wrote him a note thanking him for the copy of *Sailing Alone Around the World* that Slocum had given him before sailing home to Martha's Vineyard.

My dear Captain Slocum:
I thank you for your interesting volume, which you know I prize. By the way, I entirely sympathize with your feeling of delight in the sheer loneliness and vastness of the ocean. It was just my feeling in the wilderness of the west.
Sincerely yours,
Theodore Roosevelt

No doubt the Vineyarders had heard about his time in jail. Grace Brown recalled the family whisperings concerning the Riverton incident, and wrote to Walter Teller, "That yellow journalism was so awful at the time and our family's so shocked over it that they soft pedalled whenever we younger ones were around. As I recall it was something that happened or was reported to have happened . . . The matter was aired in the papers and there it died out . . . We who had known the Captain had found him affectionate to a degree with young things just as I know my own dad was. We never heard of any dalliance with the fair sex. When you recall as I do hearing of ministers, doctors, and dentists being nothing but Don Juans in their home town's estimation, one wonders how this all comes about?"

On his return home, there was no mention of the affair in the press. According to the August 16, 1906, Vineyard *Gazette*, "Captain Joshua Slocum, master of the *Spray*, was in town on Monday." But all who observed him after that summer noticed his unshakable sadness. Grace Brown speculated about his depression: "I think he was bitter . . . some folk are born . . . never being satisfied with half measures. I don't believe he allowed what certain people thought of him to bother him, only as annoyance and his contempt could be very potent. If any sadness, it was for a career which he felt did not justify his inherent ability." One islander recalled, "He was lazy and mentally sluggish . . . the captain suffered from the

229

disadvantage of not having enough to do." His three sons were concerned about their father's emotional health. Garfield remembered a moment of their time sailing together when his father seemed lost in the past: "Beside the bowsprit the *Spray* was in the sea though father saw a huge wave coming and headed the *Spray* into it. I held on to the bowsprit and when it was recovered from the baptism father laughed heartily. I remember hearing father sing 'We Shall Meet on That Beautiful Shore'. I think he was thinking of mother."

Virginia had been dead for over twenty years, but Garfield sensed that her spirit was alive to his father at that moment. Slocum did not have the comfort of a loving partner in Hettie, nor did she find a loving partner in him. Victor reflected, "Father was a changed man when he returned from his lone voyage — he acted to me like he wanted to be alone. That voyage was a terrible strain on him. Father was so different when he returned from sailing alone, he did not talk to me much. He appeared to be deep in thought so I stayed far." On Slocum's return to Martha's Vineyard, he and Hettie continued their pattern of spending time apart. He roamed the shores and coastlines, and she spent long spells and her winters away with friends and relatives. Grace Brown recalled one instance when Hettie and Josh were forced to share time under the same roof, in the same bed. Even as a child, she had sensed the awkwardness of the situation: "When he returned sometimes Hettie would be at our house and one time he came in unheralded and wanted a bed. We had only half the house — eight rooms and Hettie was in a small room with a single or two thirds bed. But where mother wanted to rearrange things, he said, 'Now Alice I haven't seen my wife in several months and if I can sleep in a bunk the size of a coffin I guess I can find room with Hettie.' I don't know how Hettie stood it but she laughed it off and they stayed several days before going in the *Spray* to the Vineyard."

The islanders were attuned to this unusual relationship, and the general impression was that Joshua and Hettie had reached an agreement to lead separate lives. One Vineyarder, Alice Longaker, said, "It was a long time before I became aware that he had a wife and though I have nothing concrete upon which to pin the fact it seemed, for many reasons, to be evident that he carried the relationship buoyantly. He was always the visitor and never seemed aware of ties." In reporting the comings and goings of the captain and his wife, the Vineyard *Gazette* stopped referring to Hettie as Mrs. Joshua Slocum. In 1906 she was almost always "Mrs. H. M. Slocum." The West Tisbury "Miscellanies" section may have been having a little fun at the couple's expense when it noted on July 30, 1908, that "Capt. Joshua Slocum of the sloop *Spray* is on the Island and has been a recent guest of Mrs. Slocum at West Tisbury." Another islander, H.L. Coggins, remarked, "I don't think that the Captain and wife were very close and the whole family seemed relieved when he took any of his trips."

These were Captain Slocum's twilight years: like the *Spray*, he was falling apart physically, and struggling to remain seaworthy — to be worthy of the waters one more time. He made short daytrips, and then every winter — with the tangible excuse of minding the cold and doing a little business — he escaped boredom in a trip south. The *Spray* would leave with a ballast of cement or stone and return loaded with shells, coconuts and sundry items, which he could peddle as he sailed along the New England coast.

The winter of 1907 found Slocum in Jamaica — the second visit reported by the local newspaper, the *Gleaner*, which referred to him as "the Lone Navigator." This was the year of the great earthquake in Kingston, Jamaica, and Slocum was there. He met up with a Philadelphia newspaper reporter named Louise B. Ward. Ward found the old captain to be coping well, but she also sensed his melancholy. As he sat on his boat in the harbor of a city that had almost come to ruin, Slocum may have felt personally shaken. He made an unusual remark: "I can patch up the *Spray*, but who will patch up Captain Slocum?"

That winter and the next, Slocum kept himself "patched up" enough to make safe passage from southern ports to home. These trips still gave him a sense of purpose and achievement. He still had ambitions, and told a local newspaper his latest plan: "The *Spray* shall be the first boat to go through the [Panama] Canal, and thence to

China and Japan." That adventure never materialized, and January 1908 found him still at work lecturing. He had to keep the old dream alive through stories. His brochure for the Miami audience claimed, "He will tell of his escape from raging storms, from savage cannibals off the Patagonia coast, from dangers of the deep that were met by him alone in mid-ocean. He will tell of trying to enter Havana harbor while the seas were rolling over Morro headland, and of his turning and running to Miami. Some of these things he will show you upon a curtain by a magic lantern." When he returned north in June, he delivered a piece of green coral weighing nearly two tons to the American Museum of Natural History in New York. It was at that time the largest and most valuable piece of coral in any institution in the world.

Oyster Bay on Long Island was one place that still found the old eccentric charming, in a quaint sort of way. On his return in May 1907, a local paper commented, "The captain is as full of yarns as Oyster Bay is of horseshoe crabs. Sitting snugly in his little cabin, he reels them off by the yard to the gaping landsmen, and they have come to look upon him as one of the wonders of the deep." Likewise, the New York *World* welcomed the captain back: "Once a year sea-battered, kindly old Captain Joshua Slocum puts in the harbor here with his weatherbeaten, snub-nosed, tight little yawl, the *Spray*." Archie Roosevelt met the captain and took him to the White House. As Slocum told the story, when he shook Roosevelt's hand

233

the president said, "Captain, our adventures have been a little different." Slocum responded with his usual understated humor: "That is true, Mr. President, but I see you got here first." The captain had planned to take Archie sailing after this White House meeting, but this second trip never happened. Slocum had been careless with his answer to a theological question posed by a minister from Groton, the strict Episcopalian school that Archie attended. Slocum returned to Martha's Vineyard without his young apprentice sailor and salesman.

Years later in his memoirs, Archie Roosevelt wrote about Slocum and the *Spray*: "The boat was the most incredibly dirty craft I have ever seen . . . Obie went ashore, and returned with his own money, and jettisoned the filthy old relic [a stove] that had served the captain, I don't know how many years . . . In mild, warm weather, the Captain often cooked on deck, and he had a most ingenious contrivance . . . He had an old fashioned laundry tub, in the bottom of which he coiled a piece of heavy anchor chain. On top of the chain he built a fire of driftwood. As a diet, he was fond of salt fish, and every so often he would make us enormous pancakes, 'as thick as your foot', he would tell us." Some of Archie's memories were as vivid as only those linked to smell can be. Remembering the hold of the *Spray*, he wrote, "There was a quantity of miscellaneous equipment, an enormous number of conch shells, which he got when he was down in the West Indies. Some of these had not been too carefully cleaned, and there was a fine ripe odor permeating the center part of the ship."

After 1906, Slocum's neighbours on Martha's Vineyard began to notice how neglected and run down the *Spray* was looking. Some made note of the inside of Slocum's cabin, with its jumble of books and badly corroded sextant lying about from his "trip round." Others pointed out the slack rigging and the fact that *Spray* needed tarring. One visitor described the atmosphere aboard as "pungent with the odor of tarred ropes and the salty mildew a boat collects while sailing the seven seas." The boat Slocum had lovingly rebuilt was now languishing uncared for. The *Spray*'s renewal fifteen years before had mirrored Slocum's; her deterioration now reflected his own. According to Ernest Dean, a Vineyarder who had known both Slocum and the *Spray* for many years, "they both were neat, trim, seaworthy, but as the years rolled along there were signs of wear and exposure."

Decades of nomadic wanderlust had worn Slocum down. He was now suffering from prolonged headaches. One neighbor noted, "Slocum was much run down physically and perhaps mentally — exceedingly lazy and indifferent to his surroundings." Author and sailor Vincent Gilpin was struck by Slocum's appearance in 1908: "He was thrifty and usually hard up — which didn't bother him, for his wants were few. Spray . . . was simply fitted out, rather bare, and very damp, from many soakings with salt water, and Slocum kept a little wood-stove going to help dry her out. I remember seeing him lunching one day on what looked like a half-baked potato, from which he sliced pieces with his jack-knife. He was rather shabbily dressed in civilian clothes, with a ragged black felt hat."

Slocum had once said that even the worst sea is not so terrible to a well-appointed ship, but by 1907 neither he nor his ship were well appointed. He was distracted and disheveled-looking in his shabby clothes; she was ramshackled, badly in need of paint, leaking at the deck-line, cracked and full of rust stains. But there is an under-standing a sailor has of his boat after years of sailing together. It's a feeling that somehow the boat is lucky, and has to have been so to survive the many dangers she has sailed through. Sailors believe that a boat's luck rubs off on the people involved with her — that if a sailor gives his best to a vessel, she will reciprocate.

Whether the *Spray* was seaworthy or not, Slocum had faith in her abilities and his own. He was still filled with wanderlust. Grace Brown had this view of his melancholy and his need to be constantly on the move: "I do not ascribe any sadness to anything less than for more worlds to conquer, as it were. You know that divine discontent we have heard about, that urge that would not let him give over." Slocum told family, friends, neighbors and the newspapers that he was planning a final adventure: he was planning a voyage of exploration to Venezuela, up the Orinoco River to the Rio Negro, and then into the Amazon. He joked that he intended to take his Victrola so that if he was mistaken for a god, he would not disappoint the natives.

As his neighbors watched the old salt prepare for this adventure, they must have shaken their heads. Horace Athearn, a trap fisherman at Menemsha at the time, watched the *Spray* sail off on what he thought would be her last voyage. He and others had remarked on the sad condition of the *Spray*; the general consensus was that everything looked worn, especially the standing rigging. They thought the captain was slipping, that in his best days he never would have started out in such a sorry state. Vincent Gilpin remembered that "her sails and rigging would have been renewed more than once, and would have always had weak spots." Thomas Fleming Day, editor of *The Rudder*, thought the *Spray* was "considerably dozy . . . certainly seaworthy, though slow." Captain Nat Herreshoff cast the captain's last line aboard and later remarked on the *Spray*'s worn sails and frayed lines. And Vineyarder Reginald Norton remembered people's dire predictions before Slocum set sail: "Folks used to say he would plant his bones in that boat." Those words were prophetic: Captain Joshua Slocum and the *Spray* left Vineyard Haven for the Orinoco River and were never heard from again.

Two mysteries surround Slocum's fate: What happened to him? and When did it happen? There is even some confusion regarding the year he left Vineyard Haven. By all legal and historical accounts the date was November 14, 1909. That was the date Hettie put on a petition to the

Probate Court of Dukes County. The petition stated that Joshua Slocum "disappeared, absconded and absented himself" on that day and further stated, "He sailed from Tisbury, Massachusetts in the Sloop 'Spray' . . . encountered a very severe gale shortly afterwards and has never been heard from since." And Slocum's son Victor claimed to have received a letter from his father dated September 4, 1909, wherein the captain wrote, "I am on the *Spray* hustling for a dollar." However, that date conflicts with a news item from the Fairhaven *Star* dated September 30, 1909, which referred to a mysterious piece of mail:

FEARED THAT CAPTAIN SLOCUM IS LOST

It is feared that Captain Joshua Slocum of West Tisbury, formerly of Fairhaven, owner of the famous yawl *Spray*, in which the noted lecturer and sailor has circumnavigated the globe, has been lost at sea in the little 33 foot craft, the smallest boat that ever sailed around the world.

The return of Captain Slocum's mail unopened from a foreign port to which he directed it to be sent when he sailed from this port last November on one of his long cruises on the *Spray*, and the fact that no word has been received from him since he sailed, has led his wife and relatives to believe that he has been lost.

It must be pointed out that Victor's accounts of his father's travels, while spirited and informative, are full of inaccuracies and undocumented anecdotes. He even gave his mother's date of death incorrectly. In his book *Capt. Joshua Slocum*, Victor wrote of his mother's death, "that was on July 25, 1885. There is no need of my looking at a calendar for the date, which sixty-five years ago was written on my heart, never in this life to be effaced." In fact, Virginia died on July 25, 1884.

Victor also wrote about the condition of the *Spray* before his father headed out on that final voyage: "In 1909 the *Spray* was fitted out at the Herreshoff works in Bristol, Rhode Island, for her Customary winter Voyage to Grand Cayman. Mr. Herreshoff (the great 'Nat') admired his visitor and said she was a good boat. While the *Spray* was in his yard he spent considerable time looking her over and also much time in conversation with her skipper, though Nat was known to be a man who wasted neither time nor words. When the *Spray* left Bristol in the fall of 1909, she was well fitted and provided for, and my father was in the best of physical health." But L. Francis Herreshoff, Nat Herreshoff's son, remembered quite differently in a letter to Walter Teller dated December 30, 1952: "The *Spray* did not have any work done on her at the Herreshoff Company but simply lay at one of the wharves in what is called Walker's Cove. She may have been given some old ropes, but the captain did everything himself in the refit. I shouldn't be surprised if I were the last one to speak to him for I saw him off on the morning that he departed." Herreshoff does not give a year, and Carlton J. Pinheiro, the present curator of the Herreshoff Marine Museum, in Bristol, Rhode Island, finds no record of Slocum's visit either in Nat Herreshoff's journal or in the company records.

A 1953 Vineyard *Gazette* account of Captain Slocum and his disappearance inspired Francis Mead to remember that he had been out fishing late in the summer of 1909 in Muskeget Channel and that he had heard Captain John Randolphe wondering where the *Spray* could be headed. Mead speculated that they were the last to see Slocum and the *Spray*, as "the water was pretty rough around Skiffs Island." Teller notes that another man, B.H. Kidder, wrote to the Vineyard *Gazette* claiming to have seen Slocum in Bridgeport, Connecticut. When he asked the captain where he was headed, Slocum told him, "Some faraway places." Teller concluded that it did not seem likely the year of that sighting was 1909.

Yet the evidence is overwhelming that in fact Slocum departed on his final voyage in 1908. Newspaper accounts for 1909 have no news reports concerning the captain except for ones that mention his disappearance, and these all confirm a 1908 departure. The Vineyard *Gazette* reported on July 24, 1909, "Captain Slocum sailed from Vineyard Haven for the West Indies more than a year and a half ago to escape the severity of the approaching winter and has not since been heard from. He sailed alone and was last seen by a passing steamship, which reported the *Spray* as making heavy weather." Hettie is quoted in another *Gazette* article from 1909: "I believe beyond all doubt that Capt. Slocum is lost . . . He sailed Nov. 12, 1908, going south for the sake of his health . . . We expected to hear from him when he reached the Bahamas and always made a point of keeping his publishers informed." Hettie again writes 1908, although with a change in the November date, in a letter to her friend Mrs. McNutt dated August 28, 1910. "I am sorry to say that there seem but little or no doubt but that something serious has happened Captain Slocum and the 'Spray'. He sailed from Vineyard Haven the Spray's home port on Nov. 14th, 1908 bound to the West Indies, and to my knowledge nothing has ever been heard from him since that date."

William A. Nickerson wrote to the editor of *Maine Coast Fisherman* that he saw Slocum in Cotuit, Cape Cod, in the summer of 1908. He sent a picture of the *Spray* with 1908 on the back. He added that he had heard the rumor later that same summer that Slocum was making an exploring trip in the Orinoco River. When nothing was heard, it was presumed by the Cape Cod fisherman that Slocum was lost in the vicinity of Cape Hatteras.

What makes the task of verifying Slocum's date of disappearance all the more confusing is that in many of the reports of a 1908 departure received by biographer Walter Teller, Teller has changed and scribbled 1909 in the margins, or made corrections. Kenneth E. Slack, author of *In the Wake of the Spray*, wrote to Teller about Nickerson's photograph and story in *Maine Coast*

Fisherman: "The letter says 1908, but I wrote Mr. Nickerson, as he said the *Spray* disappeared the same year when it was really the next year, and he said that he had been mistaken and on reflection, feels sure it was 1909."

Two other sources lend credence to a 1908 departure. Alice C. Longaker, whose family spent their summers at Lagoon Heights on Martha's Vineyard, sent Teller an excerpt from her father's record book chronicling those vacations. His entry for August 13, 1910, reads: "Capt. Joshua Slocum left Vineyard Haven on the day before Thanksgiving (1908) in the *Spray* for some southern port (Probably the Bahamas) and was never heard from to this date. Am not certain that the above is correct. He may have sailed from New Bedford." Teller wrote "1909" in the margin of her letter. Thomas Fleming Day, editor of *The Rudder*, wrote of Slocum's departure in the magazine's January 1911 edition: "I'm afraid we must give up all hope of ever seeing the old skipper again; it is *now over two years* [my emphasis] since he departed on his last voyage. He told me that he was going up the Orinoco River, and through the Rio Negro into the Amazon and home that way, and there is no news that he ever made the river or any port, and surely some of my correspondents would have seen *Spray* and sent word." *Over two years* from the publication date would establish the beginning of Slocum's final voyage as November 1908.

So, most of the evidence, including Hettie's obituary, points to November 12, 1908, as the date Slocum set sail.

That would have made him sixty-four years old. The second and more mysterious question concerns what happened to him. No evidence has ever been found. His jumble of books, newspaper clippings, curios, notebooks and charts, along with his sextant and his framed letter from President Roosevelt, all went down with the *Spray*.

Of course, everybody had a theory at the time. In his article "Quite Another Matter," which appeared in *The Rudder* in March 1968, H.S. Smith reflected, "Captain Slocum probably was the worst ship's husband I have encountered, and I wasn't a bit surprised when the *Spray* went missing about four years later. To me, this always has been something of an anomaly even though I have seen my share of craft that seemed well handled but poorly kept." He reflected on the boat's construction: "*Spray*'s planking was in poor shape. No two planks appeared to be of the same shape, size, or thickness, or even of the same kind of wood . . . the shape she was in would give the horrors to anyone who went to sea. It could be the captain took care of some of the neglect as soon as he quit the land, but there was nothing in the world he could have done for the way she had been roughly cobbled together in the first place."

Captain Levi Jackson was one of those who contended for last man to see the *Spray*. He was fishing for cod off the Muskeget Channel shoals when he spotted Slocum's boat. He considered it an unwise time for a sailing boat to be heading southeast, as there was a heavy wind coming from that direction. Jackson could only assume that Slocum was lost on the shoals, where many ships had been wrecked. A local paper reported, "The last person known to have seen the *Spray* is Captain Levi Jackson of Edgartown, Massachusetts on November 12th, 1908 when the *Spray* sailed for the West Indies. On that night a severe gale sprang up from the southeast hauling to the southwest, making a heavy cross sea and the sloop is thought to have been caught in a tide rip and tripped foundering before an offing was made. No wreckage was ever found."

The theory that the *Spray* had gone down suddenly near landfall was supported by a Vineyarder, Captain Donald Lemar Poole, who became a close confidant of Walter Teller. It was a speculation that Slocum would have appreciated, as he knew how real a possibility such an outcome was. After his return from the circumnavigation voyage, Slocum had written, "I had sailed over oceans. I have since completed a course over them all and sailed around the whole world without so nearly meeting a fatality as on that trip on the lagoon through a squall which sent us drifting helplessly to sea where we should have been incontinently lost."

Victor Slocum considered it most likely that his father was run down in the shipping lanes by a steamer. Hettie had her own theory, which she expressed in her letter to Mrs. McNutt: "I am always deeply impressed that some thing serious has happened. Nor do I consider it strange if the 'Spray' has not met her fate at sea . . . Captain Slocum's love for adventure I have always believed led him beyond all reason, for his own good, and the well being of his family . . . I really think that the voyage to West Indies was more than he was physically able to stand." Indeed, Slocum's physical condition was far from peak. It is possible that he collapsed or blacked out and fell overboard, or became despondent and allowed the sea to take him. He might also have died in a remote port or settlement.

Garfield Slocum said his father had always wanted to be buried at sea. Garfield's older brother, Ben Aymar, mused awkwardly about this in a letter to Teller: "Have been picturing the last hours of Capt JS and the *Spray* this way: Captain J was a quick striker, practical to the core as he sailed southward alone, he may have had a deep thinking spell on his trip only a few hours out from Martha's Vineyard. He could visualize correctly. In a vision he could see the *Spray* as his final answer to all attempts he had made to regain his forever hard earned reputation as a sailor . . . I pictured him on first study-ing on how to completely rob the sharks of any chances to profit from his proposed [illegible]. He decides to clean deck, no drifting telltales . . . heavy etching on deck . . . he sails on awaiting a final answer to his contemplated exit — the coast is clear, beautiful weather report — that perfect mystery and he was equal to perfecting his final act on earth. He heard this courtly still voice and obeyed."

For years afterward there were unconfirmed sightings of Slocum in the Caribbean and South America. The New Bedford *Standard* ran this story on May 27, 1911: "Lone mariner reported: White man seen on the Orinoco River, maybe Captain Slocum, commander of the famous sloop *Spray* [who] planned to explore the headwaters of the South American River when he landed here in November 1908. When he left here in November, 1908, Captain Slocum never reported at West Indies where he intended to stop." In a 1913 journal entry, Alice C. Longaker's mother noted, "Mr. O.J. Slocum stopped in to see us a while on Labor Day . . . He says he had heard that his brother, the Captain was alive and down in the Orionoco Country. He says that if he is alive he will 'turn up' at the celebration of the completion of the Panama Canal."

Because Slocum had been such a larger-than-life sea-dog, there were bound to be unbelievable accounts. Years later a tall tale emerged that someone had seen a man who looked exactly like Slocum in Washington, D.C., the only difference being that the Slocum look-alike had a wooden leg. Others felt that a showman like Slocum would just turn up one day with another wild tale of adventure to tell. Reports in a New York paper told of an explorer sighted along the Amazon River who people were positive was Captain Slocum. The explorer said that he was living with the natives. When the rumors reached Hettie, all she could say was, "No one can make me believe that because first of all Josh would not go native, he just would not mix with them in any sense expecially living among them . . . If it were so he must have lost his mind and is really lost." Another strange rumor was that Slocum was living like French painter Paul Gauguin — on a tropical island with three or more wives.

Over the years, no authenticated claims developed, and it was accepted that Captain Slocum had gone down in the *Spray*. Hettie filed the Absentee petition concerning Slocum's disappearance to the Dukes County Court on April 22, 1912. On January 15, 1924, he was declared legally dead on the day he supposedly had last set sail — November 14, 1909.

Since then, another theory has surfaced that, if valid, would solve the mystery of Slocum's disappearance once and for all. In a 1959 article in the Quincy, Massachusetts, *Patriot Ledger*, "Capt. Slocum Story: Solution of Sea Mystery Indicated in New Facts," Edward Rowe Snow declared, "One of the world's greatest sea mysteries, the loss of the *Spray* . . . may have been solved yesterday at the offices of the *Quincy Patriot Ledger* by the disclosure that Capt. Joshua Slocum, who vanished at sea in 1909, may have been run down by a steamer off one of the Lesser Antilles within a relatively few hours after he had left the home of a farmer of the vicinity." The source of the revelation was Captain Charles H. Bond, whom Snow considered unimpeachable, having checked into his background and references. Bond had heard the story from

247

Felix Meinickheim, a planter on the islands. According to Meinickheim, Slocum arrived on Turtle Island, Lesser Antilles, and visited with him for a few days. Then he left to explore the Orinoco River as he had planned. Captain Bond continued his story to Snow: "But Captain Slocum was destined never to complete his plans, and here is how it happened. Two nights after Captain Slocum left, Felix Meinickheim was sailing on the little mail steamer which took passengers and freight island to island." Meinickheim observed something not quite right about the mail boat: just above the waterline there was a deep cut in the stem. The captain of the mail boat told him they had run down a native boat the night before. Meinickheim asked how he could be sure it was a native boat. The answer "Who else could it be?" left the planter uneasy. On further questioning, he learned that the boat had been run down between midnight and four a.m. As Bond told the story to Snow, the second mate on that graveyard watch admitted to Meinickheim that "it had been a terribly dark night, overcast, and at the moment of contact with the other craft, there definitely was no one at the wheel of the other vessel . . . In the few seconds when I saw the other craft, I made out that she was not a native of this area."

Meinickheim pieced the puzzle together. The *Spray* was the only non-native boat cruising the waters, and the timing of the accident coincided with where Slocum would most probably have been. The planter and the steamer's officers decided to keep the story quiet. It came out fifty years later because, as Bond explained, "There is no one now alive today who will suffer from my revelation of what really took place to send Captain Slocum to his death aboard the *Spray*." This story can never be proven, but it has the ring of truth, or at least probability, to it.

Thomas Fleming Day's tribute to the lost captain in *The Rudder*'s January 1911 edition ended on a meditative note: "Peace to Captain Slocum wherever he may sleep, for he deserves at least one whispered tribute of prayer from every sailorman for what he did to rob the sea of its bad name; and for such a man, who loved every cranny of her dear old blue heart, who for years made her windswept stretches his home and highway, what is more fitting than an ocean burial?"

Joshua Slocum's life story has adventure, passion, tragedy, loss, scandal and a mysterious end. Its hero was part poet, philosopher, dreamer, hustler and adventurer. He was a pioneer, an explorer and a wonderful spinner of tales. But not far beneath his surface was a troubled, misunderstood and desperately insecure man. Hardheaded, irascible and eccentric as he was, Captain Slocum lived his life the only way it made sense to him, and in so doing accomplished a transcendent feat of seamanship. Slocum lived his life with little compromise, and where he knew he could live it best — on the sea. And in the end, the sea claimed him as her own.

On Brier Island, where Slocum as a child was lulled to sleep by the rhythm of the waves, in Westport Baptist

Church, there is a verse inscribed on a bronze plaque on Pew 13. The verse is from an ancient psalmody that was found in a Westport home, and seems a fitting requiem for an old sailor who had always listened to and could never ignore the sea's calling.

> Not in the churchyard shall he sleep,
> Amid the silent gloom;
> His home was on the mighty deep,
> And there shall be his tomb.
> He loved his own bright, deep blue sea;
> O'er it he loved to roam;
> And now his winding sheet shall be
> That same bright ocean's foam.
> No village bell shall toll for him
> Its mournful, solemn dirge;
> The winds shall chant a requiem
> To him beneath the surge.

Appendix 1

A "Log" of Joshua Slocum's Circumnavigation aboard the Spray, 1895–98

1895

April

24   Sets sail from Boston harbor.

May

7   *Spray* sails from Gloucester, Mass.

13   Visits boyhood home of Brier Island, N.S.

July

1   *Spray* sails from Yarmouth, N.S.

10   Making 150 miles a day, *Spray* 1,200 miles east of Cape Sable.

19   Flores Island, in the Azores.

20   Arrives in Faial, Azores.

24   Sets sail from Horta, Faial.

26   J.S. ill from meal of plums and white cheese.

August

4   Arrives Gibraltar.

24   U.S. Consul at Gibraltar visits *Spray*.

25   Sails from Gibraltar, chased by pirates.

31   End of three days of squalls.

September

2   "Scudding her for the channel between Africa and the island of Fuerteventura" in the Canaries.

10	"Then leaving the Cape Verde Islands out of sight astern, I found myself once more sailing a lonely sea and in a solitude supreme all around."
16–20	Becalmed by mid-Atlantic doldrums; only 300 miles sailed in ten days.
26	Latitude 5° North, longitude 26° 30' West.
30	Crosses the equator at longitude 29° 30' W.

October

5	Casts anchor in Pernambuco harbor, forty days out from Gibraltar.
6–23	Repairs and adjustments made to the *Spray*.
24	Sets sail for Rio de Janeiro.

November

5	Arrives Rio de Janeiro.
6–27	"As I had decided to give the *Spray* a yawl rig for the tempestuous waters of Patagonia, I here placed on the stern a semicircular brace to support a jigger mast."
28	Sails from Rio de Janeiro.

December

11	*Spray* beached north of Montevideo, Uruguay; "I suddenly remembered that I could not swim."
12	Anchors in Maldonado Bay.
?	Sails to Montevideo. Dock and repair, free of charge by Royal Mail Steamship Company; carpenters mend keel and dory.
29	*Spray* sails to Buenos Aires with Captain Howard, a friend from Cape Cod, aboard.
30	Arrives Buenos Aires.

Appendix 1

1896
January

?   "I unshipped the sloop's mast at Buenos Aires and shortened it by seven feet. I reduced the length of the bowsprit by about five feet . . ."

26   Sails from Buenos Aires.

27   Up the River Plate against a headwind.

February

11   *Spray* rounds Cape Virgins; enters the Strait of Magellan, battles rain squalls for thirty hours.

14   Anchors at Punta Arenas, Chile; warnings about hostile Fuegian settlements.

19   Sails from Punta Arenas, "into the country and very core of the savage Fuegians."

20   Celebrates fifty-second birthday with a cup of coffee south of Charles Island. *Spray* stays anchored in bed of kelp for two days of heavy winds.

March

3   Sails from Port Tamar for Cape Pillar; gathering storm in the northwest.

7   Fourth day of gales; *Spray* driven southeast toward the pitch of the Cape.

8   *Spray* in the midst of the Milky Way of the Sea. Having sighted and steered for Fury Island, she sails in through the Cockburn Channel.

9   A williwaw carries the sloop out of the cove into deep sea.

10   Reaches St. Nicholas Bay, "where I had cast anchor February 19," having circumnavigated the "wildest part of desolate Tierra del Fuego."

April

13   *Spray* leaves Port Angosto for the seventh and last time.

26   *Spray* makes landfall by night at Juan Fernández.

May–June

5   *Spray* sails from Juan Fernández.

Sailing "with a free wind day after day."

July

16   Arrives in Samoa after seventy-two days without a port.

17   Mrs. Robert Louis Stevenson visits the *Spray*.

August–September

20   *Spray* sails from Samoa; sets course north of the Horn Islands and Fiji, instead of south and down west side of the archipelago.

October

2   Arrives in Newcastle, Australia, after a forty-two-day stormy passage.

10   *Spray* arrives in Sydney.

Mid-October–November

Remains docked in Sydney, where J.S. receives many visitors and is feted by admirers.

December

6   Leaves Sydney, planning to sail to Mauritius by way of Cape Leeuwin on Australia's west coast.

20   Anchors at Waterloo Bay for three days for protection from fierce winds.

25   Christmas Day at a berth in Melbourne harbor.

1897

January–March

Jan 24 Leaves Melbourne; waits out bad summer weather in Tasmania. Forced to abandon plans to sail around Cape Leeuwin. Gives first public lecture, in Tasmania in February.

April

16 Weighs anchor to head round Cape Howe and up to Cape Bundoora.

22 Arrives again in Sydney, after clear passage.

May

9 Sets sail from Sydney for Port Stevens.

20 Rounds Great Sandy Cape and picks up the trade winds.

24 Sails through the islands near the Barrier Reef.

26 *Spray* anchors at Port Denison, Queensland.

28 Public lecture in Bowen, illustrated by stereopticon.

29 Sets sail for Cooktown.

31 Arrives Cooktown.

June

6 Sets sail, heading north.

10 Mid-channel in Torres Strait.

22 Only American ship represented at Queen Victoria's Diamond Jubilee on Thursday Island, off Australia's northern tip.

24 Sets course for Keeling (Cocos) Islands, 2,700 miles away.

26 "Latitude by observation at noon, 10° 23' S."

27 "133 miles on the log. Latitude by observation at noon 10° 25' S."

28 Continues sailing west on parallel of 10° 25' S., "as true as a hair."

July

2 Island of Timor in view.

11 Christmas Island in sight.

17 Casts anchor at Keeling (Cocos) Islands; twenty-three days out from Thursday Island.

August

22 Sets sail from Keeling (Cocos) Islands in a rugged sea.

September

8 *Spray* mistaken by Rodriguez Islanders for the arrival of the Antichrist.

16 Sets sail from Rodriguez Island.

19 Arrives at Mauritius, where J.S. pauses to enjoy a rest in good weather.

October

26 Sails from Mauritius.

November

9 Fourth day in the Mozambique Channel; hard south-west gale and heavy electrical storm.

17 *Spray* arrives in Port Natal (Durban), South Africa.

December

14 *Spray* sets sail toward the Cape of Good Hope; eight hundred miles of rough sea anticipated, sailing on course to Table Bay.

25 *Spray* at the pitch of the Cape; gets a Christmas dunking in rough seas.

27 Passes Cape Agulhas; next to "beat around the Cape of Good Hope."

1898

January–March

Spray arrives in Cape Town, South Africa; stay of three months in dry dock. J.S. travels by railway throughout South Africa, lecturing and attending receptions along the way.

March

26   *Spray* leaves South Africa, heading across the South Atlantic for home.

30   *Spray* rides on a southeast wind at her best speed.

April

11   *Spray* arrives in St. Helena, where J.S. is a guest of the governor and gives public lectures.

27   *Spray* arrives at Ascension Island, where J.S. maroons the chart-eating goat.

30   Sets sail after fumigation and invited inspection for certification of *Spray*'s solo crew status.

May

8   "She crossed the track, homeward bound, that she had made October 2, 1895 on the voyage out . . . the *Spray* had encircled the globe."

10–13   *Spray* making 180 miles a day for several days.

14   *Spray* just north of the equator signals U.S. warship *Oregon*; J.S. learns that America is at war with Spain.

17   "Devil's Island two points on the lee bow."

18   "Tonight, in latitude 7° 13' N., for the first time in nearly three years I see the North Star."

20   The island of Tobago in sight.

22   Arrives in Grenada.

28   Sets sail from Grenada.

30   Arrives on the island of Dominica.

June

4   "The *Spray* cleared from the United States consulate, and her license to sail single-handed, even round the world, was returned to her for the last time."

10–17 Becalming in the horse latitudes; sets sail on 18th into southwest gale.

20   Gale and turbulent cross-seas; *Spray*'s jibstay breaks at the masthead, with jib and all falling into the water.

25   Off Fire Island in the midst of a powerful tornado accompanied by a severe electrical storm, "the climax storm of the voyage." *Spray*, under bare poles, changes sights from New York harbor to the coast of Long Island.

27   Reaches Newport, Rhode Island.

July

3   "With a fair wind, she waltzed beautifully round the coast and up the Acushnet River to Fairhaven, where I secured her to the cedar spile driven in the bank to hold her when she was launched. I could bring her no nearer home."

Appendix 2:

Previously Unpublished Letter Written by Joshua Slocum to Westport, Nova Scotia, Postmaster, August 1895

This letter, missing the first two pages, came to Slocum biographer Walter Teller, author of *The Search for Captain Slocum*, through Mrs. Melvin Tibert (née Florence Wallis) of Freeport, Nova Scotia. The letter is missing a return address and the salutation, so its point of mailing and addressee remained a mystery. It has never before been published. It was originally thought that Slocum must have written the letter to his friend J.J. Wallis (Florence's father), editor of the *Yarmouth Light*. It was also assumed that Slocum posted the letter from Faial in the Azores, during his stop there in July 1895, on the first leg of his circumnavigation.

Phillip D. Shea, author and past director of the Joshua Slocum Society International, first brought the letter to public attention in an article that ran in both Halifax newspapers, the *Chronicle-Herald* and the *Mail Star*, on November 15, 1996. Entitled "Slocum's Lost Letter Found," Shea's article attempts to decipher the captain's mysterious allegation of "treachery" during his stopover in Yarmouth, Nova Scotia. He reflects: "What could have caused Slocum's outrage? His letter doesn't give details of the insult nor does he even mention it in his book, but it annoyed Slocum so much he fantasized a visit to

Halifax to challenge the perpetrator . . . What was the 'treachery' or was it only an imagined slight that enraged the thin-
skinned skipper? A search of Nova Scotia newspapers for that
period has revealed a front-page story in the Halifax *Herald* of
June 24, 1895 that undoubtedly raised his ire. The short item
was headed 'Another Brilliant Nova Scotian'; unfortunately, it
was not about the captain of the *Spray*, but about the election
of Professor Simon Newcomb, a native of Wallace, N.S., as a
foreign associate of the Academy of Science in Paris."

Shea further deduces: "Underneath, in the same column, ran
a story from Yarmouth with the headline: 'Another Crank At
Large.' The report, which appears innocuous itself, gives details
of Slocum's proposed voyage in 'his little vessel.' It also mentions
'Captain Slocum feels confident of the success of his voyage, as
he has been for many years voyaging in these diminutive crafts'
— certainly a demeaning description of a master mariner who in
30 years at sea had been captain of some of the largest and finest
vessels afloat. The so-called 'Crank' was not amused." Phillip
Shea also notes: "The misspellings and grammatical errors [in
the letter] resemble those in other Slocum correspondence."

When Shea's article appeared in the newspapers, Westport
resident Robert McDormand found a copy of the same letter
in his brother's papers, with the first two pages intact. The letter was posted from Gibraltar, but was not addressed to
Wallis. Slocum was writing to Mr. Ruggles, who was postmas-
ter at Westport, Digby County, Nova Scotia.

The Spray,
Gibraltar, August 10th, '95
Dear Mr. Ruggles:
According to promise, I write or try to write you a letter:

The *Spray* "discovered" Spain Aug. 2nd, 29 days sail from Cape Sable, having called at Fayal to which port she was 18 days from Cape Sable.

I have been quite well throughout except in one night a sort of cholera from green fruit and goat cheese after leaving Fayal, and such an attack as I had then might have killed me had it overtaken me ashore.

John Bull is doing the handsome thing by the *Spray*. The old craft is now the guest of Admiral ships and among guns of great calibre. The Senior officer of the port, having taken charge of the sloop, brought her into the arsenal. Gunboats made room for her — yes Sir, they did.

Captain Prince in command put everything at my disposal. H.B.M. will have quite an interest in the voyage, hence yours, etc. is not slighted! Not at all!

(Page 3, where letter in the Teller Collection begins):
The *Spray* came across the little old pond, it may interest you to know; as quickly as possible; Had there been, even ten men onboard sailing her she could not have come more quickly. I made a good voyage and know it one that may stand a long time unbeaten by any one man: "Be not however vain glorious" is the admonition of my thoughts. There is perhaps little in it to speak of at all but people are interested so let it stand!

Every body was very kind to me at Westport. I saw many very smart young men there, too, some of my old school mates and chums. Will you kindly remember me to all Briar Island? — The whole island has to come to you for letter! and for the news!

A chap in Halifax tried to do me harm: In Yarmouth

his representative enjoyed a half hour of the *Spray*'s "hospitality" — the best she had — And he the next day, in Halifax a hundred miles off fired a shot — at my back.

A South Sea Islander could not have shown greater treachery. Upon leaving Yarmouth, therefore, I beat a course in for Halifax, for, said I, this educated gentleman being such as appears it will be worth my while to enter the port and study the characteristic of the people — one object of the voyage being, as you are aware sir, to gather information.

Night was coming on when the *Spray* entered the mouth of their harbor.

Perceiving the natives preparing a fire on the beach where I made signs I would land: and not knowing their number or their mode of attack: I hauled off! From the hour till I arrived at Fayal the *Spray* never ceased going! It was wonderful how well she kept her course, even before the wind. Indeed I didn't do much on the voyage except make, take in, and trim sails.

Some one warned me that I would loose my voice, too, I was told I had a musical voice. So it would be a pity to lose that!

Now few of my friends ever heard me sing but it occured to me that I might by the aid of song keep my voice intact.

I was surprised at my success. I believe that my voice is, even, improved: "Home Sweet Home" "Annie Laurie" and "God Save the Queen" went rolling free over the ocean. Turtle and sea lions poked their heads up to catch the air: One morning when I was singing my favorite song a porpoise jumped clean over the bowsprit — and it wasn't a very good day either for jumping! But that is no matter!

Perhaps you didn't hear that the *Spray* rescued a deacon at Yarmouth, well she did: A real live, and good, deep-water baptist deacon!: But he was tickled to get on deck and out of the water for all that! I wish your reporter for the Digby paper would mention to my friends that I am well and — mentioning, too, my escape at Halifax if not too much trouble and I am sure there are still, on the hospitable side of the dear old Province, those who will be glad to hear that I am still alive. One at least I know as he scans this my poor scrawl and looks back over the past: over the joys and sorrows, will not "Thurst for my blood."

Will you please rember me very kindly to your family, all!

> Sir I remain
> Very Sincerely
> Joshua Slocum

Appendix 3:

Letters Written by Henrietta Slocum to Mrs. Alfred McNutt, 1889 and 1910

The following three letters were written by Hettie Slocum to Mrs. Alfred McNutt in Colchester County, Nova Scotia. The Slocums met Captain and Mrs. McNutt when the *Liberdade* was in Barbados. Hettie wrote the first about the voyage home in the *Liberdade*, and the other two about the disappearance of her husband on "November 14, 1908." All three letters are kept in the Public Archives of Nova Scotia. (All spellings reproduced here are from the originals.)

Washington D.C.

Jan. 28th 1889

Mrs. McNutt

Dear Friend —

Long befor this reaches you, you will no doubt have heard of our safe arrival in America do Norte.

We first touched American soil at South Santee, S.C. Oct. 29th.

We left Barbados Oct. 7th made Mayatuez Porto Rico the 11th. Sailed again the 15th.

Just touched at Lobo Quay for water. Sailed over the Great Bahamas banks. Called at one of the Bimini Islands for shells and sponges.

Crossed the Gulf Oct. 25th. The first light we sighted on the coast was at Cape Canaveral Florida.

First port of regstry was South Port, S.C. We spent two weeks there and at Wilmington, sailed again Nov. 16th was only outside a few hours when the wind came ahead again.

We run into New River Inlet with bar breaking bad, got over without any trouble and layed snug inside nine days while one of the bigest northeasters of the season on the coast was blowing. The storm raised the rivers and ditches so much that we were able to go inside the rest of the way.

We went through drawing 2 feet 4 inches of water where at ordinary time it was a rare thing to have more than twelve inches.

We were very glad for we had already had enough of it outside. Spent one day at Beaufort, N.C.

The next port we made was Norfolk Va. where we stayed until Christmas Eve. We set sail for Washington, D.C. Xmas day was spent in the Chesapeake bay.

We ate our Xmas on board the Liberdade. The weather was fine and wind fair So we enjoyed our sail up the Chesapeake with Potomac very much.

Arrived here Dec. 27th sound and well making Washington winter quarters for "Liberdade" and crew.
You may imagine we were all very glad to haul up for the winter after our long and tiresome voyage.

The "Liberdade" did her part well. I think lots of the little craft now.

I have thought of you and your good husband very many time since I last saw you.

How I did dread starting out again from Barbados on our little ship that feeling soon left me and I felt quite happy as we sailed along. We had a big storm off the coast of Cuba and some bad weather on this coast.

We came through everything nicely.

It surprises me more and more when I think of all we have come through.

Our voyage is full of interest to us. I look back with pleasure over it now.

We will remain here until after Inauguration and then go to Baltimore. Will get to New York in due time.

I have not been to see my folks yet. hope to get a chance to go from Baltimore.

There is a big interest taken here in our voyage.

Ther people in Baltimore are very anxious to see the little craft. We will give them all a chance to see her.

This is a very fine city.

I should like to know very much where you are now. I want you to write me. I want to hear from you very much. I look back with pleasure to the days spent on board you ship. If you should get this soon you may address me at Washington D.C. Foot of 6th Street (Liberdade). Anytime you write me at East Boston I will get it. If I am not there my folks will forward to me wherever I am. We are all in good health. As soon as I learn where you are I will send you some photographs of the boat, and our own.

I do hope Mrs. McNutt that we will have the pleasure of meeting you and Captain McNutt again. Josh say to tell you he is enjoying the stockings you gave him more than anything else this winter. He thinks they are splendid. Josh sends his best wishes to you and Capt. McNutt. With kind regards to your husband. I am your friend, Hettie M. Slocum

P.S. This address will always find me. H.M.S.

Appendix 3

Address. 69 Saratoga Street
East Boston
Mass

1910/ Aug 28
Windham Depot
Box 54 Cobbett's North Shore
New Hampshire

Dear Mrs. McNutt —

Your kind letter received at above address.

I am sorry to say that there seem but little or no doubt but that something serious has happened Captain Slocum and the "Spray". He sailed from Vineyard Haven the Spray's home port on Nov. 14th, 1908 bound to the West Indies, and to my knowledge nothing has ever been heard from him since that date. When a day or two out from the Vineyard the "Spray" was sighted by a passing fishing vessel who reported the "Spray" making heavy weather in a gale.

Captain Slocum asked me to write him at Nassau to be called for. It was his purpose to spend the winter in the West Indies to escape the cold weather at home and to do some business while there as he had done before here to fore.

I have tried to persuade myself that he might have decided after sailing to undertake some new adventure and keep out of touch with the outside world for a time. But all things considered I do not feel that this atal probable, I am deeply impressed that something serious has happened. Nor do I consider it strange if the "Spray" has met her fate at sea.

I have tried to find out if possible the fate of the "Spray", but as yet have not learned anything that would throw any light on it as yet.

I tried to persuade my husband not to go for it seemed so hard for him to undertake such a voyage alone. He said he knew he could not stand the cold weather at home through another winter, he felt the cold very much.

I really think that the voyage to West Indies was more than he was physically able to stand. He was very anxious for me to go with him, said he knew I would have a good time when I got to the West Indies. I could not think of such a thing now. I have not as much courage as I had when we made the Voyage in the Liberdade.

Captain Slocum's love for adventure I have always felt led him beyond all reason for his own good and the well being of his family.

He was in good spirits when he sailed, and talked a lot about things he intended to do at home when he returned in the Spring to Early Summer.

Some people are inclined to think that Captain Slocum has gone on some new adventure and will show up at some future time. If he was a younger man I would think this very probable. But under the circumstances and all things considered I do not believe this atal likely.

He was not any hand to talk or dwell on the narrow escapes he had had.

But he told me of a narrow escape he had on the trip before goint to West Indies of being smashed to pieces on a coral reef, and also of being run down at night by a steamship.

Victor at the present time is on a whaling cruise. I think he went as much for the adventure as anything. He does not follow the sea for a living. Garfield is married and has two children lives in New York State.

Appendix 3

I have been spending a few weeks here with my sister at her summer cottage,

I have not spent much time at my Vineyard home, since Capt Slocum went away, When I am there I cannot help but keep looking for his return. I shall probably spend the winter in Boston as I have done for the last few winters. Now that I am left alone, our property at West Tisbury, Martha's Vineyard is a very poor investment, and I shall never be able to get anything like the money it cost back. And I cannot live alone there. I am fortunate to have the deeds of property there in my own name. I am up against legal difficulties by the disappearance of my husband without any proof of what has happened. For instance I cannot collect any royalties from Captain's book "Sailing Alone" for seven years, so I am tied up more or less by legal complications. A gentleman in Washington, a good friend of Captain Slocum's has written me of late, since he saw the report of the supposed disaster in the papers, That he was going to try and find out if possible some thing of the fate of the "Spray" By way of inquiry through the "New York Herald". "London Times" and Australian papers. I shall be very thankful if this man is able to learn something of the "Spray's" fate.

It is distressing to say the least the suspense of not knowing what has happened. Any thing definate would be a satisfaction to know the worst would be a relief, rather than not knowing.

I was very glad to hear from you and Capt McNutt. I am sure it was very kind of you to write me at this time.

I am sorry I cannot give you more hopeful news.

I have not forgotten how kind you were to us when we were in Barbados, on the Liberdade voyage. I would be very

269

glad if I could have better news to write you at some time in the near future. I have no faith myself that my husband is now alive.

Thanking you for your kind letter.

Very sincerely —

Henrietta M. Slocum

69 Saratoga Street

East Boston

Mass.

Sept. 22/1910

My Dear Friend Mrs. McNutt —

Your letter of so long ago is unanswered.

It was delayed some time in reaching me. I had left New Hampshire when it arived there.

I am delighted to hear from you and to know that you have been settled on land all these years. I think the sea faring life is a hard one; there are some very attractive features about it of course.

I have not heard anything new since I wrote you last.

I have little or no hope of ever even hearing any thing more.

Some time some wreckage may be seen that would indicate the fate of the "Spray". I get a good many letters from people who have known Captain Slocum or have read his book "Sailing Alone" and have seen the report that he is missing and write me like yourself to know what about it and so on.

I shall be at this address for the Winter. I am working for my bread and butter. I am left without support so am obliged to earn my own living. I cannot draw on royalties for seven years, at the end of seven years if Captain Slocum is still missing I can demand an accounting from the Publishers through the Probate Court. If in the mean time I should get proof that my husband was dead. I could apply to Probate Court then at any time for a settlement. My real estate as a little home if my husband was living or at home, it would be alright, but as an investment it is of little value to me. I have kept hens before now. and probably will do so again. But it is the being alone; living alone. I do not know how to endure it, only for that I could make my living there easier than in the city. My folks all live about Boston, that is the most of them. I have a brother in Lynn[?], two sisters in Wakefield, and a sister in Brighton (greater Boston) and cousins, all about here. I have one sister in Hantsport Nova Scotia married to Rev. L. J. Tingley Baptist Minister, he used to own a place at Wolfville has sold and has bought at Hantsport. I have never been there myself. I seldom go to Nova Scotia. If I should ever go that way I should surrly look you up, it would surrly be a great pleasure to meet you and Captain McNutt after all these years.

Your little poem is beautiful and I appreciate it very much. I fear you may have made your visit to Beverly[?] before this time I have delayed so long. If you have not, and do come later I should be delighted to see you.

I could arrange to see you for a little while any how. I am very busy my time not being my own I am sorry to say. I am glad to be able to support myself and not be dependant on any one. My health is good although I am no longer young, 48 years old now.

> With very kind wishes I am
> Very Sincerely
> Henrietta M. Slocum

Appendix 4:

Joshua Slocum Society International

The Joshua Slocum Society was founded in 1955 by Richard McClosky and incorporated as a non-profit corporation in 1972. Now known as the Joshua Slocum Society International, it is dedicated not only to preserving the memory and legacy of Captain Joshua Slocum but to honoring circumnavigators and solo voyagers.

In addition to descendants of Captain Slocum, its members include circumnavigators, experienced yachtsmen, and sailors of all types, including the armchair variety. Its annual journal, *The Spray*, and periodic newsletter, *Spray Ahoy!*, feature activities and accomplishments of members as well as information relating to Joshua Slocum.

Membership information can be obtained by writing to Joshua Slocum Society International, c/o Commodore Ted Jones, 15 Codfish Hill Road Ext., Bethel CT 06801, USA. The Joshua Slocum Society International website address is http://www.mcallen.lib.tx.us/orgs/SLOCUM.HTM

Notes on Sources

The *New York Herald Book Review* for September 6, 1953, ran the following letter of inquiry from Walter Magnes Teller: "As I am at work on a biographical study of Captain Joshua Slocum — 1844 to 1908 — circumnavigator and author — I would appreciate hearing from anyone with documents and information or recollection pertaining to him." He also published his request in the *New York Times*, the *Sydney Morning Herald*, and *The Age* of Melbourne, Australia. Walter Teller's correspondence and notes of interviews from people who responded to the inquiry and who remembered Slocum are part of the Teller Collection, which is housed in the Old Dartmouth Historical Society New Bedford Whaling Museum, New Bedford, Massachusetts.

I have looked through the boxed files of letters and rough notes that led to Teller's first book, *The Search for Captain Slocum*, published by Charles Scribner's Sons in 1956. Some of the material is undated and not clearly identifiable. Wherever possible in these source notes, I have included dates of letters and interviews, and names of individuals who supplied information to Teller, as gleaned from the biographer's notebooks, and from photostats of letters sent and received by Slocum. A major correspondent was Grace Murray Brown, a cousin of Slocum's and the family historian and storyteller. Her letters and genealogy notes, although not always clearly dated, were written between 1952 and 1956. Another important link in

Teller's search was Donald Le Mar Poole, a captain from Martha's Vineyard who had clear impressions and memories of Slocum on the Vineyard. He also provided technical advice to Teller, and the two men shared a friendship that developed in correspondence from 1953 to 1960 and again from 1972 until 1976.

Teller kept notes of his visits with Hettie Slocum, then Mrs. Ulysses E. Mayhew. There are letters and records of interviews with other immediate Slocum family members, including Benjamin Aymar (letters written between September 11, 1952, and March 23, 1955), Jessie Slocum Joyce (letters written between September 1, 1952, and April 2, 1959), and J. Garfield Slocum (letters written between September 1 and April 21, 1953). Letters from Victor, who died in 1949, were given to Teller by Victor's niece, Catherine Woodruff. Lorimer B. Slocum provided letters Slocum had written to other family members.

When Teller's book was revised for a 1971 edition published by Rutgers University Press, it was titled simply *Joshua Slocum*. This augmented edition includes information gleaned from correspondence with Kenneth E. Slack, author of *In the Wake of the Spray*, published in 1966. Leon Fredrich's diligent research material on Captain Slocum was brought to my attention by the curator of the New Bedford Whaling Museum, Judith N. Lund. It has changed the Slocum story somewhat, especially with respect to shipping records that shed new light on the captain's early commands.

Other documents found in the Teller Collection (TC) include the following: copies of original Slocum letters 1872–1904; photostats of Slocum letters 1894–97 from originals at the Peabody Museum, Salem, Massachusetts; photostats of Slocum letters, 1897–1902, originals at the New York Public Library;

copies of Slocum letters 1885– 1906, originals at the Smithsonian Institution, Washington, D.C.; copies of Slocum letters to writer Clifton Johnson; copies of records of the Department of State, originals in the National Archives, Washington, D.C.; and correspondence with psychologist Carl Binger, M.D., and graphologist Meta Steiner, 1953–54, both of whom were asked by Teller to examine Slocum's nature and psychological makeup. Teller also corresponded with Duncan J. Spaeth, professor of American Literature at Princeton University, who lent his opinions on Slocum as a literary stylist.

The Teller Collection also contains newspaper clippings, many undated and unidentified. The major sources are the *Vineyard Gazette*, Edgartown, Martha's Vineyard, the *New Bedford Standard, Times*, and *Mercury*, the *Boston Herald*, the *Boston Globe*, the *New York Times*, the *New York Tribune*, the *Sydney Daily Telgraph*, the *St. Helena Guardian*, the *Mount Holly News*, the *New Jersey Mirror*, and the *New Era* of Riverton and Palmyra, New Jersey. I have been as specific and accurate as information allowed.

The copy of *Sailing Alone Around the World* (SAAW) I have used for reference and pagination was published by W.W. Norton & Company in 1984. Reference notes and pagination also come from *The Voyages of Joshua Slocum* (VJS), edited and with commentaries by Walter Magnes Teller, Special Anniversary Edition, reissued in 1995 by Sheridan House, originally published in 1985 (contains complete texts of "Rescue of Some Gilbert Islanders," *Voyage of the Liberdade, Aquidneck* Correspondence, *Sailing Alone Around the World*, and *Voyage of the Destroyer from New York to Brazil*). Slocum's son Victor's book, *Capt. Joshua Slocum: The Adventures of America's Best Known Sailor* (CJS), was reprinted by Sheridan House in 1972.

The previously unpublished letters written by Henrietta M. Slocum, which appear in Appendix 3, are housed in the Public Archives of Nova Scotia (PANS).

Prologue—*On Beam Ends*
Pg. 1
"I had been cast . . ."
   — SAAW, p. 4
Pg. 2
"one of the finest American
   . . ." — PANS
Pg. 3
"naturalized" Yankee — Ibid.
Pg. 4
"elegant bark" — Ibid.
"going steam" — Ibid.
Pg. 5"
One day when I was . . ."
   — Slocum interviewed
   in undated newspaper
   article (around 1908),
   probably *Providence
   Journal*, TC
"Come to Fairhaven . . ."
   — SAAW, p. 4
Pg. 6
"ship" — Ibid., p. 4
"Poverty Point . . . " — Ibid.,
   p. 4
"cast up from old ocean . . ."
   — Ibid., p. 4

Pg. 7
"No, going to rebuild her . . ."
   — Ibid., p. 4
Pg. 8
"something tangible appeared
   . . ." — Ibid., p. 4
"much-esteemed stem-piece
   . . ." — Ibid., p. 4
"The *Spray* changed her
   being . . ." — Ibid., p. 5
Pg. 9
"What was there for an old
   sailor to do?" — Ibid.,
   p. 4

Chapter One — *The Call of
   the Running Tide*
Pg. 11
"On both sides my family . . ."
   — SAAW, p. 3
Pg. 12
"The wonderful sea . . ."
   — Ibid., p. 3
Pg. 14
"There's all tide rips . . ."
   — PANS
Pg. 15

"I was born in a cold spot . . ."
— SAAW, p. 3
"lovely, gentle soul" — PANS
"too many children . . ."
— Letter from Grace
Murray Brown to Walter
Teller (TC)
Pg. 16
"the island of plenty" — JS's
letter to Roberts Brothers,
May 13, 1895, written
aboard the *Spray* at
Westport, Brier Island
"howling and fighting"
— CJS, p. 32
Pg. 17
"You sail by the Grace . . ."
— PANS

Chapter Two — *Learning
the Ropes*
Pg. 21
"I had a fair schooling . . ."
— SAAW, pp. 156, 157
Pg. 22
"I came 'over the bows' . . ."
— Ibid., p. 3
"I was not long in the galley
. . ." — Ibid., p. 3
Pg. 24
"in through the cabin

windows" — Ibid., p. 3
"over the bows" — Ibid., p. 3
Pg. 25
Victor's description of sextant
found in CJS, p. 39
Pg. 26
"working the ice cargo . . ."
— JS in letter to R.U.
Johnson dated July 23,
1899 (TC)
"he found a good friend . . ."
— CJS, p. 39
"husky youth" — Ibid., p. 40
"He was on the upper topsail
. . ." — Undated clipping
(before voyage, probably
April, 1895), *Boston
Herald*; segment reprinted
in *New Bedford Standard-
Times*, December 21,
1944 (TC)
Pg. 27
"the goal of happiness . . ."
— PANS
"a naturalized Yankee"
— SAAW, p. 3
"Next in attractiveness . . ."
— Ibid., p. 3
Victor's description of his
father's early journals
— CJS, p. 43

Pg. 28
"The lure of his inshore . . ."
 — Ibid., p. 44
"come up through the hawse
 hole" — PANS
Pg. 29
"Virginia was heard to
 remark . . ." — CJS, p. 48
Pg. 30
Shipping Records — *Daily
 Alta* California Shipping
 Intelligence, San
 Francisco, October 4, 9,
 16, 1869; October 7, 1870;
 May 7, 1871; August 21,
 1873; August 22, 1873
 — from Walter Teller's
 correspondence with Leon
 Fredrich in the Teller
 Collection (TC)

Chapter Three — *True Love
and a Family Afloat*
Pg. 31
"Mrs. Slocum sat busily
 engaged . . ." — Excerpt
 from "An American
 Family Afloat,"*New York
 Tribune*, June 26, 1882,
 page 8, column 1.

Pg. 32
"Father took the wheel . . ."
 — Ben Aymar Slocum,
 correspondence to Teller,
 TC
Pg. 33
Information on shipping
 records — Teller corre-
 spondence with Leon
 Fredrich, TC
Pg. 35
"never missed, no matter . . ."
 — CJS, p. 68
Pg. 36
"The cry arose at once . . ."
 — Recollection of second
 mate, Frederick Hinckley,
 as cited by Suzanne J.
 Stark in "Mates at Sea,"
 Seaport, Spring, 1986,
 p. 29.
"blackbirding" — CJS, p. 69
Pg. 37
"Up through the cracks . . ."
 — Ibid., p.87
Pg. 38
"Only in forests . . . — Ibid.,
 p. 87
"Indian blood" — Ben Aymar
 Slocum to Teller, TC

"was trained to ride horses
. . ." — Ibid.

Pg. 39

"Two of my children . . ."
— JS in a letter to John
W. Edmonds, New York,
May 3, 1890, TC

Pg. 40

"a great success" — Ibid., TC

"the ocean is no place . . ."
— Ben Aymar Slocum to
Teller, TC

"made all comfortable outfits
. . ." — JS in a letter to
John W. Edmonds, New
York, May 3, 1890, TC

"all in twenty gold pieces . . ."
— Ibid., TC

Pg. 41

Virginia's letter — photostat
in Teller Collection

Pg. 42

"Father took the wheel . . ."
— Ben Aymar Slocum to
Teller, TC

"Any man who can sail . . ."
— Ibid., TC

"the lady who stood beside"
— Ibid., TC

Pg. 43

"As beautiful as her name"
— JS in letter to cousin,
Joel Slocum, May 4,
1899, TC

"his best command"
— SAAW, p. 3

"I had a right to be proud
. . ." Ibid., p. 3

Pg. 44

"very much like the study . . ."
CJS, p. 147

"He simply revelled . . ."
— Ibid., p. 147

Victor's recollection of comic
book — Ibid., p. 128

"a lot of chuckling over them"
— Jessie Slocum in corre-
spondence with Teller, TC

"Father and mother always
encouraged us . . ."
— Ibid., TC

Pg. 45

"field day" — CJS, p. 146

"How I loved to see her . . ."
— Ben Aymar Slocum in
letter to Teller, TC

"She was an excellent cook
. . ." — Jessie Slocum in
correspondence with
Teller, TC

"Mother was a remarkable woman . . ." — Ibid., TC

"deck piled with yams . . ." — CJS, p. 137

Pg. 46

"We had monkeys" — Ibid., p. 138

"typical American sailor . . ." — Excerpt from "An American Family Afloat"

Pg. 47

"Virginia was most kind to me . . ." — Emma Slocumb [sic] Miller in correspondence with Teller, October 28, 195?, TC

"Two incidents come to mind . . ." — Ibid., TC

Pg. 48

"two striking thoughts . . ." — excerpt from "An American Family Afloat" *New York Tribune*, June 26, 1882.

Pg. 50

"at the scant mercy . . ." — "Rescue of Some Gilbert Islanders," VJS, p. 387 [Originally published as an appendix to the 1890 edition of *Voyage of the Liberdade*]

"When we behold . . ." — Slocum quoting Sinbad the Sailor — Ibid., p. 390

"slop chest" — CJS, p. 164

"at a loss to know . . ." — VJS, p. 391

Chapter Four — *Ebb and Flow*

Pg. 53

Letter from Slocum to Mrs. Walker (Virginia's mother), TC

Pg. 54

"When she died, father never . . ." — Garfield Slocum in letter to Teller, TC

Pg. 55

"not a martinet . . ." — *Boston Sun*, August 3, 1894, TC

"My brother met . . ." — Grace Murray Brown in letter to Teller, December 14, 1952, TC

Pg. 56

"I now see . . ." — Special dispatch to the *Boston Herald*, New York, June

12, 1884, TC

"Slater said he came voluntarily . . ." — Ibid.

Pg. 57

"ignominiously towed by the nose . . ." — SAAW, p. 3

"the nearest in perfection of beauty" — Ibid.

Pg. 58

"constant alarms" — CJS, p. 180

"Her heart was not strong . . ." — Jessie Slocum in Teller correspondence, TC

"the stateroom doors . . ." — Garfield Slocum, memories in letters to Teller, TC

"The deck house was . . ." — Ibid.

Pg. 59

"as close to a yacht . . ." — Victor Slocum, noted in Teller correspondence, TC

"She left her needle . . ." — Garfield Slocum in Teller correspondence, TC

Pg. 60

"she often fainted . . ." — Ben Aymar Slocum in

Teller correspondence, TC [Walter Teller advanced a theory regarding Virginia's death in *The Search for Captain Slocum* (1956), but not in the revised 1971 edition: "In such sanitation as a sailing ship could spare for a woman in childbirth, would not be unlikely to lead to infection, and to a rheumatic heart."]

"Thy will be done . . ." — noted in Teller correspondence, TC [According to Ben Aymar Slocum, his father brought down the family bible (Virginia's), as he had for other shipboard deaths. Ben Aymar wrote Teller that he'd seen "more than once when weighted bodies went sliding along a plank or board over the main deck bulwark."]

"Mother's eyes were a brilliant . . ." — Ben Aymar Slocum in Teller correspondence, TC

"on many occasions . . ." — Ibid.

"learned to understand . . ." — Ibid.

"ill fortunes gathered rapidly . . ." — Ibid.

Pg. 61

Snapping of piano wires . . . — Garfield Slocum in Teller correspondence, TC

"a ship with a broken rudder" — Ibid., TC

Pg. 62

"Hettie was no doubt bedazzled . . ." — Grace Murray Brown, TC

"for out on the Atlantic . . ." — VJS, *Voyage of the "Liberdade,"* Ch. 1, p. 42

Pg. 63

"Crew were picked up . . ." — Ibid., p. 55

Pg. 64

"A change of rats . . ." — Ibid., p. 58

"looming up like . . ." — Ibid., p. 58

"fearfully out of tune" — Ibid., p. 59

"suffering, I should say . . ." — Ibid., p. 59

Pg. 65

"Arming myself, therefore . . ." — Ibid.

"gang of cut-throats" — Ibid.

"I could not speak . . ." — Ibid.

"A man will defend . . ." — Ibid.

Pg. 66

"his chills turned to . . ." — Ibid., p. 66

"wet, and lame and weary . . ." — Ibid., p. 68

Pg. 67

"I listened to the solemn splash . . ." — Ibid., p. 69

"drifting pest house" — Ibid., p. 70

"what it cost me . . ." — Ibid., p. 71

"We came to a stand . . ." — Ibid., p. 72

Pg. 68

"Currents and wind caught her foul . . ." — Ibid., p. 74

"Father lost all of his money . . ." — Garfield Slocum in Teller correspondence, TC

"This was no time . . ." — VSJ, *Voyage of the Liberdade*, p. 74

Pg. 69

"she should sail well . . ."
— Ibid., p. 76

"a megre kit" — PANS

Pg. 70

"But all that . . ." — Ibid.,
p. 77

"Madam had made the sails
. . ." — Ibid., p. 80

Pg. 71

"The old boating trick . . ."
— PANS

"Father had a lot of nerve
. . ." — Garfield Slocum in
Teller correspondence, TC

"the thin cedar planks . . ."
— VJS, *Voyage of the
Liberdade*, p. 93

"the most exciting . . ."
— PANS

Pg. 72

"Oh, I hope not . . ." — Ibid.,
TC

"left those of the south . . ."
— Ibid., p. 104

"A phantom of the stately
Aquidneck . . ." — Ibid.,
p. 104

Chapter Five — *What Was
There for an Old Sailor*

to Do?

Pg. 73

"Mine was not the sort of
life . . ." — SAAW, pp. 3, 4

Pg. 74

"With all its vicissitudes . . ."
— VJS, *Voyage of the
Liberdade*, p. 122

"She was canoe-shaped . . ."
— Joseph Chase Allen,
Directory Edition,
Vineyard Gazette, undated
clipping 195?, TC

Pg. 75

"full brow, bright hazel eyes
. . ." — *New York World*,
May 19, 1889, TC

"wee cabin on a plank . . ."
— Ibid.

Pg. 76

"comfortable apartment
ashore" — From "An
American Family Afloat,"
New York Tribune.

"'Just there' . . ." — *New York
World*, May 19, 1889, TC

"Xmas day was spent . . ."
— Hettie Slocum's letter
of January 28, 1889, to
Mrs. Alfred McNutt,

Masstown, Colchester County, Nova Scotia — PANS

Pg. 77

"We had a big storm . . ." — Ibid.

"brave enough to face . . ." — VJS, *Voyage of the Liberdade*, p. 122

"Hettie found she was not wholly . . ." — Grace Murray Brown, letters to Teller (1952–56), TC

"Father did not come to the house" — Garfield Slocum, correspondence with Teller, TC

"His love for Hettie . . ." — Grace Murray Brown, letters to Teller (1952–56), TC

Pg. 78

"More than any other event . . ." — Joseph Conrad, *Mirror of the Sea*, p. 61

Pg. 79

"spent much of his time . . ." — Ben Aymar Slocum, correspondence with Teller, TC

"a hand alas! . . ." — Title

page, *Voyage of the Liberdade*, 1890, Robinson & Stephenson

"It is a very interesting narrative . . ." — *Yarmouth Herald*, July 2, 1895, gleaned from research sent by Leon Fredrich to Walter Teller, TC

Pg. 80

"a record of skilful seamanship . . ." — Ibid.

"The book is written . . ." — Ibid.

"I would have to get used to steamships . . ." — Garfield Slocum, correspondence to Teller, TC

"It didn't seem to suffice . . ." — Slocum, in undated newspaper interview (around 1908), probably *Providence Journal*, TC

Pg. 81

"the first ship . . ." — PANS

"Frankly it was with a thrill . . ." — VJS, *Voyage of the Destroyer from New York to Brazil*, Introduction, p. 171

Pg. 82

"Confidentially: I was
burning to get a rake . . ."
— Ibid., p. 189
"Being a man of a peaceful
turn . . ." — Ibid., p. 173
"navigator in command"
— Ibid., p. 173
"This Department . . ."
— Department of State
letter, Washington, D.C.,
December 9, 1893, TC
Pg. 83
"Alas! for all the hardships
. . ." — VJS, *Voyage of the
Destroyer*, p. 194
"ridiculed and defamed him
. . ." — *Boston Sun*,
August 3, 1894, TC
"anywhere at any time . . ."
— Ibid.
Pg. 84
"duellists should . . ."
— Ibid.
"My wife would . . ."
— Ibid.
"she sat on the water . . ."
SAAW, p. 6
"a smart New Hampshire
spruce" — PANS
"What was there . . ." — Ibid.,
p. 4
Pg. 85

"I'm glad you're quite frank
. . ." — Letter from Teller
to William Sloane at
Rutgers University Press,
TC
"Joshua, I've had a v'yage"
— Slocum's comments to
reporters, *Boston Globe*,
April 16, 1895; also
appeared in "The Voyage
of the Aquidneck and its
Varied Adventures in
South American Waters,"
Outing, April 1903, TC
"The object of the trip?"
— *Boston Globe*, undated
clipping, TC
pg. 86
"My Syndicade is filling up,
. . ." — Letter to Eugene
Hardy, Roberts Brothers,
TC
"I can not contract with you
. . ." — Letter to Slocum
from Alf Ford, managing
editor of the *Louisville
Courier Journal*, January
3, 1894, TC
[Ralph Shoemaker, librarian
of the *Courier Journal*, wrote
to Walter Teller that he could
find no articles written by

Slocum. Teller records in his notes about correspondence with Shoemaker, "Looks as though in Louisville they never bought a line. In fact, the only paper I know that did, is the Boston Globe, and as we shall see they didn't buy much. I expect part of the trouble may have been that Slocum was too busy and hard-working to write." TC [Travel letters from Slocum's *The Spray* appeared as Monday columns in the *Boston Globe* as follows: October 14, 1895, p. 6; October 21, 1895, p. 5; November 11, 1895, p.4]
"Mr. Wagnalls of the house . . ." — Undated letter from JS to Eugene Hardy, TC

Pg. 87
"a shop-worn . . ." — Ibid.
"A thousand thanks"
— Letter from JS to Eugene Hardy, January 9, 1895, TC
"Rarely if ever . . ."
— H. Rider Haggard's foreword to *A Strange Career*, a biography of John Gladwin Jebb by his widow, William Blackwood and Sons, 1895
"The library of the Spray . . ."
— *Boston Herald*, April 16, 1895, TC

Pg. 88
"I don't go out . . ." — Ibid.
"Capt. Josh is a kinky salt . . ." — Undated clipping, (before voyage, probably April 1895), *Boston Herald*, TC
"very easily managed . . ."
— Ibid.
"the suicide squad" — John Hanna, *The Rudder*, May 1940, p. 51, TC
"A big lurching sea . . ."
— Ibid.

Pg. 89
"they flop right over . . ."
— Ibid.
"the Spray was a . . ."
— Howard Chapelle, *Maine Coast Fisherman*, June 1965

Pg. 90

"I laid in two barrels . . ."
— Clifton Johnson, "The
Cook Who Sailed Alone,"
Good Housekeeping,
February 1903

Pg. 91

"To Sail Around World . . ."
— *Boston Daily Globe*,
April 16, 1895, p. 4, TC

"builder, owner, skipper, . . ."
— Ibid.

"There now lies a little sloop
. . ." — Ibid.

"Her present rig . . ." — Ibid.

Pg. 92

"From New York I shall . . ."
— Ibid.

"sleep in the day time . . ."
— Ibid.

Pg. 93

"an adventure . . ." — Ibid.

"Capt. Slocum . . ." — Ibid.

"The enterprise the old knight
. . ." — *Joshua Slocum*,
Walter Teller, p. 77

"Do you think . . ." — Letter
to Teller from Walter
Sloane, TC

Pg. 94

"Waves dancing joyously . . ."
— SAAW, Capt. Joshua

Slocum, Ch. 2, p. 8

Chapter Six — *All Watches*

Pg. 95

"I used to soak . . ." — In
Clifton Johnson, "The
Cook Who Sailed Alone,"
Good Housekeeping,
February 1903.

Pg. 96

"Sleeping or waking . . ."
— SAAW, p. 31

"thrilling pulse" — Ibid., p. 8

"weigh the voyage . . ."
— Ibid.

Pg. 97

"fisherman's own" — Ibid.

"I perceived, moreover, . . ."
— Ibid.

"the worst tide-race . . ."
— Ibid., p. 11

"He dodged a sea . . ." — Ibid.

Pg. 98

"fierce sou'west rip" — Ibid.,
pp. 11, 12

"I think Pernambuco . . ."
— Letter from JS in
Westport to Eugene
Hardy, May 21, 1895, TC

"In our newfangled notions
. . ." — SAAW, p. 9

Pg. 99
"The price of it was . . ."
    — Ibid., p. 12
"an attack of malaria at
    Gloucester . . ." — Letter
    from JS in Yarmouth to
    Roberts Brothers, June 20,
    1895, TC
"After all deliberations . . ."
    — Ibid.
"let go my last hold on
    America" — PANS
Pg. 100
"[I have] been trying to
    scribble . . ." — Letter
    from JS in Horta Faial to
    Eugene Hardy, July 23,
    1895
"I send one more letter . . ."
    — Letter from JS in
    Pernambuco to Eugene
    Hardy, October 8, 1895.
[Slocum also sent a personal
letter to Hardy from
Pernambuco, in which he let
off a little steam. The note
has prophetic overtones: "The
Sun printed trash of mine
freely enough on more than
one occasion when it came
for nothing and I suspect that

a case of murder or rape
would find space for all the
particulars in all of the
papers, But I cant [sic] go to
war with them. I lived awful
hard coming down: But dont
say anything about it."]
Pg. 101
"A navigator husbands the
    wind" — SAAW, p. 140
Pg. 102
"The *Spray* had barely . . ."
    — Ibid., p. 87
Pg. 103
"To know the laws that
    govern . . ." — Ibid., p. 76
"I saw antitrade clouds . . ."
    — Ibid., p. 109
"I wished for no winter
    gales . . ." — Ibid., p. 104
Pg. 105
"It never took long . . ."
    — Ibid., Appendix, p. 154
"During those twenty-three
    days . . ." — Ibid., p. 110
Pg. 106
"I found no fault . . ." — Ibid.,
    p. 23
"a contrivance of my own . . ."
    — In Clifton Johnson,
    "The Cook Who Sailed

Alone," *Good Housekeeping*, February 1903

"My way is to cook my victuals . . ." — Ibid.

"Ground coffee . . ." — Ibid.

Pg. 107

"I had much difficulty . . ." — SAAW, p. 23

"The only fresh fish . . ." — Ibid., p. 30

Pg. 108

"hermetically sealed the pores" — In Johnson, *Good Housekeeping*

"butter that will keep . . ." — Ibid.

"I was determined to rely . . ." — SAAW, p. 58

Pg. 109

"set to work with my palm and needle . . ." — Ibid., p. 58

"If it was not the best-setting sail afloat, . . ." — Ibid., p. 58

"Between the storm-bursts . . ." — Ibid., p. 66

Pg. 110

"I . . . mended the sloop's sails . . ." — Ibid., p. 66

"carefully top and bottom" — Ibid., p. 94

"unshipped the sloop's mast . . ." — Ibid., p. 40

Pg. 111

"In the days of serene weather . . ." Ibid., p. 106

Chapter Seven — *High Seas Adventures*

Pg. 113

"But where the sloop avoided — SAAW, p. 45

Pg. 114

"For under great excitement, one lives fast." — Ibid.

"Take warning, Spray . . ." — SAAW, p. 8

"It was the 13th of the month, . . ." — Ibid., p. 12

Pg. 115

"whirled around like a top" — Ibid.

"I now saw the tufts . . ." — Ibid., p. 28

"the sons of generations of pirates" — Ibid.

Pg. 116

"shook her in every timber" — Ibid.

"You can just imagine . . ."
  — PANS
"I perceived this theiving . . ."
  — Ibid., p. 28
"too fatigued to sleep"
  — Ibid., p. 29
Pg. 117
"heartsore of choppy seas"
  — Ibid., p. 44
"I will not say . . ." — Ibid.,
  p.44
"where the sloop avoided . . ."
  — Ibid., p. 45
Pg. 119
"I had only a moment . . ."
  — Ibid., p. 45
Pg. 120
"At this point where the tides
  . . ." — Ibid., p. 63
"the waves rose and fell . . ."
  — Ibid., p. 53
"as squalid as contact . . ."
  — Ibid., p. 46
"fire-water" — Ibid.
"poisonous stuff . . ." — Ibid.
Pg. 121
"You must use them . . ."
  — Ibid.
"It was not without thoughts
  . . ." — Ibid., p. 47
"savages" — Ibid.

"yammerschooner" — Ibid.
"into the cabin, . . ." — Ibid.,
  p. 48
Pg. 122
"So much for the . . ." — Ibid.
"I reasoned that I had all . . ."
  — Ibid.
Pg. 123
"business end" — Ibid., p. 55
"like a pack of hounds"
  — Ibid.
"They jumped pell-mell . . ."
  — Ibid.
Pg. 124
"a Fuegian autograph" —
  Ibid., p. 67
Pg. 133
"one eye over my shoulders
  . . ." — Ibid., p. 60
"the worst murderer . . ."
  — PANS
Pg. 126
"I was so strongly impressed
  . . ." — SAAW, p. 46
"the terror of Cape Horn"
  — Ibid., p. 46
"compressed gales of wind
  . . ." — Ibid., p. 47
"A full-blown williwaw . . ."
  — Ibid.
Pg. 127

"Here I felt the throb . . ."
— Ibid.
Pg. 128
"feeling his way . . ." — Ibid.,
p. 54
"Any landsman . . ." — Ibid.,
p. 54 (as cited by Slocum
in Charles Darwin, *The
Voyage of the Beagle*,
Everyman's Library 104,
1906, pp. 229–31)
"the greatest sea-adventure
. . ." — SAAW, p. 54
Pg. 129
"God knows how my . . ."
— Ibid.
Pg. 130
"humoring my vessel"
— Ibid., p.69
"All my troubles . . ." — Ibid.,
p. 70

Chapter Eight — *Walden at
Sea: A Solitude Supreme*
Pg. 131
"Still in dismal fog . . ."
— Ibid., p. 15
Pg. 132
"Even when I slept . . ."
— Ibid., p. 31
Pg. 133

"I watched light after light
. . ." — Ibid., p. 14
"lowered over the sea like a
pall . . ." — Ibid., p. 14
"In the dismal fog I felt . . ."
— Ibid., p. 15
"The acute pain of solitude
. . ." — Ibid., p. 16
Pg. 134
"While the days go thus . . ."
— Ibid., p. 82
"sense of loneliness . . ."
— Ibid., p. 87
"How could one tell . . ."
— Ibid., p. 50
Pg. 135
"All distracting uneasiness
. . ." — PANS
"Then was the time . . ."
— Ibid., p. 70
Pg. 136
"For days she sailed . . ."
— Ibid., p. 105
"The weather became fine
. . ." Ibid., p. 45
Pg. 137
"The false appearance . . ."
— Ibid., p. 36
"a sort of Calvary . . ."
— Ibid., p. 64
Pg. 138

"large red cap . . ." — Ibid.,
p. 21

"Yonder is the Pinta . . ."
— Ibid., p. 21

"pains and calentura"
— Ibid., p. 22

"You did wrong, captain . . ."
— Ibid., p. 21

Pg. 139

"smiling full moon" — Ibid.,
p. 14

"many long . . ." — Ibid.,
p. 14

"there was no end . . ." Ibid.,
p. 79

"the spider and his wife . . ."
— Ibid., p. 136

"In my cabin it met . . ."
— Ibid., p. 60

Pg. 140

"where I drew . . ." — Ibid.,
p. 118

"When I found myself . . ."
— Ibid., p. 68

"Moreover, she had discovered . . ." — Ibid., p. 68

Pg. 141

"Eight bells" — Ibid., p. 15

"sounded hollow in . . ."
— Ibid., p. 15

"[I] pitched my voice . . ."
— Ibid., p. 15

"The porpoises were . . ."
— Ibid. p. 15

Pg. 142

"after a worthy literary friend
. . ." — Ibid., p. 68

"gossiping waves" — Ibid.,
p. 70

"doffed their white caps
beautifully" — Ibid., p. 69

"gam" — Ibid., p. 31

"There are no poetry-
enshrined . . ." — Ibid.,
p. 31

Pg. 144

"I had almost forgotten . . ."
— Ibid., p. 146

Pg. 145

"I sailed with a free wind . . ."
— Ibid., pp. 75, 76

Pg. 146

"self-reliance unshaken . . ."
— Ibid., p. 77

"I found from the result . . ."
— Ibid., p. 76

"There is nothing in the
realm . . ." — Ibid., p.77

Pg. 147

"I was en rapport now . . ."

— Ibid., p. 77

"To kill the companions . . ."
    — Ibid. , p. 154

"Nothing is more dreadful
    . . ." — Ibid., p. 79

Pg. 148

"I was destined to sail . . ."
    — Ibid., PANS

"Everything in connection
    . . ." — Letter from JS to
    Clifford Johnson, April 17,
    1903, TC

Pg. 149

"Old sailors may have odd
    ways . . ." — Letter from
    JS to cousin, Joel Slocum,
    May 4, 1899, TC

"I sailed alone with God."
    — SAAW, p. 70

Chapter Nine — *Ports of Call*

Pg. 151

"Captain Slocum was what
    . . ." — Thomas Fleming
    Day, *The Rudder*, January
    1911, p. 62

Pg. 152

"Though I do not feel . . ."
    — PANS

Pg. 153

"To be alone forty-three days
    . . ." — SAAW, p. 79

"I expected to see this . . ."
    — Ibid., p. 110

Pg. 154

"My vessel being moored . . ."
    — Ibid., p. 80

"I preferred to remain . . ."
    — Ibid., p. 127

Pg. 155

"plucky Yankee" — *Daily
    Telegraph*, Sydney, January
    9, 1897, TC

"the hero of . . ." — *Sydney
    Morning Herald*, undated
    clipping, TC

"So much interest . . ."
    — *North West Post*,
    Tasmania, undated
    clipping, TC

"the news of her arrival . . ."
    — *St. Helena Guardian*,
    undated clipping, TC

Pg. 156

"the gallant Captain's . . ."
    — *Gibraltar Chronicle*,
    August 23, 1895

"An Intrepid Navigator"
    — *North West Post*,
    February 23, 1897,

Tasmania
"Five minutes in his company
   . . ." — Ibid.
"During his sojourn . . ."
   — Melbourne newspaper
Pg. 157
"By the way, some one . . ."
   — JS quoted in *Daily
   Telegraph*, Sydney, January
   29, 1897, p. 3, col. 4
Pg. 158
"when she heard . . ."
   — PANS, p. 115
"destroyer of the world"
   — Ibid., p. 115
"The captain is eating . . ."
   — Ibid., p. 112
Pg. 159
"The heart of a missionary is
   all . . ." — JS, in letter to
   Joseph B. Gilder, written
   from "The Spray tied to a
   palm tree," Keeling Cocos,
   August 20, 1897
"He didn't want your . . ."
   — Ben Aymar Slocum, in
   correspondence with
   Walter Teller, TC
"I myself do not care . . ."
   — JS, in letter to cousin,
   Joel Slocum, May 4, 1899,

TC
"instead of proceeding . . ."
   — PANS
"to feast [his] eyes . . ."
   — SAAW, p. 101
Pg. 160
"of course made a pilgrimage
   . . ." — Ibid., p. 74
"blessed island" — Ibid., p. 74
"Why Alexander Selkirk . . ."
   — Ibid., p. 74
"made the hills ring . . ."
   — Ibid., p. 72
"She told me that . . ."
   — Ibid., p. 81
Pg. 161
"To Captain Slocum . . ."
   — Ibid., p. 81
"at once amusing . . ."
   — Ibid., p. 82
"saw nothing to shake . . ."
   — Ibid., p. 82
"I had a curious . . ."
   — Johnson, in "The Cook
   Who Sailed Alone," *Good
   Housekeeping*, February
   1903.
Pg. 162
"to the unconventional . . ."
   — SAAW, p. 84
"You don't mean *round* . . ."

— Ibid., p. 127

Pg. 163

"one of the party . . ." — Ibid., p. 123

"losing himself in a passion . . ." — Ibid., p. 123

"The next day . . ." — Ibid., p. 123

"in the land of napkins . . ." — Ibid., p. 115

"the ghosts of hempen towels . . ." — Ibid., p. 115

Pg. 164

"What an example . . ." — Ibid., p. 122

"He showed me . . ." — Ibid., p. 127

"Man, man . . ." — Ibid., p. 94

"had to do something for . . ." — PANS

Pg. 165

"Boston to Bowen . . ." — Ibid., p. 100

"proceeded to exhibit . . ." — *Cape Town Argus*, undated clipping (prob. early March 1898)

"a large number . . ."— J.R. Whitton, Rector of the Normal College, Cape Town, March 4, 1898.

"accounts of perilous travels . . ." — PANS

Pg. 166

"When I got out . . ." — Slater, in *Daily Telegraph* (Sydney), October 9, 1896

"At first my daily fare . . ." — Ibid.

Pg. 167

"I ask the public . . ." — Ibid.

"Captain Slocum declined . . ." — Ibid.

"a pluck into anchorage" — SAAW, p. 88

"gathered data from . . ." — Ibid., p. 88

Pg. 168

"disgusted" — Slocum, in *Daily Telegraph* (Sydney), October 9, 1896 (from Newcastle)

"This Captain Slocum . . ." — Ibid.

"Slater: You have been . . ." — Records of cross-examination of Slater by Slocum in The Courts, *Slater v. Slocum*, in *Sydney Morning Herald*, October 12, 1896.

Pg. 169
"As I sailed farther . . ."
— SAAW, p. 81
Pg. 170
"received a new coat . . ."
— *Gibraltar Chronicle*,
August ?, 1895
"repairs to hull . . ."
— Shipyard reports, Leon
Fredrich research, TC
"intrepid water tramp"
— Heman Hagedorn, *The
Roosevelt Family of
Sagamor Hill*, N.Y.,
Macmillan, 1954, p. 245
[He writes of Slocum: "The
intrepid water-tramp, Captain
Joshua Slocum, had all his
adult life sailed the seven
seas in his forty-foot sloop,
alone, with no crew, surviving
by a succession of miracles,
which in themselves gave
him a kind of oblique
significance."]
"Captain Slocum . . ." — *St.
Helena Guardian*, PANS
Pg. 171
"I soon found that . . ."
— Ibid., p. 134
Pg. 172

"PROBABLY LOST . . ."
— *New Bedford Standard*,
August 24, 1897
"If there was a moment . . ."
— SAAW, p. 95
Pg. 173
"I have not yet decided . . ."
— *Daily Telegraph*
(Sydney), January 29,
1897

Chapter Ten — *Booming
Along Joyously for Home*
Pg. 175
"Differing in many respects
. . ." — Undated clipping,
possibly *Providence
Journal*, TC
Pg. 176
"I had a desire . . ." — SAAW,
p. 150
"a succession of impulses
. . ." — Igor Stravinsky,
cited in *Harvard Dictio-
nary of Music*, Second
Edition,Willi Apel,
Belknap Harvard, 1974,
p. 823
Pg. 177
"a morning land-wind"
— SAAW, p. 123

"Cape of Storms" — Ibid.,
 p. 128
"One gale was much . . ."
 — Ibid.. p. 126
"The *Spray* was trying . . ."
 — Ibid.
"The voyage then seemed . . ."
 — Ibid.
"the dividing-line of the
 weather" — Ibid., p. 126
Pg. 178
"the land of distances . . ."
 — Ibid., p. 126
"'Tis the fairest . . ." — Ibid.,
 p. 130
"The *Spray* soon . . ." — Ibid.,
 p. 130
"ran along steadily . . ."
 — Ibid., p. 130
Pg. 179
"just leaping along . . ."
 — Ibid., p. 130
"One could not be . . ."
 — Ibid., pp. 130, 131
"island of tragedies" — Ibid.,
 p. 133
Pg. 180
"Let what will happen . . ."
 — Ibid., p. 137
"strange and forgotten . . ."
 — Ibid., p. 139

"the handsome day's work
 . . ." — Ibid.. p. 139
"Are there any . . ." — Ibid.,
 p. 139
Pg. 181
"Let us keep together . . ."
 — Ibid., p. 139
"pondered long . . ." — Ibid.,
 p. 139
"was startled by . . ." — Ibid.,
 p. 141
"I taxed my memory . . ."
 — Ibid., p. 142
Pg.182
"imaginary reefs" — Ibid.,
 p. 142
"I could have nailed . . ." —
 Ibid., p. 142
"The *Spray* was booming . . ."
 — Ibid., p. 146
"was jumping like . . ."
 — Ibid., p. 146
Pg. 183
"The great King Neptune . . ."
 — Ibid., p. 147
"I was tired, tired . . ."
 — Ibid., p. 127
"climax storm . . ." — Ibid.,
 p. 147
"hugged the rocks along . . ."
 — Ibid., p. 150

Pg. 184
"after the cruise . . ." — Ibid.,
　p. 150
"early yesterday morning
　. . ." — *Newport Herald*,
　June 28, 1898, p.3
"The solitary occupant . . ."
　— Ibid., p.3
Pg. 185
"The first name . . ."
　— SAAW, p. 150
"musical story" — Letter
　from Mabel Stevenson
　(Secretary, The Wagnalls
　Memorial) to Walter
　Teller, October 31, 1953,
　TC
[Miserere " a musical story,"
Mabel Wagnalls, Funk &
Wagnalls, New York, 1892,
pp. PANS]
"A thousand thanks . . ."
　— Ibid., TC
"Was the crew well . . ."
　— SAAW, p. 150
Pg. 186
"return to the very beginning"
　— Ibid., p. 150
"I secured her . . ." — Ibid.,
　p. 150

Chapter Eleven — *That
　Intrepid Water Tramp*
Pg. 187
"Occasionally lapsing . . ."
　— Undated clipping,
　probably *Providence
　Journal*
Pg. 188
"I am longing . . ." — JS in
　letter to the *Standard*,
　New Bedford, July 3,
　1898. TC
"I want to give . . ." — Ibid.
Pg. 189
"But my heart is . . ." — Ibid.
"the time to be spent . . ."
　— JS in letter to the
　Boston Sun, October 31,
　1898, TC
"to equip [his students] . . ."
　— Ibid.
Pg. 190
"induce people . . ." — Ibid.
"In fact, just as . . ." — Ibid.
"I am not ashamed . . ."
　— *Morning Mercury*,
　July 4, 1898
Pg. 191
"several tons of freight . . ."
　— Letter from JS to the
　Times of London, written

from St. Helena on April 31, 1898, mentioned in *New Bedford Standard*, Summer of 1898
"Curiosities of all sorts . . ."
— *New York Herald*, July, 1898
Pg. 192
"Captain Slocum is . . ."
— *New York Times*, August 5, 1898, p.12, col. 2
"It is not 'the greatest . . .'"
— Letter from JS to the *Times of London* written from St. Helena on April 31, 1898, mentioned in the *New Bedford Standard*, Summer 1898
Pg. 193
"Press Comments . . ."
— Lecture publicity pamphlet, with quotes of reviews of lectures given by JS along his world voyage, 1897 and 1898, TC
"Talks — 100 slides" — Ibid.
"The Captain has a droll . . ."
— Ibid., cited from *Natal Mercury*, November 24, 1897, TC
"called first class . . ."

— Letter from JS to Richard Gilder, July 1, 1898, TC
"The views were very . . ."
— *New Bedford Evening Standard*, July 3, 1898, TC
"I soon found that people . . ."
— Letter from JS to Richard Gilder, July 1, 1898
Pg. 194
"blow the hair . . ." — *St. Helena Guardian*, April 3, 1898, p. 3, col. 1
"I left my hat there" — Ibid.
"because 'her' . . ." — *Cape Argus*, January 16, 1898, TC
"because he could not . . ."
— Ibid.
"I have a fund . . ." — Letter from JS to editor, *Century*, TC
"Without say Slocum Slocum . . ." — Ibid.
Pg. 195
"one or two short letters"
— Letter from JS to Richard Gilder, July 1, 1898, TC
"These I discontinued . . ."

— Ibid.

"vessel has in a cargo . . ."

— Ibid.

Pg. 196

"There were indeed features . . ." — Ibid.

"My 'type-writer' and I . . ." — Letter from JS to C.C. Buel, January 1899, TC

"Mr. Johnson . . ." — Letter from JS to *Century*, TC

Pg. 197

"make it not the worst . . ." — Ibid.

"When you see an error . . ." — Letter to Slocum from editors, TC

"a prominent part . . ." — Letter to Walter Teller from Constance Buel Burnett, TC

"I write to assure you . . ." — Letter from JS to editor, Johnson, August 12, 1899, TC

Pg. 198

"I find it rather difficult . . ." — Letter from JS to editor, Johnson, August 14, 1899, TC

["Sailing Alone Around the World" was serialized in *The Century Illustrated Monthly Magazine* between September 1899 and March 1900. On November 11, 1899, Slocum wrote to the editor of the *New York Times* regarding "a criticism from an old salt." The disgruntled and thin-skinned captain of the *Spray* wrote this to the disbeliever: "This unpretentious sloop built by one pair of hands, after circumnavigating the globe is sound and snug and tight. She does not leak a drop. This would be called a great story by some; nevertheless it is a hard fact." In defense of his story in the *Century*, Slocum continued: "The story of the voyage is contructed on the same seaworthy lines; that is, it remains waterproof, which your navigating officer will discover, I trust, if only he exercise to the end that patience necessary on a voyage around the world."]

"I congratulate the Century

. . ." — Letter from JS to C.C. Buel, October 30, 1900, TC

"To the one who said . . ." — *Sailing Alone Around the World*, The Century Company, 1900

"To Mabel Wagnalls . . ." — Letter from Mabel Stevenson (Secretary, The Wagnalls Memorial) to Walter Teller, October 31, 1953, TC

[Mabel Wagnalls later wrote a short review of *Sailing Alone Around the World*, which the Century Company used for their advertising pamphlet. She wrote: "Round the World Alone" — a mighty motto this; and in all the world's history it applies to only one man, Captain Joshua Slocum. Amid solitude and silence, with the keel of his little boat he has traced the great circle — the emblem of eternity."]

Pg. 199

[The following are as quoted in a three-page publicity brochure launching *Sailing Alone Around the World*, The Century Company, New York, 1900, TC]

"one of the most . . ." — *The Bookseller*, New York

"a nautical equivalent . . ." — Van Wyck Brooks

"The tale is true . . ." — Sir Edwin Arnold

"Absence of literary . . ." — *New York Evening Post*

Pg. 200

"There is no question . . ." — *The Nautical Gazette*, April 20, 1900

[Dr. Edward R. Shaw, School of Pedagogy, New York, edited *Sailing Alone Around the World* for schools. In his foreword to *Around the World in the Sloop Spray*, (Scribner, N.Y., 1903), Shaw declared the captain's story to be "a story of adventure and a lesson in geography all in one." Copies of the old reader are in the Maritime Museum of the Atlantic, Halifax, N.S., and the Old Dartmouth Historical Society Whaling Museum, New Bedford,

Mass.]

"You see I had . . ." — Letter from JS to Joel Slocum, May 4, 1899, TC

"I hope that the *Century* . . ." — Letter from JS to C.C. Buel, The Century Co., March 30, 1899, TC

Pg. 201

"I am not the old fossil . . ." — Letter from JS to Professor Otis Tufton Mason, February 27, 1901, TC

"I consider the human . . ." — Ibid. TC

"I assume that he . . ." — Garfield Slocum's correspondence with Walter Teller, TC

"The cabins of the Spray . . ." — *New York Post*, undated clipping, TC

Pg. 202

"a hold full of curiosities . . ." — *Morning Mercury*, July 4, 1898, TC

"A Daring New England Yankee . . ." — *Bennett Illustrated Souvenir Guide*, Pan-American Exposition,

1901 (edited and compiled by Mark Bennett, United News Edition, The Goff Co. Buffalo, N.Y.), TC

Pg. 203

"The captain made ports . . ." — Ibid.

"A piece of her original mainsail . . ." — Sloop Spray Souvenir, booklet by Henrietta M. Slocum, The Gillis Press, Copyright 1901 by Joshua Slocum

"an old work horse . . ." — 1901 story, Buffalo newspaper

Pg. 204

"The horse that furnished . . ." Ibid.

Chapter Twelve — *Swallowing the Anchor?*

Pg. 205

"But he was one . . ." — excerpt from H.S. Smith, *Quite Another Matter*, in *The Skipper*, March 1968

Pg. 206

"Ports are no good . . ." — *The Mirror of the Sea*,

Joseph Conrad, Chapter
XXXIV, p. 115
[H.S. Smith sent his thoughts
on this quote to Walter Teller
and made this comparison
to Slocum's situation: "I do
not think that 'Spray' was
benefited [sic] by her long
lay-up, or her owner either."]
Pg. 207
"Capt. and Mrs. Slocum . . ."
    — *Vineyard Gazette,*
    November 13, 1902
"Of late the captain . . ."
    — Clifton Johnson,
    Outing, October 1902,
    Vol. 41, p.35
Pg. 208
"it was his own taste . . ."
    — Undated clipping from
    the *New Bedford Standard,*
    TC
"marine flavor" — Walter
    Teller's notes of a visit
    with Percy Chase Miller,
    July 8, 1953, TC
"Rudder Ranch" — Letter
    from JS to Clifton
    Johnson, September 21,
    1902
"In a single season . . ."

— Clifton Johnson,
    Outing, October 1902,
    Vol. 41, p. 35, TC
Pg. 209
"has a temper . . ." — Walter
    Teller, *Joshua Slocum,*
    p. 209, Rutgers University
    Press, 1956, 1971
"capable of letting . . ."
    — Grace Murray Brown,
    correspondence with
    Walter Teller, TC
"be as independent . . ."
    — Ibid.
Pg. 210
"I can not be . . ." — Ibid.
"a terrible row . . ." — Ibid.
Pg. 211
"very quick in his movements
    . . ." — Teller's notes on
    an interview with Joseph
    Chase Allen, summer
    1953, TC
"I was on the front . . ."
    — Ibid.
Pg. 212
Shouting poetry by Robbie
    Burns — Grace Murray
    Brown in letter to Walter
    Teller, TC
"he burst upon . . ." — Ibid.

"an account of his voyage
. . ." — *West Tisbury News*,
PANS
"a little alienated . . ."
— unidentified notes in TC
Pg. 213
"It did not hurt . . ." — Teller's
recollections of visits with
Hettie Slocum, July 9,
1952, TC
"Josh, Joshua, or . . ."
— Ibid.
"A winter would be . . ."
— Letter from Grace
Murray Brown to Walter
Teller, TC
"Father was a changed . . ."
— Letter from Garfield
Slocum to Walter Teller,
TC
Pg. 214
"carried a small round . . ."
— Teller's notes from an
interview with Joseph
Chase Allen, summer
1953, TC
"hustling a dollar" — Letter
from JS to Victor, with
September 1909 date, not
in TC
[Teller notes that the letter is

in the possession of B. Aymar
Slocum, but B. Aymar's
granddaughters, Carol
Slocum Jimerson and Gale
Slocum Hermanet, told me
they have not seen the letter
and have no recollection
of it.]
"lectured to a small . . ."
— *The Gleaner*, January
22, 1906
"the audience was . . ."
— *Daily Telegraph*,
January 9, 1906
Pg. 215
"Had all this occurred . . ."
— Major James Pond,
Eccentricities of Genius,
New York, 1900.
"absolutely charms . . ."
— Ibid.
Information about JS's
storytelling — Carol W.
Saley's correspondence
with Teller, August 10,
1953, TC
"how to blow the . . ."
— Ibid., TC
Pg. 216
"I became so . . ." — Letter
from JS to William Tripp,

March 18, 1904, West
Tisbury, TC

"He is now on . . ."
— Unidentified clipping,
TC

"was bound west to pick up
. . ." — *Providence Journal*,
October 15, 1906

Pg. 218

"Capt. Slocum in Trouble . . ."
— *Boston Herald* (Special
Dispatch to the *Sunday
Herald*), May 27, 1906.
[The account of Slocum's
arrest appeared in a number
of papers, but not in the
Vineyard *Gazette*.]

Pg. 219

"lean and hungry looking . . ."
— Percy Chase Miller in
letter to Walter Teller, TC

"a little dippy" — Ibid.

"a good hand . . ." — *New Era*
of Riverton and Palmyra,
N.J., undated clipping

"The old sailor was . . ."
— Ibid.

"There was no . . ." — *New
Era*, June 1, 1906, p. 2,
col. 5

Pg. 221

"Senator John G. Horner
. . ." — *Mount Holly News*,
July 10, 1906

"I am very sorry . . ."
— Mount Holly Court
notes, Judge Gaskill,
Mount Holly News, July
10, 1906.

Pg. 222

"scared to death . . ."
— Teller's notes from
interview with Mrs.
Walter Mayhew (née
Doris Flanders), August
31, 1953, TC

"because on further
investigation . . ." — Ibid.

Pg. 223

"almost a Greek tragedy"
— Ibid.

Chapter Thirteen —
*Seaworthy for the Last
Time*

Pg. 225

"He looked like . . ." — Letter
from H.S. ("Skipper")
Smith to Walter Teller,
March 6, 1953, TC

Pg. 226

"I can patch up . . ." — JS to

305

Louise B. Ward, Jamaica,
1907, as recalled in letter
to Walter Teller, July 10,
1957, TC
Pg. 227
"Archie is off . . ." — *The
Letters of Theodore
Roosevelt*, selected and
edited by Elting E.
Morison, Harvard Univer-
sity Press, Cambridge,
Mass., 1952, Vol. 5, p. 347
"Archie is one . . ." — *New
Bedford Standard*,
September 10, 1906
"Of course we saw . . ."
— Archie Roosevelt,
Memorandum for Walter
Teller, "My Recollections
of Capt. J. S.," February
2, 1953, TC
[Archie Roosevelt recalled his
time with the JS as "a mar-
vellous adventure for a child."]
Pg. 228
"My dear Captain Slocum
. . ." — Ibid., and *New
Bedford Standard*,
September 10, 1906
[In a letter to Walter Teller
dated February 17, 1953,

Winfred Scott Clime recalled
that Slocum had the letter
from the president framed
and hung on the wall of the
Spray's cabin: "On the left
hand side as I went below I
saw a framed letter from
President Theodore Roosevelt,
written from the White
House." TC. The framed
letter probably went down
with the *Spray*.]
Pg. 229
"That yellow journalism . . ."
— Grace Murray Brown,
letter of December 14,
1952, to Walter Teller, TC
"Captain Joshua Slocum . . ."
— *Vineyard Gazette*,
August 16, 1906
"I think he was bitter . . ."
— Grace Murray Brown,
TC
"He was lazy and mentally
sluggish . . ." — Letter
from H.S. Smith to Walter
Teller, March 10, 1953, TC
Pg. 230
"Beside the bowsprit . . ."
— Letter from Garfield
Slocum to Walter Teller,

TC

"Father was a changed man
. . ." — Victor Slocum,
correspondence with
Walter Teller, TC

"When he returned . . ."
— Grace Murray Brown
in undated letter to Walter
Teller, TC

Pg. 231

"It was a long time . . ."
— Alice Longaker, in
undated correspondence
with Walter Teller, TC

"Captain Joshua Slocum . . ."
— *West Tisbury Miscella-
nies*, July 30, 1908

"I don't think . . ." — H.L.
Coggins, in undated cor-
respondence with Walter
Teller, TC

Pg. 232

"the Lone Navigator" — *The
Gleaner*, January 29, 1907

"I can patch up . . ." — JS to
Louise B. Ward, Jamaica,
1907, as recalled in letter
to Walter Teller, July 10,
1957, TC

"The *Spray* shall be . . ."
— *New Beford Times*,

September 10, 1906

Pg.233

"He will tell . . ." — Letter
from Vincent Gilpin to
Walter Teller, December
8, 1956. "The dodger on
his lecture read Thursday,
January 23, 8 p.m. This
letter fixes JS's visit to
Miami, as Gilpin relates
that Slocum signed his
copy of *Sailing Alone
Around the World*, January
10, 1908, "aboard the
Spray." Gilpin sent Teller
two prints of the *Spray* in
Miami, including the one
showing the exposed
hull.]

"The captain is as full of . . ."
— May 1907, newspaper
article out of Oyster Bay,
TC

"Once a year . . ." — Undated
clipping, *New York World*,
TC

Pg. 234

"Captain, our adventures . . ."
— as cited in PANS

"This boat was the most . . ."
— Archie Roosevelt,

Memorandum for Walter
Teller, "My Recollections
of Capt. J.S.," February
2, 1953, TC
"There was a quantity . . ."
    — Ibid.
Pg. 235
"pungent with the odor . . ."
    — PANS
"they both were neat . . ."
    — Ernest J. Dean in
    correspondence to Walter
    Teller, TC
[Dean also wrote: "It was
most interesting and educational, to lay out the proposed
courses with him, and also
amusing to see him run his
index finger (I think every
finger and thumb on both
hands was knuckle busted,
set back or crooked — they
looked worse than the fingers
of an old time ball player)
over miles and miles of ocean
chart, and listen to his running chatter of his experiences in different parts
shown on the chart . . ."]
[Dean Wrote to Teller of his
memories of JS in Nassau

harbor. Of Slocum's strength
in his last years, Dean commented: "I had one of my
sailors row me alongside [the
Spray], and when Slocum
recognized me, he let out a
loud, 'Come aboard!' grabbed
me by the arms and fairly
swung me on deck. I was
amazed (and still am) at his
strength. Dean also witnessed
Slocum's ornery side, when
Slocum got into a scrap with
a Bahamian. "Slocum seemed
all nerved up. I asked him
what had happened, and here
is his reply: 'I was splicing
some rigging on deck when
they came along — ginned up
some — and started talking
about the Spray and its size
and running it down in general. One of them said loud
enough for anyone to hear,
'Any mon that says he sailed
around the world in that
thing is a goddom liar.' I
looked up in time to see
which one said it, made a
pier head leap, and with a
couple of side-winders,

unshipped his jaw."]
"Slocum was much run down
. . ." — Letter from H.S.
Smith to Walter Teller,
March 6, 1953.
[Smith recalled a comment
made by one of his compan-
ions also visiting JS aboard
the *Spray*: "I would hate to
sail that old trap across Long
Island Sound if a stiff wind
was blowing."]
"He was thrifty and . . ."
— Letter from Vincent
Gilpin to Walter Teller,
December 8, 1956
Pg. 236
"I do not ascribe . . ."
— Grace Murray Brown
in undated letter to
Walter Teller, TC
Anecdote about the Victrola
— Mentioned in letter
from Pierce D. Brown to
Teller, October 24, 1952
Talk about seeing JS last set
sail — Teller's notes of
talking with Horace
Athearn, June 30, 1953,
TC
Pg. 237

"her sails and rigging . . ."
— Letter from Vincent
Gilpin to Walter Teller,
December 8, 1956
"considerably dozy . . ."
— Thomas Fleming Day,
The Rudder, January 1911,
p. 62
"Folks used to say . . ."
— Letter from Reginald
Norton to Walter Teller,
August 12, 1953, TC
Pg. 238
"disappeared, absconded . . ."
— Probate Court of Dukes
County, TC
"He sailed from . . ." — Ibid.
[The Absentee Petition and
Decree was filed April 1912,
and allowed July 21, 1913.
Recorded in General Book
29, p. 432, Dukes County
Court House, Edgartown,
Mass. Hettie was appointed
receiver of JS's assets: real
estate and personal estate
(royalties due).]
"I am on the Spray . . ."
— Letter from JS to
Victor, supposedly dated
September 4, 1909, not

in TC. Teller wrote in his notes that letter was in possession of Ben Aymar Slocum. His grand-daughters, Carol Slocum Jimerson and Gale Slocum Hermanet have other artifacts belonging to Ben Aymar, but have not seen the letter.]

"Feared that Captain . . ."
— *Fairhaven Star*, Thursday, September 30, 1909

[The obituary for Hettie Slocum, by Mrs. Ulysses E. Mayhew, was presented as a special in the October 20, 1952, edition of West Tisbury's *Standard-Times*: "Sea veteran, 90, Dies on Vineyard." It noted, "In 1908 Captain Slocum left without his wife in the Spray for a journey from which he never returned."]

Pg. 239

"that was on July . . ." — CJS
"In 1909 the *Spray* . . ."
— Ibid., p. Ibid.

"The *Spray* did not . . ."

— Letter from L. Francis Herreshoff to Walter Teller, December 30, 1952, TC [L. Francis Herreshoff also ventured an opinion as to cause of death: "His son says in his book that he thought the Spray was run down and sunk, but my opinion is that he was going to visit the Amazon River and I believe very likely was overtaken by fever up some of the unexplored creeks."]

Pg. 240

"the water was . . ." — Letter from Francis Mead, Edgartown, Mass., to Henry Hough, *Vineyard Gazette*, June 19, 1953

"Some faraway places"
— Letters to the editor, *Vineyard Gazette* — B.H. Kidder, Friday, July 17, 1953.

"Captain Slocum sailed . . ."
— *Vineyard Gazette*, July 24, 1909

Pg. 241

"I believe beyond all doubt . . ." — Hettie, in the *New*

Bedford Standard, July 24, 1909

"I am sorry . . ." — Hettie's letter to Mrs. Alfred McNutt, Nova Scotia, August 28, 1910, PANS

William Nickerson — Letter to *Maine Coast Fisherman*, April 1959

Pg. 242

"The letter says 1908 . . ."
— Letter from Kenneth E. Slack to Walter Teller, March 7, 1960

"Capt. Joshua Slocum . . ."
— Letter from Alice Longaker to Walter Teller, August 6, 1953

"I'm afraid we must . . ."
— Thomas Fleming Day, *The Rudder*, January 1911, p. 62

Pg. 243

"Captain Slocum probably . . ." — H.S. Smith, "Quite Another Matter", *The Skipper*, March 1968

"*Spray*'s planking . . ." — Ibid.

[In a letter to Teller dated March 4, 1953, Smith adds, "To tell the truth, Slocum

was very much what I term a 'hammer and nails' carpenter . . ." Apparently he never made repairs until their absolute necessity became apparent and on going below I found many evidences of serious deterioration.]

Pg. 244

"The last person . . ."
— Teller's notes from an interview with Captain Levi Jackson on August 13, 1952, Edgartown, Martha's Vineyard, TC

"I had sailed over . . ."
— Ibid.

"I am always deeply . . ."
— Hettie's letter to Mrs. Alfred McNutt, Nova Scotia, August 28, ?1910, PANS

Pg. 245

"Have been picturing . . ."
— Letter from Garfield Slocum to Teller, TC

Pg. 246

"Lone mariner reported . . ."
— *New Bedford Standard*, May 27, 1911

"Mr. O. J. Slocum . . ."

— Letter from Alice
Longaker to Walter Teller,
August 6, 1953
Story of Slocum with a
wooden leg — PANS
"No one can make . . ."
— Ibid.
Pg. 247
Story of three or more wives
— Ibid.
Capt. Slocum Story —
Edward Rowe Snow,
Quincy Patriot Ledger,
1959
"One of the world's . . ."
— Ibid.
Pg. 248
"But Captain Slocum . . ."
— Ibid.
"it had been a . . ." — Ibid.
"There is no one . . ." — Ibid.
"Peace to Captain Slocum
. . ." — Thomas Fleming
Day, *The Rudder*, January
1911, p. 62
Pg. 250
"Not in the churchyard . . ."
— Poem on plaque on
Pew 13, the Southern
Family Pew, in Westport
Baptist Church

[An old leatherbound
Psalmody was found in the
attic of what JS called the
"little church on the hill." In
the book was an anonymous
verse (from which the
stanza is taken) entitled "The
Sailor's Grave."]

Index

A

Acushnet River, 6
Aden, 99
Africa, 145
Agra, 26
Aiken, James, 65
Airy, Captain, 26
Alan Erric Island, 142
Alaska, 38
Allen, Joseph Chase, 74, 211–213
America, 189
American Museum of Natural History, 233
Amethyst, 40, 41, 43
Amoy, 34, 35
Annapolis County, 62
Annapolis Valley, 15
Antigua, 181
Antonina, 66, 67
Aquidneck, 57, 58, 59, 60, 61, 62, 63, 64, 65, 66, 67, 68, 69, 70, 72, 78, 82, 83
Arnold, Sir Edwin, 199
Ascension, 171
A Strange Career, 87

Athearn, Horace, 237
Atkinson, Prosecutor, 213
Australia, 159, 203
Aymar, 34, 35, 37

B

Bahamas, 216, 241, 242
Baltimore, 61
Barbados, 76
Batavia (now Djakarta), 26
Bay of Fundy, 12, 14, 15, 16, 97
Beagle, 128
Bichard, Nicholas, 28, 29, 33
Black Pedro, 124
Blue Mountains, 38
Bond, Captain Charles H., 247
Boston, Massachusetts, 5, 56, 57, 61, 62, 77, 78, 80, 81, 85–87, 91, 94, 99, 139, 165, 172, 185, 196, 203
Boston Daily Globe, 85, 91, 93
Boston Herald, 56, 87, 88, 92
Boston Sun, 83, 109
Bowen, Australia, 164
Brazil, 81, 83, 100, 180

313

Bridgeport, Connecticut, 240

Brier Island, 12, 14, 15, 16, 19, 24, 47, 97, 114, 180, 249

Bristol, Rhode Island, 239, 240

British Columbia, 27

Brooklyn Bridge, 46

Brown, Grace Murray, 55, 209, 273

Buel, C.C., 196, 200

Buenos Aires, 59, 60, 110, 197

Buffalo, New York, 198, 202–204, 206

Burlington County Prison Register, 212

Burnett, Constance Buel, 197

Burrard Inlet, 34

Buzzards Bay, 82

C

California, 99

Cape Agulhas, 177

Cape Bundaroo, 169

Cape Cod, 159

Cape Hatteras, 241

Cape Horn, 109, 111, 117, 126, 128, 130, 148, 196, 200

Cape Leeuwin, 172

Cape of Good Hope, 54, 103, 111, 172, 174, 176, 198

Cape Pillar, 127

Cape Town, 148, 154, 165, 170, 178, 180, 191

Cape Town Normal College, 165

Cardiff, 43

Caribbean, 71, 216, 246

Carmen Island, 29

Carnegie Hall, 189

Carolinas, 71

Century Illustrated Monthly Magazine, 193, 194

Ceylon, 99

Chapelle, Howard, 89

Cheney, 23, 24, 25, 26

Chesapeake Bay, 76

China, 25, 34, 99, 188, 233

China Sea, 99

Cockburn Channel, 122, 128

Coffee Island, 142

Coggins, H.L., 231

Columbia River, 27

Columbus, Christopher, 137

Concord, New Hampshire, 200

Coney Island, 47

Conrad, Joseph, 78

Constitution, 28, 29, 33, 34

Cook, Captain, 159

Cook Inlet, Alaska, 30

Cooktown, Australia, 159

Cottage City, Massachusetts, 196

Cotuit, 241

Cuba, 77

D

Daily Alta, 34

Daily Astorian, 40

Darwin, Charles, 128

Day, Thomas Fleming, 237, 242, 249

deal drogher, 23

Dean, Ernest, 235
Defoe, Daniel, 160
Delaware Bay, 6
Destroyer, 81–83
Devonport, 155
Dexter, 184
Digby, Nova Scotia, 14
Drake, Sir Francis, 178
Dublin, 23, 25
Dukes County Court, 247
Durban, 163
Dutch West Indies, 26

E

East China Sea, 36
Eccentricities of Genius, 215
Edgartown, Massachusetts, 244
Epitome of Navigation, 25
Erie Canal, 202, 203

F

Faial, 138
Fairhaven, Massachusetts, 1, 6,
  8, 80, 82, 83, 91, 186, 193, 198
Fairhaven Star, 237
Fiji, 29, 102
Flying Dutchman, 177
fo'c'sle, *see* forecastle
Fogarty, Thomas, 198
forecastle, 24
Fortescue Bay, 121
Foy, Mark, 170
Funk and Wagnalls, 86, 93
Fury Island, 129

G

Gaskill, Judge, 221
Gates, Naomi Slocombe, 77
Gauguin, Paul, 247
Gibraltar, 100, 115, 138, 151,
  156, 170
Gilbert Islanders, 49
Gilder, Richard Watson, 194,
  195, 196
Gill, David, 164
Gilpin, Vincent, 235, 237
Gloucester, Massachusetts, 96,
  97, 99
Good Housekeeping, 95, 106, 161
Grand Caymans, 191
Green Head Cliffs, 19
Grenada, 182
Griffin, 27
Groton, 234
Guam, 189
Guayamas, Mexico, 29
Gulf of California, 29

H

Haggard, H. Rider, 87
Half Moon Bay, 28
Hanna, John, 88
Hardy, Eugene, 86, 87, 98–100
Harper Publishing House, 47
Hathaway's Wharf, 34
Havana, 233
Hawaii Public Archives, 40
Hayes, Bully, 36

Herreshoff, Captain Nat, 237, 239, 240
Herreshoff, L. Francis, 239
Herreshoff Marine Museum, 240
Hettie, 3, 5, 62, 63, 64, 66, 68, 70–72, 75–77, 81, 85, 93, 172, 185, 194, 196, 198, 200, 201, 206, 213, 216, 230, 231, 237, 240–242, 244, 246, 247
Hong Kong, 26, 34, 39, 42–44, 99
Honolulu, 40
Horner, Senator John G., 221
Horn Islands, 102
Horta Faial, 100
Hudson River, 202

I

Ilha Grande, 63, 82
India, 99
Indian Ocean, 105, 157
In the Wake of the Spray, 241
Irishtown, 16
Irving, Washington, 137
Isthmus of Panama, 99

J

Jackson, Captain Levi, 243
Jamaica, 216, 232
Japan, 50, 51, 99, 188, 233
Jebb, John Gladwin, 87
Johannesburg, South Africa, 195
Johnson, Clifton, 148, 196, 207–209, 275
Josh, *see* Slocum, Joshua

Juan Fernández, 139, 160, 162, 169

K

Keeling (Cocos) Islands, 103, 111, 153, 158
Keeling Harbor, 105
Kenney, Captain, 43
Kidder, B.H., 240
Kingston, Jamaica, 232
Kodiak, 30
Kohala, 40
Krakatoa, 51
Kruger, President Paul, 151, 162

L

Lagoon Heights, 242
Laguemanac, Philippines, 41, 43
Langley, Samuel Pierpont, 201
Lesser Antilles, 247
Liberdade, 7, 70–72, 74–76, 79, 80, 82, 88, 207
Life of Columbus, 137
Liverpool, 25, 26, 46, 51
Living Age, 36
Lodge, Henry Cabot, 227
London, 193
Longaker, Alice C., 231, 242, 246
Long Island, 226, 233
Long Island Sound, 89
Lunenburg, Nova Scotia, 47

M

McKinley, President, 188

McNutt, Captain and Mrs. Aflred, 76, 241, 244

Maine Coast Fisherman, 241

Maldonado, Uruguay, 66

Maloney, Thomas, 65

Manhattan Beach, 47

Manila, 37, 38, 45

Marquesas Islands, 190

Martha's Vineyard, 74, 196, 204, 206, 207, 211, 228, 230, 234, 235, 242, 245, 269, 274, 275

Martin, Captain, 26

Martini-Henry rifle, 91

Mason, Professor Otis, 201

Massachusetts, 43, 61, 62, 77, 194

Massachusetts Bay, 94, 114

Mauritius, 140, 157, 164

Mead, Francis, 240

Meinickheim, Felix, 248

Melbourne, Australia, 34, 156, 157, 169

Menemsha, 222, 237

Miami, 216, 233

Mills, Dr. C.S., 218

Miserere, 93

Montana, 28

Montevideo, 62, 66, 67, 106, 151, 159

Morning Oregonian, 190

Morning Star, 51

Morocco, 115

Mount Hanley, Nova Scotia, 15

Mount Holly, 219, 220

Mount Holly News, 220, 275

Muscaget Shoals, 243

Muskeget Channel, 240

mutiny, 48, 55

N

Nansen, Dr., 115

Napoleon, 179

Natal Mercury, 193

Nautical Gazette, 56, 200

New Bedford, 242

New Bedford City Hall, 193

New Bedford Evening Standard, 299

New Bedford Standard, 188, 214, 246, 275

Newcastle, New South Wales, 165, 219

New Hampshire, 84

New Hebrides, 35

New Jersey, 217, 221

New London, Connecticut, 48

Newport, Rhode Island, 183, 185, 227

Newport Herald, 184

New South Wales, 165, 167

New York, 36, 46, 47, 55, 62, 75, 81, 83, 92, 183, 191, 193, 196, 198, 200, 246

New York Evening Post, 199

New York Herald, 191

New York Post, 201

New York Times, 192

New York Tribune, 46

New York World, 75, 195, 233
Nickerson, William A., 241, 242
Norfolk, 72
Norie, J.W., 25
Northern Light, 2, 4, 43, 45, 46,
   48–51, 55–58, 75, 92, 166, 167
North Mountain, 15
North West Post, 155
Norton, Reginald, 237
Nova Scotia, 46, 62, 79, 98, 133
Nukahiva, 153, 190

O

Okhotsk, Sea of, 39
Olongapo, 37, 39
Oregon, 27, 39, 40
Oregon, 180, 181
Orinoco River, 236, 237, 241,
   242, 246, 248
Orionoco Country, 246
Osborn, B.S., 56
Outing, 207, 208
Oxford Point, 6, 7, 8, 9, 10, 89
Oyster Bay, 240, 242, 249

P

Panama, 92
Panama Canal, 246, 232
Pan-American Exposition, 201,
   202
Paranaguá, 65, 66
Paranaguá Bay, 66, 67
Pato, 39, 40, 57
Patriot Ledger, 265

Pernambuco, Brazil, 59, 61, 69,
   98, 100, 197
Petropolanska, 39
Philadelphia, 218, 219, 233
Philippines, 37, 38, 41, 51, 188
Pierce, Captain Eben, 5, 6, 81,
   84
Pinheiro, Carlton J., 240
"pinkies", 16
Pinta, 138, 179
Pinzòn, Martin Alonso, 138
Pond, Major James B., 215
Poole, Captain Donald Lemar,
   244
Port Angosto, 109, 123, 129, 197
Port Tamar, 127, 134
Potomac, 75, 76
Poverty Point, *see* Oxford Point
President of the United States, 68
Pretoria, 162, 163, 178
Probate Court of Dukes County,
   238
Providence Journal, 172, 216
Punta Arenas, Chile, 119, 120,
   126, 129

Q

Queensland, 105
Quincy, Massachusetts, 43, 247

R

Randolphe, Captain John, 240
Red Sea, 99
Rime of the Ancient Mariner, 44

Rio de Janeiro, 63, 64, 67, 68, 69, 252
Rio Negro, 236, 242
River Plate, 67, 159
Rivers, Lieutenant Carlos A., 83
Riverton, 218, 219, 222, 223, 228
Riverton New Era, 218
Riverton Yacht Club, 217
Roberts Brothers, 86, 99
Robertson, Captain, 33
Robinson Crusoe, 160, 182, 199, 201
Rodriguez, 157
Roosevelt, Archie, 226, 227, 233, 234
Roosevelt, President Theodore, 217, 223, 228, 243, 227
Rosario, 63

S

Sagamore Hill, 217, 226
Sailing Alone Around the World, 94, 124, 148, 171, 198, 228, 275
St. Helena, 155, 170, 172, 179, 182
St. Helena Guardian, 275
Saint John, New Brunswick, 23
St. Kilda, 156
St. Marys, 18
St. Marys Bay, 17
Salem Witch Trials, 223
Saley, Carol W., 215
Samblich, Captain Pedro, 120, 123

Sambro, 133
Samoa, 102, 134, 139, 147, 153, 154, 158, 160–162, 169, 190
San Francisco, 27, 28, 29, 30, 40, 42
Santa Catarina, 67
Santa Catarina Island, 59
Santa Maria, 151
Selkirk, Alexander, 160
Shanghai, 36, 40
Shinn, Samuel W., 221
Simons Bay, 177
Singapore, 99
Slack, Kenneth E., 241
Slater, Henry A., 55, 56, 166, 167, 168
Slocombe, John, 14, 15, 16, 18, 27, 47
Slocombe, Sarah, *see* Southern, Sarah Jane
Slocum, Benjamin Aymar, 32, 33, 35, 38, 40, 42, 45, 51, 59, 60, 61, 77, 78, 81, 159, 171, 245, 274
Slocum, James Abram Garfield, 2, 41, 43, 45, 54, 58–60, 62, 64, 68, 71, 77, 80, 170, 200, 208, 213, 228, 230, 244, 268
Slocum, Jessie Lena, 37, 44, 45, 57, 58, 61, 72, 77, 274,
Slocum, Joel, 149, 200
Slocum, Joshua
  name change, 27; American citizenship, 27; birth, 15;

Brazil, 4; brothers, 41, 210, 246, 260; and crew, 3, 4; early life, 3; in Fairhaven, 2; father, 10, 17, 22; finances, 3, 4; fur trading, 27; marriage, 32, 58; mother, ; Native people, 26; sea otter hunting, 27; second marriage, 4, 60; shipbuilding, 26; sister, 57, 61; sons, 4, 16, 31, 41, 45

Slocum, Victor, 4, 14–16, 22, 26, 28, 34, 35, 37, 44, 46, 58, 61, 65, 66, 70, 88, 172, 191, 230, 238, 239, 244

Smith, H.S., 243

Smithsonian Institution, 201

Snobtown, 16

Snow, Edward Rowe, 247, 248

Solomon Islands, 35

Soushay, 26

South Africa, 163, 164, 170, 179, 193

South America, 71, 79, 120, 125, 246

South Brooklyn, 196

Southern, Sarah Jane, 14, 15, 23

Southwest Point Light, 14

Spain, 180

Spray, 6-10, 80, 81, 84–91, 93, 94, 96–98, 102, 104–106, 109–111, 114–119, 121, 123–130, 140–142, 146, 147, 149, 152, 155, 157–160, 163, 164, 165, 169, 170, 172, 173, 175, 176, 178–186, 190–192, 195, 197, 198, 200–208, 213, 215, 229, 230, 232–249

Stanley, Henry Morton, 164

Staten Island, 29

Stevenson, Fanny, 160, 161

Stevenson, Robert Louis, 87, 160

Straits of Magellan, 92, 98, 107–109, 116, 119, 125, 129, 134, 140, 142, 147, 194

Stravinsky, Igor, 176

Suez Canal, 99

Sunda Strait, 51

Sweetcake Cove, 16

Sydney, Australia, 29, 35, 59, 155, 165–167, 169, 170

Sydney Morning Herald, 273

Sylph, 227

T

Table Mountain, 176

Tagals, 38, 39

Tanjore, 25, 26

Tasmania, 110, 155, 164, 169

Teller, Walter, 58, 85, 93, 198, 208, 210, 222, 223, 229, 239–242, 244, 245

The Gleaner, 232

The Louisville Courier Journal, 86

The Rudder, 88, 151, 225, 237, 242, 243, 249,

Thieves Bay, 122

Thoreau, 199
Thursday Island, 105, 161, 164
Tierra del Fuego, 124, 130, 139, 212
Times of London, 192
Tisbury, Massachusetts, 238
Tobago, 181, 182
Torres Straits, 173
Transvaal, 162, 163, 176
Treasure Island, 199
Tripp, William, 216
Troy, 202
Turks Island, 18
Turtle Island, 248

U

United Empire Loyalist, 27
United States, 68–71, 74, 182
Uruguay, 62, 66, 117, 137

V

Varian, George, 198
Venezuela, 236
Vineyard Gazette, 207, 229, 231, 240
Vineyard Haven, 210, 237, 240–242
Voyage of the Destroyer, 83
Voyage of the Liberdade, 71, 79, 80

W

Wagnalls, Mabel, 93, 185, 198
Wagnalls, Mr., 86
Walker, Virginia, 3, 4, 29, 30, 32–39, 41, 43–47, 49, 53, 57–60, 75, 159, 230
Walker's Cove, 239
Ward, Louise B., 232
Washington, 30, 33
Washington, D.C., 246
Watterson, Mr., 86
West Indies, 171, 182, 216, 217, 234, 240, 241, 244, 247
Westport, Nova Scotia, 12, 15-18, 98
Westport Baptist Church, 249, 250
West Tisbury, 204, 207, 208, 210–212, 216, 231, 238
West Tisbury News, 212
William, John, 35
Woods Hole, Massachusetts, 197
Wright, Charles D., 218–221
Wright, Elsie, 218, 219, 222, 223

Y

Yarmouth, Nova Scotia, 98, 99
Yarmouth Herald, 79
Yokohama, 48